for John
with admiration & friendship
David

EMBATTLED RIVER

EMBATTLED RIVER

The Hudson and Modern American Environmentalism

DAVID SCHUYLER

CORNELL UNIVERSITY PRESS
ITHACA AND LONDON

First published 2018 by Cornell University Press

Printed in the United States of America

Library of Congress Cataloging-in-Publication Data

Names: Schuyler, David, author.
Title: Embattled river : the Hudson and modern American
    environmentalism / David Schuyler.
Description: Ithaca : Cornell University Press, 2018. | Includes
    bibliographical references and index.
Identifiers: LCCN 2017051164 (print) | LCCN 2017053547 (ebook) |
    ISBN 9781501718069 (epub/mobi) | ISBN 9781501718076 (pdf) |
    ISBN 9781501718052 | ISBN 9781501718052 (cloth ; alk. paper)
Subjects: LCSH: Environmentalism—Hudson River Valley (N.Y.
    and N.J.)—History. | Environmental protection—Hudson River
    Valley (N.Y. and N.J.) | Hudson River Valley (N.Y. and N.J.)—
    Environmental conditions.
Classification: LCC GE198.H83 (ebook) | LCC GE198.H83 S34 2018
    (print) | DDC 333.91/4097473—dc23
LC record available at https://lccn.loc.gov/2017051164

For Kenneth T. Jackson

CONTENTS

ILLUSTRATIONS

ACKNOWLEDGMENTS

I am grateful to Franklin & Marshall College for the sabbatical during which I wrote most of the pages that follow, and also for the college's support of my research and teaching over the course of thirty-eight years. During that time many F&M students have helped me in my research on different scholarly endeavors, largely through our wonderful Hackman Scholars program, endowed by alumnus William Hackman, which supports students in collaborative research with faculty. In writing this book I have been fortunate to have two Hackman Scholars work with me. Molly Cadwell helped with the research at the beginning of this project, and I am proud that she transformed what she learned into a superb honors thesis on Storm King's significance to American environmentalism. Wyatt Behringer also contributed to the research and was instrumental in the early stages of checking the text and notes.

For financial support in conducting research I am indebted to the Archives Partnership Trust, which enabled me to conduct research in the New York State Archives, especially the records of the Hudson River Valley

Commission, and to the Rockefeller Archive Center, where I consulted the Hudson River Valley Commission records and, more revealingly, two boxes of Laurance Rockefeller's papers that had not been cataloged. I am grateful to archivist Monica Blank for finding and making accessible the Laurance Rockefeller papers relevant to this book, and to Jim Folts for his help during my visit to the state archives.

Many people in the Hudson River Valley have also been extraordinarily helpful. I am deeply indebted to Thomas Wermuth, dean of the faculty and director of the Hudson River Valley Institute at Marist College, where I was the first Barnabas McHenry Visiting Scholar during the fall semester of 2015. I am also indebted to John Ansley and the staff at Rare Books and Special Collections, James A. Cannavino Library, especially Ann Sandri, for making its terrific Hudson River environmental collections accessible. Harvey Flad, a friend for many years and now retired after a distinguished career at Vassar College, generously shared his research files on the Cementon case, gave me the benefit of his encyclopedic knowledge of other environmental battles in the valley, and commented on a draft of this book. Ned Sullivan and Reed Sparling of Scenic Hudson have done so as well. Paul Gallay of Riverkeeper welcomed me to his office and answered innumerable questions that helped me frame that chapter. He too commented helpfully on an earlier draft.

I could not have written this book without the help of many individuals in the Hudson River Valley who shared their knowledge of important developments. J. Winthrop Aldrich, now retired but the longtime deputy commissioner for historic preservation in New York, knows most of these issues firsthand, as he was involved in many of the conservation and environmental battles I analyze. Wint answered innumerable questions as I was struggling to understand those issues, and also commented on the entire typescript in draft. I had never met Albert K. Butzel, who is one of the individuals most responsible for the development of U.S. environmental law, but when I sent him an e-mail he responded welcomingly, and since that first exchange his thoughts have guided me as I have written many of the pages that follow. Al also read a draft of this book, and I am indebted to him for his thoughtful, constructive criticism. John Cronin shared with me his vast knowledge of many of the organizations and issues I have written about, and commented helpfully on an earlier version of this book. Adam Rome's reading of a draft challenged me to place the environmentalism of the Hudson River Valley into a national context.

Tom Daniels and Steve Schuyler also read this in draft and helped me in many ways.

Betsy Garthwaith, formerly *Clearwater*'s boat captain and now president of the organization's board of directors, read the Clearwater chapter and helped me when I was assembling the illustrations; Karl Beard and Barnabas McHenry offered sage advice on the Greenway and NHA chapter; and John Mylod shared his recollections of the years in which he was executive director of Clearwater and offered helpful comments on that chapter.

Others who have helped include Mark Castiglione, who for many years headed the Hudson River Greenway / Hudson River National Heritage Area; John Doyle, formerly director of the Heritage Task Force of the Hudson River Valley; and Frances Dunwell of the Hudson River Estuary Program. Maynard Toll put me in touch with his old friend Leon Billings, who gave me invaluable insight into the politics surrounding adoption of the National Environmental Policy Act. Conversations or correspondence with Hayley Carlock, Carl Petrich, Tom Whyatt, Frederic C. Rich, and Loretta Simon were very helpful in my understanding of important issues I have written about. Sam Pratt's knowledge and advice helped me analyze the St. Lawrence Cement controversy, as did conversations with Sara Griffen. Peter Brown shared with me his copy of *Nuclear Power in the Hudson Valley: Its Impact on You.*

My colleagues at Shadek-Fackenthal Library were enormously helpful in my research, especially Meg Massey and Jenn Buch in Interlibrary Loan. American Studies colleagues Louise Stevenson, Alison Kibler, Carla Willard, and Dennis Deslippe were supportive in many ways during this scholarly journey.

I spent most of the fall of 2015, when I was at Marist, as a guest of my oldest brother, Barry, and his wonderful spouse Jodi. They gave me their extra bedroom and a smaller one where I hooked up my computer and worked many nights. They have also welcomed me on subsequent research trips as well as visits home for the holidays. Their house overlooks the Hudson just north of Newburgh, the same vista, looking east toward Mount Beacon and south toward Storm King and Breakneck Ridge, that I came to love as a child. Visits to their home, and their welcoming embrace, as well as the scenery so remarkable from their windows and porches, remind me of why I still, after so many years away, consider the Hudson Valley home.

To all I am deeply grateful.

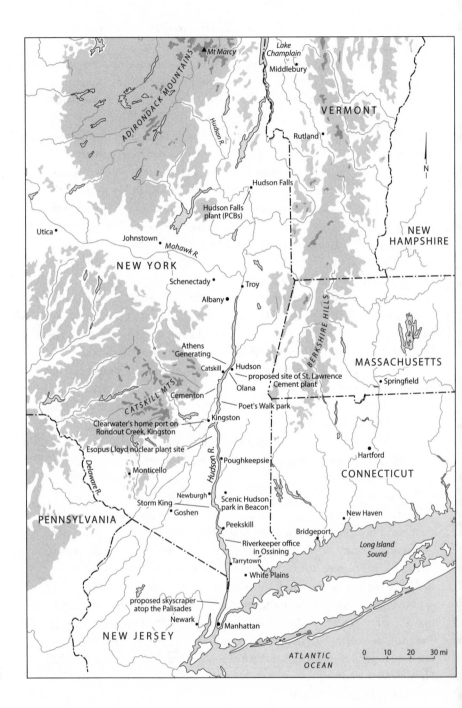

Mt Marcy

Lake
Champlain

Middlebury

ADIRONDACK MOUNTAINS

Hudson R.

VERMONT

Rutland

N

Hudson Falls

Hudson Falls
plant (PCBs)

NEW
HAMPSHIRE

Utica

Johnstown

Mohawk R.

NEW YORK

Schenectady

Troy

Albany

BERKSHIRE HILLS

MASSACHUSETTS

Athens
Generating

Catskill

Hudson

proposed site of St. Lawrence
Cement plant

Olana

Springfield

CATSKILL MTS.

Cementon

Poet's Walk park

Clearwater's home port on
Rondout Creek, Kingston

Kingston

Esopus Lloyd nuclear plant site

Delaware R.

Monticello

Hudson R.

Poughkeepsie

Hartford

CONNECTICUT

Newburgh

Storm King

Goshen

Scenic Hudson
park in Beacon

New Haven

PENNSYLVANIA

Peekskill

Bridgeport

Riverkeeper office
in Ossining

Long Island
Sound

Tarrytown

White Plains

proposed skyscraper
atop the Palisades

Newark

Manhattan

NEW JERSEY

ATLANTIC
OCEAN

0   10   20   30 mi

INTRODUCTION

Since 1962 the Hudson River Valley has been a key battleground in the development of modern environmentalism in the United States. What began with a small group of individuals opposed to Consolidated Edison's plan to construct a pumped-storage power plant at Storm King Mountain, the northern gateway to the Hudson Highlands, quickly attracted supporters in the region and across the nation. That small group organized as the Scenic Hudson Preservation Conference and successfully waged a legal and public relations campaign against the powerful utility that established the foundations for environmental law. Other groups organized as well, sometimes in response to a specific threat, at other times with a broader mission to defend water quality, such as Riverkeeper, or to promote environmental education, the replica nineteenth-century sloop *Clearwater*'s mission. Through their collective efforts, these organizations have defended the valley's environment and worked to promote the quality of life and the economic vitality essential to its residents.

The Hudson is a comparatively short river. It flows south from Lake Tear of the Clouds on Mount Marcy, the highest peak in the Adirondacks, for 315 miles until it reaches the Atlantic Ocean. It flows by the Catskills, which attracted the first generation of artists who defined an American landscape tradition, named after the river itself, as well as the Highlands, a visually spectacular fifteen-mile stretch where the river courses through the mountainous Appalachian spine. It broadens into a bay three miles wide at the Tappan Zee, memorialized in Washington Irving's prose, and flows past the Palisades and New York City before reaching the sea.

Writers and policy makers trying to explain or analyze the Hudson often divide the river into two, sometimes three, stretches: the upper Hudson, from its source to the Federal Dam at Troy, and the lower river—itself sometimes divided into a lower and middle river—from Troy south to the Atlantic Ocean. I have accepted what might be called the two-stretch river, as the Hudson is navigable as far north as the dam and is a tidal estuary for much of that distance. Each section has experienced different stages of economic development, urban growth, post–World War II decline, and, in most places, a revival in recent years. The human presence along the river—the buildings, factories, extractive industries, and pollution—has affected its ecosystem as well as the lives of residents in the valley.[1]

Although environmentalism is a relatively recent development, the Hudson planted the seeds for an appreciation of the natural world throughout much of its history. In the nineteenth century it claimed a powerful hold on the American imagination. Our national sense of the importance of landscape and scenery began in the Hudson River Valley. A group of landscape painters, led by Thomas Cole, Asher B. Durand, and Frederic E. Church, captured the beauty of the valley on their canvases, many of which now hang in the nation's foremost museums. Engravings after drawings by William Henry Bartlett, originally published in *American Scenery*, which disproportionately represented the Hudson River Valley and the Catskills, were frequently framed and graced the walls of parlors throughout the nation. So were lithographs published by Nathaniel Currier and James Ives. These images helped make the valley the archetypal American landscape. The writings of Irving, James Fenimore Cooper, Nathaniel Parker Willis, and others also contributed to the widely shared recognition that the Hudson River Valley was an iconic place. Through the memory of the importance of the valley in the American Revolution and the beginnings of historic preservation in the first half of the nineteenth century, the Hudson was a key in fostering a sense of national identity.[2]

Generations of residents—fishermen, swimmers, recreational boaters, hikers, and those who appreciated its scenery—have developed a strong attachment to the Hudson River, which has resulted in the widely shared belief that the valley is a special place and has led many who grew up along the river or lived on its banks, over more than a half century, to defend the landscape. As the rising generation of environmentalists discovered in the 1960s, the work of artists and writers who a century earlier had painted, written about, and cherished the Hudson River Valley became a foundation for their efforts to preserve the landscape. These efforts have helped establish the modern environmental movement.[3]

In this book I focus on a number of the major conservation and preservation battles and initiatives that have taken place in the Hudson River Valley since, in 1962, Consolidated Edison proposed that pumped-storage plant at Storm King Mountain. In a previous book on the Hudson, *Sanctified Landscape*, I organized my interpretation of the emergence of the Hudson Valley as iconic landscape in the nineteenth century through the role of individuals such as Cole, Andrew Jackson Downing, and John Burroughs. Here the focus is on the organizations that have rallied to the defense of the river, who used the courts, legislation, and public opinion to challenge threats to a landscape their members cherished. Even before Scenic Hudson's momentous "Peace Treaty" with Con Ed in 1980, other battles were under way, including opposition to nuclear and conventional power plants and Governor Nelson Rockefeller's proposed expressway along the east bank of the river. In more recent years environmentalists have challenged what they considered the ineffective role of federal and state agencies in protecting the environment and struggled to force General Electric to clean up the PCBs it dumped into the river, an effort that is ongoing. Other organizations have promoted the construction of greenways to link parks and other open spaces throughout the valley, or have advocated heritage tourism as the new driver of the region's postindustrial economy.[4]

Most important, in its legal challenges to Con Ed's plan, Scenic Hudson won a critical victory: in 1965 the Second Circuit Court of Appeals ruled against Con Ed and the Federal Power Commission and stated that Scenic Hudson had standing in the court, which Con Ed had challenged, and which opened the federal judiciary to citizen suits involving the environment and a host of other issues. The court also chastised the Federal Power Commission for not considering scenic, cultural, and historic concerns in its decision making, and it effectively required the first environmental impact statement. Each of the significant points in this decision became the heart of the National Environmental Policy Act of 1969, the foundation of modern environmental law.[5]

Although I devote attention to water quality, the fisheries, and the most appropriate development along the river's banks, in the chapters that follow I attempt to tell the most important stories about how a number of organizations have fought to protect the Hudson, and the significance of those fights for American environmentalism. The Scenic Hudson decision is surely the most important of these developments, as it has shaped environmental law and policy nationwide. The battle over a proposed nuclear power plant at Cementon is also crucial: for the first time, the staff of the Nuclear Regulatory Commission recommended the denial of a license for a nuclear power plant to the Power Authority of the State of New York and based its determination on aesthetic considerations. The visual impact analysis presented by Carl Petrich, Harvey Flad, and Richard Benas in the Cementon battle, and by Flad against the proposed nuclear plant at Lloyd-Esopus, established the foundation for visual impact analysis that has been adopted by New York and other states and has been important in conservation and environmental battles elsewhere.

Other developments are also important. Pete Seeger preached a gospel of populist environmentalism, and the *Clearwater*, the sloop that he did so much to create and sustain, has become a symbol of a greener future and has emphasized environmental education. Riverkeeper has been a staunch supporter of clean water, and has courageously investigated and litigated to force elected officials and regulators to comply with the Clean Water Act. It has also successfully campaigned to ban hydraulic fracturing—fracking—in New York State. Scenic Hudson has evolved from its beginnings at Storm King Mountain to become a land conservation organization that has also developed riverfront parks and has made many other contributions to the quality of life in the Hudson Valley. Scenic Hudson has also been an effective and innovative restraint on inappropriate commercial and residential development along the river and has championed farmland preservation. All three organizations, though they have different emphases, have united in demanding that federal and state officials enforce the Clean Water and Clean Air Acts and have fought hard to hold General Electric accountable for the PCBs released into the upper Hudson, mostly illegally, with devastating consequences for the river, today the largest Superfund site in the United States. Other efforts may seem more prosaic in comparison, but they too are important. The Hudson River Valley Greenway may not own an acre of land, but as Barnabas McHenry, the longtime chair of the Greenway Council, has observed, it is an umbrella "under which New York can promote, fund, but not enforce, conservation." Other, smaller groups have been essential in preserving land or in addressing pollution or other environmental issues.[6]

In the pages that follow I have departed, admittedly somewhat uncomfortably, from my usual perch in writing about American cultural history in the nineteenth century. Here I have felt it essential to address policy and politics as they are unfolding presently. I hope that I have succeeded in using history as a foundation for analyzing contemporaneous conditions and also presenting my concerns for the future as the second decade of the new millennium nears it close.

The Hudson River's renaissance—significant improvements in water quality, stronger regulations to make development along its banks appropriate while preserving public access, the many thousands of newcomers who have found the valley a desirable place to live—is still a work in progress. There is still too much poverty in its cities, too much suburban sprawl that is consuming valuable farmland, too much inappropriate development.

Other problems persist. Construction of sewage treatment plants has dramatically reduced the amount of pollution flowing into the river, with the result that the Hudson's waters are cleaner today than at any time since the beginnings of industrialization in the valley in the mid-nineteenth century. But the water itself is poisoned, not just by PCBs but by many other chemical micropollutants that aging sewage treatment plants were not designed to treat. Moreover, those treatment plants, most of which have combined sewage and stormwater pipelines, overflow during periods of heavy rainfall or snowmelt, and pour billions of gallons of untreated sewage and polluted stormwater into the Hudson each year. Much of the middle stretch of the river is now safe for swimming, though because of PCBs and other pollutants its fish are not safe for human consumption.

Moreover, as Riverkeeper has demonstrated, some areas at certain times of the year are perilous for bathers, and a more effective and frequent water sampling program is essential.[7]

In addition, as the Clearwater organization, Scenic Hudson, and River-keeper have argued, the Hudson needs much more effective oversight, and policing, by the federal Environmental Protection Agency and the state Department of Environmental Conservation. Those agencies have at times been remiss in enforcing the Clean Water Act, as amended in 1972, and have occasionally been an obstacle to rather than a strong advocate for environmental protection. The Hudson River Estuary Program is a welcome addition to the state's efforts in protecting the river and environs. Under its energetic director, Frances Dunwell, who is a longtime advocate for the river and author of two excellent books on the Hudson, the Estuary Program promises to be precisely what the Hudson needs—a holistic, interdisciplinary agency that protects the river and its many tributaries. But the Estuary Program is a state agency, which leaves it vulnerable to the changing political climate and gubernatorial priorities in Albany.[8]

The work of Scenic Hudson, Riverkeeper, and the Clearwater organization has been essential to the recovery of the river. Scenic Hudson and Riverkeeper are led by talented and dedicated individuals, Ned Sullivan and Paul Gallay (Dave Conover, the acting executive director of Clearwater, has been a terrific educator, but staff turnover and divisions within the board in recent years demonstrate that the organization needs stability at the top and an effective board committed to fund-raising). Fortunately, with former boat captain Betsy Garthwaite as president of the board, Clearwater appears to be sailing on an even keel once again. Ultimately, these organizations are collections of individuals who support their missions, and the Hudson River has benefited from the efforts of numerous individuals. The eight people who met at Carl Carmer's octagonal house in November 1963 took on one of the most powerful utilities in the nation; they succeeded in protecting Storm King Mountain and in the process revolutionized American environmental law. Seeger's populist environmentalism was based on his belief that individuals working within their own communities were a powerful force for social change, and the *Clearwater* has become the symbolic flagship of the environmental movement. River-keeper has been the strongest advocate for clean water in New York State. Other, smaller groups have successfully opposed nuclear power plants at

Cementon and Lloyd-Esopus. Citizens often mobilized into groups such as the Mid-Hudson Nuclear Opponents or Hudson River GREEN. These and other organizations, and the passion of the thousands of citizens who joined cleanups organized by Scenic Hudson, Riverkeeper, and Clearwater, and who contacted their state and federal legislators, or wrote letters to the editor, have defended the Hudson River Valley they cherish. These are individuals who care passionately about the big stream, as Carmer once described the Hudson.

A panel discussion organized by the Olana Partnership in 2012 featured three of the environmentalists who successfully challenged construction of the proposed nuclear power plant at Cementon, at a majestic bend in the river and in the viewshed of Olana, the landscape painter Frederic Church's spectacular house and grounds, which had become a state historic site in 1966. One of the panelists, J. Winthrop Aldrich, described the Hudson River Valley as "the great national arena of the battle between the engineer and the poet" in the nineteenth and twentieth centuries. Aldrich, one of the most important leaders in conservation and historic preservation in New York over the last four decades or so, was describing the long-standing and ongoing battles between those who cherish and want to preserve the valley for its scenic beauty and those who propose nuclear power plants and other new construction that would promote economic development yet potentially threaten the valley's scenic attributes. Other than omitting the numerous individuals defending the river who don't write verse, Aldrich was absolutely correct: the Hudson River Valley has been arguably the most important arena in the battle between conservation and development in our lifetimes. Beginning in 1962, the valley has indeed been the place where many of the most important environmental battles of our time have been fought, on the ground, in the legislature, and in the courts.[9]

1

THE BATTLE OVER STORM KING

On September 27, 1962, the *New York Times* reported that Consolidated Edison, the electrical utility that provides power to New York City and Westchester County, was planning to construct a pumped-storage power plant at Storm King Mountain, on the west bank of the Hudson River fifty-five miles north of Manhattan.[1] In a remarkable coincidence, that same day Rachel Carson published *Silent Spring*, her scientific study of the consequences of pesticides, especially DDT, for animal populations.[2] These two developments profoundly shaped modern environmentalism in the United States. Carson's book demonstrated the importance of scientific research and helped popularize the nascent environmental movement. Opponents of Con Ed's proposed plant, led by the Scenic Hudson Preservation Conference, litigated the licensing of the plant in federal court and in so doing established the foundations for environmental law.

Storm King Mountain faces Breakneck Ridge on the east bank, where another utility, Central Hudson Gas & Electric, proposed locating a second pumped-storage power plant. Together Storm King and Breakneck are the northern gateway to the Hudson Highlands, a fifteen-mile stretch where the Appalachian spine crosses the river. The Highlands constitute what is undeniably the most impressive river scenery in the eastern United States. While numerous foreign and American writers waxed poetic about the beauties of the Highlands in the nineteenth century, perhaps none were more discerning than Washington Irving and the Yale theologian Timothy Dwight. Irving, whose fertile imagination invented much of the folklore of the Hudson and environs, explained in Diedrich Knickerbocker's *History of New York* that the Hudson was once a vast lake, dammed at the Highlands, that extended some forty miles to the north. The mountains were "one vast prison, within whose rocky bosom the omnipotent Manetho confined the rebellious spirits who repined at his control." There, "bound in adamantine chains, or jammed in rifted pines, or crushed by ponderous rocks, they groaned for many an age." Eventually, the waters of the lake broke through the mountains and flowed south to the ocean, along the way freeing the spirits once imprisoned there and leaving the Highlands as "stupendous ruins." According to the venerable Knickerbocker, those spirits continue to dwell in the Highlands and cry out in haunting voices that reverberate through this stretch of the river.[3]

Timothy Dwight repeated Irving's account that the Hudson was once a lake. When he visited the Highlands in 1811 he described how the river, more than a mile wide at Newburgh Bay, narrows precipitously as it passes through the mountains. "The grandeur of this scene," he wrote, "defies description." The Highlands captivated Dwight, who struggled to find a vocabulary commensurate with the grandeur of the landscape. "It is difficult to conceive of anything more solemn or more wild than the appearance of these mountains." After describing the forests whose deep brown hues he likened to universal death, and clouds at sunset that "imparted a kind of funereal aspect to every object within our horizon," Dwight concluded by observing,

There is a grandeur in the passage of this river through the Highlands, unrivaled by anything of the same nature within my knowledge. At its entrance particularly and its exit, the mountains ascend with stupendous precipices immediately from the margin of its waters, appearing as if the chasm between them had been produced by the irresistible force of this mighty current, and the intervening barrier at each place had been broken down and

finally carried away into the ocean. These cliffs hang over the river, especially at its exit from the mountains, with a wild and awful sublimity, suited
to the grandeur of the river itself.

Dwight, an astute chronicler of the American landscape, was in his travels essentially seeking evidence of the progress of civilization in the United
States, which he measured by the neatness and industry of residents and
the settling of Protestant churches in small towns and villages. But the
scenery of the Highlands inspired him in ways that no other place he visited did, just as it impressed so many others.[4]

The Hudson Highlands attracted the attention of nineteenth-century
artists and writers whose work collectively sanctified the Hudson River
Valley. Landscape painter Thomas Cole, for example, decried the cutting of trees and other developments that were defacing a landscape he
believed all Americans should cherish. James Fenimore Cooper, whose
fictional character Natty Bumppo described the view from the Catskill escarpment as embracing "all creation," also lamented the wasteful ways of
his contemporaries. Nathaniel Parker Willis gave disproportionate attention to Hudson River and Catskill landscapes in *American Scenery*, and
painter Frederic E. Church, who lived in a house overlooking the Hudson,
was perhaps the first to articulate the need to call for an end to the commercial development that was ruining Niagara Falls.[5]

Over the course of the nineteenth and early twentieth centuries several
villages grew up in the Highlands, and the state constructed a highway
along the face of Storm King Mountain that opened in 1922, but to a remarkable extent the river scenery remained much as Dwight encountered
it. Vincent Scully, an architectural historian at Yale University, thus described Storm King in his testimony before the Federal Power Commission
(FPC): "It rises like a brown bear out of the river, a dome of living gran-
ite, swelling with animal power. It is not picturesque in the softer sense
of the word, but awesome, a primitive embodiment of the energies of the
earth. It makes the character of wild nature physically visible in monu-
mental form."[6]

Consolidated Edison's plan for a hydroelectric power plant at Storm
King was an attempt to meet New York City's peak power demands.
Overnight, when electricity demand was low, the utility would pump

millions of gallons of river water through a forty-foot wide, two-mile-long tunnel to a storage reservoir at the top of the mountain. The reservoir, to be located just southwest of Storm King Mountain, would cover approximately 230 acres and hold 740 million cubic feet of water. During periods of peak demand the water would be released and, as it flowed through reversible turbines, generate some two million kilowatts of electricity for a city whose needs were increasing dramatically as more and more air conditioners hummed away on sultry summer days. It would be the largest pumped-storage plant in the world, and the Federal Power Commission and Con Ed anticipated it could be expanded to produce three million kilowatts. Con Ed conceded that it would take three kilowatts of energy to pump the water to the reservoir and generate two kilowatts of electricity upon its descent, but instead of seeing this as inefficient, the company presented it as a welcome use of its generating capacity overnight, when power plants were underutilized. The electricity generated by Storm King would also enhance the utility's profitability, as the cost per kilowatt would be cheaper than that produced by older, less efficient plants. At the time of the initial announcement, the project had an estimated price tag of $115 million—a figure that would steadily rise in succeeding years. Con Ed's chairman, Harland C. Forbes, described the Storm King project as "a gigantic storage battery on our system." He stated that the utility would soon submit to the Federal Power Commission an application to approve construction and added, according to the *New York Times*, that "no delays were expected." Con Ed filed an application for licensing to the FPC in January 1963.[7]

Predictably, elected officials and residents of Cornwall, the village where the plant would be located, embraced it as an economic boon, which would almost double the value of real estate taxes generated and enable the village to modernize its facilities without raising taxes on residents. Joseph X. Mullin, the mayor of Newburgh, a few miles north of Cornwall, supported the project, as did the Orange County Board of Supervisors and labor unions, which welcomed the construction jobs the power plant would create. Governor Nelson A. Rockefeller strongly supported Con Ed's plan, stating that "the values of this project . . . outweigh the objections which have been raised to it" and argued that the inexpensive electricity it would provide was essential to continued economic growth in metropolitan New York. The Hudson River Conservation Society and

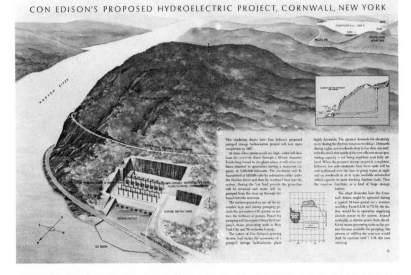

Figure 1. Schematic drawing of the pumped-storage power plant at the base of Storm King Mountain, as proposed by Consolidated Edison. Courtesy of Archives and Special Collections, James A. Cannavino Library, Marist College, Poughkeepsie, New York.

the Palisades Interstate Park Commission, the latter chaired by the governor's brother, Laurance Rockefeller, decided not to oppose the pumped-storage plant (though the conservation society later changed its position and announced its strong opposition to Con Ed's plans, as did the Palisades Interstate Park Commission when the utility proposed relocating the powerhouse to the south side of Storm King Mountain, on park land).[8]

The *New York Times*'s coverage of the Storm King project did not produce an immediate outcry against the plan, but the illustration of the project in Con Ed's 1962 annual report alarmed many conservationists and lovers of the Hudson River Valley. The schematic rendering depicted a powerhouse at the base of the mountain eight hundred feet long and fifty feet high, with eight transformers atop the powerhouse and a large crane that would be used to raise and lower screens designed to minimize harm to the fish population. A high concrete wall above the powerhouse would rise almost to the level of Storm King Highway, more than two hundred feet above the river. Not included in the rendering were the transmission lines that would cross the river and further disfigure the northern gateway to the Highlands and then extend through Putnam and Westchester Counties to connect with Con Ed's electrical grid in Yonkers. Publication of this schematic caused at least some people to realize that the proposed pumped-storage plant threatened a cherished landscape and place. A small group met at folklorist and historian Carl Carmer's residence, a remarkable octagonal house in Irvington, New York (surely inspired by the quirky phrenologist Orson Squire Fowler's *A Home for All*) and organized as the Scenic Hudson Preservation Conference on November 8, 1963. The task they faced was formidable: the Federal Power Commission was staffed by experts in utility operations, and, then as now, there was a revolving door between industry and regulatory agencies. The FPC routinely approved plans submitted by electrical utilities, and the courts had long deferred to its expertise.[9]

Scenic Hudson challenged Con Ed's plans before the FPC, but its attorney, Dale Doty, a former member of the commission, had little time to prepare for the hearing or to line up expert witnesses. In his brief Doty questioned whether cheap electricity better served the public interest than

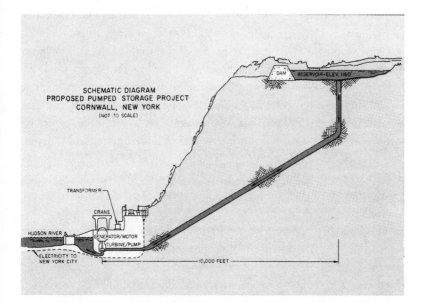

Figure 2. Schematic drawing of the powerhouse, tunnel, and reservoir at Storm King Mountain. Courtesy of Archives and Special Collections, James A. Cannavino Library, Marist College, Poughkeepsie, New York.

"preserving the beauty of one of America's great scenic and historic landscapes." At the February 25, 1963, hearing, Con Ed basically argued that the power plant would be effectively screened by landscaping and colored to blend in with the mountain. It would not, the utility insisted, impair the scenic beauty of the Highlands. Edward Marsh, the FPC's hearing officer, agreed, reporting to the commission that the project "would have relatively little adverse effect on the natural beauty of the area"—a conclusion that a *New York Times* editorial called erroneous. Oral arguments before the FPC took place in November 1964, and the following March the commission awarded Con Ed a license to construct the pumped-storage plant.[10]

Even before the FPC issued its licensing decision, R. Watson Pomeroy, a state senator from Dutchess County and chair of the Joint Legislative Committee on Natural Resources, presided at two days of hearings in November 1964. Held at the Bear Mountain Inn, in the middle of the Hudson Highlands, the hearings revealed widespread opposition to Con Ed's plans. Many of the 107 speakers highlighted the scenic beauty of the Highlands and also presented scientific evidence to rebut Dr. Alfred Perlmutter's testimony, made on behalf of Con Ed before the FPC. Perlmutter had argued that the principal spawning ground for striped bass was well north of Storm King and that the proposed plant would inflict little harm on the Hudson River fisheries. *Sports Illustrated* writer Robert Boyle effectively refuted Perlmutter's testimony and demonstrated that the river at Storm King was the center of the spawning area for striped bass and that because the river was a tidal estuary, the eggs and larvae would be drawn through the turbines at a much higher rate than Perlmutter had claimed. The Con Ed plant, Boyle argued, would be devastating for the Hudson River fishery. In addition, Alexander Lurkis, a highly regarded engineer, argued that gas turbines presented a more cost-effective alternative to the hydroelectric plant.[11]

The Pomeroy committee's report pointed to significant flaws in the hearing process for the Storm King project, especially in regard to the possibility of fish kills, the route of overhead transmission lines, especially their impact on Fahnestock State Park and the community of Yorktown, where the overhead lines would pass through a site proposed for a local school, and the impact of construction on the Hudson Highlands. The joint committee concluded that the project's impact "would be serious and contrary to the interests of the people of New York" and voted unanimously to oppose the project until Con Ed answered significant questions. Pomeroy also wrote to Joseph Swidler, chair of the Federal Power Commission, enclosing a copy of the joint committee's preliminary report and urging the commission to withhold authorizing construction until completion of a more thorough study of the plant's impact on the Hudson Valley. In later testimony before Congress, Pomeroy praised Leo Rothschild, who together with Carmer had organized the Scenic Hudson Preservation Conference, and condemned Con Ed as "the villain in the plot," as it had demonstrated "complete disregard for the permanent impairment of the scenic beauty and other natural resources of the area." Pomeroy added that his joint committee was considering a bill that would establish a Lower Hudson River Valley Heritage Commission, which would have responsibility for the river from the Adirondack Park to the Verrazano Narrows Bridge.[12]

When the committee released its preliminary report in mid-February 1965, it concluded that the Storm King plant would have "an adverse, if not disastrous" impact on the Hudson River's fisheries and on the scenic beauty of the Highlands. The report also raised troubling questions about the ability of the FPC to override state and local land-use decisions. Senator Pomeroy contacted President Lyndon B. Johnson and urged him to delay FPC approval of the project. He informed the president that the committee found that the FPC has produced "a partial record, closed to addition and correction, being used to hustle this national treasure into the hands of a private utility." Rod Vandivert, Scenic Hudson's executive director, waged a highly effective public relations campaign against Con Ed. In early September 1964, for example, a flotilla of fifty boats sailed from Cold Spring to Cornwall Landing. At the base of Storm King Mountain, three teenage boys, dressed in Continental army uniforms, planted a sign that turned Con Ed's corporate slogan on its head: "Dig You Must Not." The *New York Times* headline read "Waterborne Pickets Protest Hydroelectric Project That Might Mar the Beauty of the Hudson River Valley." A sub-headline adopted military language, describing the flotilla as an armada and the landing of the three uniformed boys as establishing a beachhead. Scenic Hudson was succeeding in generating favorable coverage in the press, especially the *Times*, and what Con Ed assumed was a local controversy that would soon die down was instead becoming regional and even national.[13]

In July 1965 Scenic Hudson and three towns in Westchester County where Con Ed would build the overhead transmission lines petitioned the U.S. Court of Appeals for the Second Circuit to overturn the FPC decision. Lloyd K. Garrison replaced Doty as Scenic Hudson's attorney, and he was joined by a recent Harvard Law School graduate, Albert K. Butzel, and other attorneys at Paul, Weiss, Rifkind, Wharton & Garrison. Butzel recalls that one of the first steps Lloyd Garrison and Judge Rifkind took was to rename the proposed power plant as the Storm King project (Con Ed had used the more innocuous "Cornwall project"). Other counsel represented the Westchester County towns opposed to the overhead transmission lines. Randall J. LeBoeuf Jr., a prominent utilities lawyer, argued on behalf of Con Ed, and four federal attorneys represented the FPC. The case was decided on December 29, 1965. In remanding the case to the FPC the appellate judges criticized the commission for not considering alternatives to the Storm King plant, for not engaging in the kind of comprehensive planning required by the Federal Power Act, and for compiling a woefully inadequate record of the basis for its decision. Specifically, the judges determined that Scenic Hudson had legal standing in the courts, which Con Ed had challenged, even though its members had not suffered economic injury; that the commission had failed to give adequate weight to the scenic, historic, and cultural significance of the Hudson Highlands; and that the commission had erred in not considering the impact of the power plant on the river's fisheries or evaluating the actual cost of burying the overhead transmission lines. In the opinion, Judge Paul R. Hays wrote, "The Storm King project is to be located in an area of unique beauty and major historical significance. The highlands and gorge of the Hudson offer one of the finest pieces of river scenery in the world." He then quoted Karl Baedeker's statement that the Hudson "is finer than the Rhine" and stated that the FPC was required by the Federal Power Act to consider the proposed power plant's impact on the landscape. The decision was a stunning victory for Scenic Hudson and a powerful rebuke to the FPC.[14]

Scenic Hudson I, as it is often called, was a major victory for environmentalism. Laurance Rockefeller, for example, observed: "This is an opinion of great historic significance because of the new status it gives to natural beauty. The court is implying than a plan cannot be 'practical' if it simply fulfills engineering and cost requirements more effectively than any other. These usual factors of superiority must now, by law, be weighed against any aesthetic problems they create." The Court of Appeals, in granting and affirming Scenic Hudson's standing, established a precedent that other environmental groups and citizen activists would use effectively in succeeding years. As Scenic Hudson's board minutes state, "our legal briefs are being used throughout the country in other conservation battles." Alexander Saunders, then vice chairman of Scenic Hudson's board, wrote friends that in its litigation Scenic Hudson had "set a legal precedent protecting our nation's natural resources and scenic beauty." The court also required federal agencies to undertake careful consideration of scenic, cultural, and historical issues in evaluating proposals before them. And, in requiring that the FPC take account of those scenic, cultural, and historical questions, and insisting that the commission measure the impact of the proposed power plant on Hudson River fisheries, the court effectively mandated the preparation of an environmental impact statement. Each of these requirements would become central components of the National Environmental Policy Act of 1969.[15]

The Scenic Hudson I decision was not the end of the dispute but the beginning of a legal, political, and public relations battle that would continue for another fifteen years. In May 1966, Con Ed amended its application to the FPC, proposing to place the powerhouse largely underground. Two months later the Hudson River Fishermen's Association and other environmental or conservation groups intervened in support of Scenic Hudson. In October 1966 the U.S. Department of the Interior recommended that the project "not be built." The following month the FPC began holding the remanded hearings, which continued through May 23, 1967. Butzel marshaled a remarkable array of individuals who testified to the historical, cultural, and environmental significance of Storm King and the Hudson Highlands, including Charles Eliot 2d, a highly regarded landscape architect and professor of city and regional planning at Harvard, Vincent Scully, and David Brower, head of the Sierra Club, among many others. Eliot and Scully were especially articulate. Eliot argued that the Highlands "represent contact with natural forces,—in contrast with urban and man-made conditions. Here, in that rugged terrain one can sense mystery and adventure, explore and discover, and experience the majesty of space and the land." The Highlands were an essential resource for millions of city dwellers for the opportunity they provided for " '*re*-creation' in the receptive sense with renewal of contact with natural forces, escape from pressures of man-made surroundings, and re-filling of spiritual well-springs." The Storm King project, Eliot testified, would "irretrievably damage those qualities and their enjoyment." Scully asserted that Storm King was a place all Americans should cherish. The mountain, he stated, "strongly reminds me of some of the natural formations which mark sacred sites in Greece and signal the presence of the Gods." Despite the formidable testimony in opposition to the project, on August 8, 1968, the FPC's senior hearing officer, Ewing G. Simpson, recommended that Con Ed's licensing application be approved.[16]

Shortly after this recommendation, New York City petitioned to intervene in the case in October, fearing that the revised plan to place the powerhouse underground would necessitate blasting that could damage the nearby Moodna Pressure Tunnel, which carried much of the city's drinking water under the Hudson River and was only 140 feet from the proposed excavation. After additional testimony the FPC hearing examiner concluded, on December 23, 1969, that the underground powerhouse was not a real threat to New York's water supply and also that a second proposed site, on land in Palisades Interstate Park, was unacceptable.[17]

The FPC's hearings subsequent to the remand were much more exhaustive than the first round. There were one hundred days of testimony from approximately sixty expert witnesses, some 675 exhibits were presented, and the hearing record consisted of more than nineteen thousand pages. On August 19, 1970, the FPC voted to approve Con Ed's license.[18]

In January 1971, Scenic Hudson, joined by New York City, the Palisades Interstate Park Commission, the Sierra Club, the Wilderness Society, the Izaak Walton League of America, the National Audubon Society, and the National Parks and Conservation Association, among many other groups, filed an appeal with the Second Circuit Court in what became known as Scenic Hudson II. Garrison and Butzel represented Scenic Hudson, while David Sive litigated on behalf of the Sierra Club, among the many attorneys involved.[19]

This time, however, the appellate court ruled against Scenic Hudson and the other intervenors in a divided opinion, and in a tie vote the full court refused to grant a rehearing before the entire court. Based on a review of the massive amount of testimony the FPC had received in the rehearings, and its full report, the court ruled that the FPC had adequately addressed the principal points in its 1965 opinion—that the commission had considered alternatives to the Storm King plant, that the plant's impact on natural resources, scenic beauty, and historic sites would be minimal, that the commission had adequately addressed the fisheries issue, and that Con Ed had demonstrated that the cost of burying the overhead transmission lines would be prohibitive. In its new ruling, the justices determined that the commissioners had carefully considered the possible impact of the underground powerhouse on a key part of New York City's water supply and found that it presented "no appreciable hazard to an aqueduct."[20]

The Second Circuit opinion did not endorse the FPC's findings. Instead, it recognized that the commission had fulfilled the specific instructions of the remand. While clearly sympathetic to the petitioners' arguments, the court ruled: "We find, however, that the Commission has fully complied with our earlier mandate and with the applicable statutes and that its findings are supported by substantial evidence." The court then conceded that as a matter of regulatory law, it was required to respect the expertise and findings of the commission. "In view of the extensive powers delegated to the Commission and the limited scope of review entrusted to this court, it is our duty to deny the petitions."[21]

As was true of the 1965 decision, the 1971 ruling was not the end of the battle over Storm King Mountain. Scenic Hudson and other petitioners continued on, dragging Con Ed through a series of legal proceedings and a continuing public relations disaster for the utility. Scenic Hudson and the Fishermen's Association challenged the redesign of the Con Ed plant, claiming that its filling in of the river shoreline required a permit from the Army Corps of Engineers (under the terms of the Rivers and Harbors Act of 1899). In 1973 the Court of Appeals accepted a Fishermen's Association petition and ordered the FPC to reopen its hearings on the fisheries question, and also ordered a halt to construction until that issue was resolved. In the new hearings, experts testifying on behalf of Scenic Hudson and the Fishermen's Association demonstrated that a report on which the FPC had relied in relicensing the Storm King plant, which concluded that the plant would have a minimal impact on fisheries, was wrong. This report, which had been commissioned by the state Conservation Department and the federal Fish and Wildlife Service but paid for by Con Ed, had failed to account for the fact that the Hudson was a tidal estuary at Storm King and that the larvae and newly hatched fish would pass before the plant's intake valve eight times each day, not once, as the report had assumed. Instead of an estimated loss of 2 to 3 percent of the striped bass population, which the report had asserted, these experts agreed that 40 percent was a more realistic number, which would devastate the population of striped bass within two years of commencement of operations.[22]

At the time these new hearings were proceeding, Con Ed's financial situation had become dire, causing it to suspend the dividend it had paid regularly over many years, and only the purchase by the Power Authority of the State of New York of two Con Ed power plants then under construction saved the utility from bankruptcy.[23]

Even worse for Con Ed, the Fishermen's Association continued to raise concern over the massive fish kills at Indian Point, the nuclear power plant the utility operated in Buchanan, on the east bank of the river. Robert Boyle had obtained photographs of thousands of striped bass killed at Indian Point, which had been trucked to a nearby dump, and published a searing article in *Sports Illustrated* that denounced Con Ed and the state Conservation Department, which had tried to confiscate the photographs and minimized the extent of the fish kills. During the 1970s the Fishermen's Association and the Natural Resources Defense Council (NRDC) persisted in raising legal issues about the role that Indian Point and other power plants played in the river's ecosystem, and challenged the licensing of the second and third Indian Point nuclear plants. Concerned that tens of millions of eggs, larvae, and juvenile fish were being sucked into power plants each year, the U.S. Environmental Protection Agency (established in 1970) required Con Ed and other utilities to construct cooling towers at their facilities along the river as a condition of granting or renewing licenses. The environmentalist and conservationist communities were divided over the cooling towers: although they would protect Hudson River fisheries, the towers would be a blight on the landscape. To an already financially strapped Con Ed, the cost of constructing those cooling towers at its Hudson River plants would have been enormous—the utility claimed $240 million—which ultimately forced Con Ed into talking with the Fishermen's Association and the other intervenors.[24]

Russell Train, a respected conservationist and former judge, was chosen as mediator. Train, then president of the World Wildlife Fund, had formerly headed the Conservation Foundation and was a member of the board of the Natural Resources Defense Council, itself an outgrowth of the Storm King litigation and which was representing the Fishermen's

Association. He had also served as the second head of the Environmental Protection Agency. In secret negotiations that extended over eighteen months, Train maintained a constructive, apparently trustful atmosphere and gained agreement on key points. In what the *New York Times* quoted Train as calling the "Hudson River Peace Treaty," on December 19, 1980, the mediator announced a historic compromise. The electric utilities would not be required to construct the cooling towers but would install state-of-the-art equipment to minimize fish kills. They would also temporarily cease operations at key Hudson River power plants, on a rotating basis, during the peak spawning season, another measure to protect the fisheries. Con Ed would in turn scrap plans for the power plant at Storm King Mountain, give the approximately four hundred acres of land it had assembled at Storm King to the Palisades Interstate Park Commission, and establish a $12 million endowment to support research on the Hudson River's ecology, which became the Hudson River Foundation and which has been an essential source of scientific information about the river over more than three decades. Train described the settlement as a "historic achievement." "We all gain from this landmark agreement," he continued. "It protects the environment, conserves energy, protects consumers, fights inflation, while helping protect the unique scenic resources of the Hudson River."[25]

Scenic Hudson, the Fishermen's Association, the NRDC, and a host of others had taken on Goliath and won.

The battle over Storm King Mountain was important for a number of reasons. One key to Scenic Hudson's success was its insistence on the importance of the Hudson River Valley to the emergence of American culture. Longtime board chair Frances Reese persuaded John K. Howat, then a curator and later Fleischman Chair of the American Wing at the Metropolitan Museum of Art, to write *The Hudson River and Its Painters* (1972), a lavishly illustrated history of the long-neglected American landscape tradition. Howat dedicated the book to Storm King Mountain and the Hudson River Gorge, and contributed all royalties to Scenic Hudson. After reviewing the careers of the most important of the Hudson River School painters, Howat expressed admiration for the "landscape pioneers who worked in the studios of New York for their remarkable contributions to American art as well as for their sympathetic presentation of a simpler world," a yet unspoiled American landscape. Howat's book, along with the pioneering work of David Huntington on Frederic E. Church, provided great impetus to a renewed appreciation of the Hudson River School and the centrality of the valley to the nation's cultural identity. Huntington also led the campaign to preserve Olana, Church's exotic house and 250-acre estate, which is now a state historic site.[26]

In a larger sense Storm King fundamentally shaped American environmental law and policy. Robert Lifset and Albert K. Butzel have demonstrated that as the case wound its way through the appeals process, ecological science—especially concern over the Hudson River fisheries—supplanted scenic, cultural, and historical questions in the court's decision making. As Robert Boyle wrote in 1969, eleven years before the peace treaty, "the battle to stop the Storm King plant has been one of the most fierce and publicized in the history of American conservation." In its magazine the National Audubon Society concurred, describing Storm King as "the symbol of an historic fight by citizens to save a majestic landscape from the opening wedge of industrialization." The Storm King case, the journal *Audubon* predicted, "will affect conservation crises of today and tomorrow throughout the nation."[27]

The environment became a compelling issue in the United States throughout the 1960s. President Lyndon B. Johnson exemplified this in his 1965 State of the Union address, in which he pledged to "end the poisoning of our rivers and the air that we breathe." Calling America's natural beauty our common heritage, he advocated "a massive effort to save the countryside and to establish—as a green legacy for tomorrow—more large and small parks, more seashores and open spaces than have been created during any other period in our national history." A month later, in his Special Message to the Congress on Conservation and Restoration of Natural Beauty, Johnson urged the need for "a new conservation." "We must not only protect the countryside and save it from destruction," he stated; "we must restore what has been destroyed and salvage the beauty and charm of our cities. Our conservation must be not just the classic conservation of protection and development, but a creative conservation of restoration and innovation" that would enhance the "dignity of man's spirit." The president called for federal funding to help cities increase the number of parks and playgrounds, full funding of the Land and Water Conservation Fund to enable the federal government to acquire national parks and recreational areas, and new measures to control the pollution fouling the nation's air and water. He paid particular attention to rivers, though he did not specifically mention the Hudson: "Every major river system is now polluted. Waterways that were once sources of pleasure and beauty and recreation are forbidden to human contact and objectionable to sight and smell."[28]

During his presidency Johnson signed almost three hundred laws concerning beautification and conservation. Perhaps most important of these was the Wilderness Act (1964), which authorized the involvement of citizens and groups in the legislative process and, as historian John A. Andrew III has written, "virtually guaranteed stronger environmental protection legislation in the future." It also gave the federal government broad authorization to protect wilderness. The Water Quality Act of 1965 marked a major change from previous laws, as it attempted to prevent pollution at its source rather than downstream. Most legislation enacted during the 1960s, however, allowed the states to set standards, which ultimately weakened the effectiveness of those new laws.[29]

Johnson also convened a White House Conference on Natural Beauty in May 1965, which was chaired by Laurance Rockefeller. Congressional leaders, especially Senators Henry Jackson and Edmund Muskie, who chaired the Subcommittee on Air and Water Pollution of the Public Works Committee and introduced the Environmental Quality Improvement Act of 1969, and Representatives John Dingell and Emilio Daddario, held hearings on the need to protect the environment and introduced far-reaching legislation—the National Environmental Policy Act of 1969 (NEPA), the Clean Air Act (1970), and the Clean Water Act Amendments of 1972 (usually referred to as the Clean Water Act)—that fundamentally reshaped American environmental policy.[30]

The 1960s was also the decade when both the federal and state governments embraced the open space movement perhaps most closely identified with William H. Whyte. Whyte, who despaired at the suburban sprawl that was disfiguring the Chester County, Pennsylvania, of his youth, wrote a series of influential articles that decried the vanishing American countryside. In 1960 New York State initiated a $75 million program to help local governments acquire open space, and several other states followed suit. Secretary of the Interior Stewart Udall stated that the greatest challenge he faced was "to hold open spaces against the sprawl of suburbia." Across the nation, spending for park and open space acquisition rose significantly during these years.[31]

Equally important, and perhaps essential to the passage of the clean air and water acts, was the popular outpouring of support nationwide for the first Earth Day, held on April 22, 1970. In New York City, an estimated 250,000 people thronged Fifth Avenue from Fourteenth to Fifty-Ninth Streets, while an estimated 100,000 others gathered at Union Square and listened to speeches by a group of luminaries including the composer and conductor Leonard Bernstein, and, on the stage with him, a grave-digger who headed the Hudson River Fishermen's Association, Richie Garrett. Garrett told the crowd that the fight to save the Hudson was the most important undertaking in his life and asserted that "clean water and clean air and a clean earth is the most important issue of all. If we lose our rivers, the other social problems will be dwarfed," he stated, because our nation would collectively "drown in garbage up to our eyeballs." Residents of other cities held smaller but important festivals that first day, which collectively made environmentalism a powerful cause.[32]

What role the Storm King case played in this legislative agenda and the popular embrace of environmentalism is difficult to determine precisely. Although key elements of the Storm King I decision became the heart of NEPA, scholars, lawyers, and activists have differed in their assessment of its significance. Most writers who have analyzed the congressional debates about the evolution of NEPA followed the lead of Lynton Keith Caldwell, a consultant to the Committee on Interior and Insular Affairs, chaired by Senator Jackson, who basically ignored the significance of Scenic Hudson I in constructing its history. Caldwell, who wrote his book *The National Environmental Policy Act* (1998) with financial support from the Henry M. Jackson Foundation, and who dedicated the book to Jackson for his "foresight and statesmanship," simply doesn't mention the Storm King case as important in the development of NEPA. Neither have other policy scholars, including Daniel L. Mandelker, Matthew J. Lindstrom, and Zachary A. Smith. Caldwell attributed the enactment of NEPA to Jackson's political skill as a senator and minimized the role that Muskie, in particular, played in the development of environmental legislation.[33]

Caldwell also claims credit for the inclusion of the required environmental impact statement in section 102 of NEPA. Leon Billings, a longtime member of Muskie's staff, disagrees. He recalls that Jackson favored language that would have required a "finding" but that Muskie insisted on an "environmental impact statement." In tense negotiations with William

Van Ness, Jackson's counsel on the Interior and Insular Affairs Committee, and also with Jackson himself, Billings carried the day, and NEPA as enacted included the provision for an environmental impact statement that explains what resources would be affected by the proposed action, irreversible loss of resources that would result, and alternatives to the proposed action, as well as provided for public participation in the process of evaluating the conclusions of the statement. Billings believes that the environmental impact statement requirement grew out of Muskie's concern that Jackson's version of NEPA was "an attempt to get around Scenic Hudson," though the published record of numerous congressional committees fails to include any mention of the 1965 Scenic Hudson decision. This is not dispositive: NEPA was rushed through Congress late in the legislative session. The House of Representatives approved the conference version of the bill on December 22, 1969, two days after the Senate adopted the measure and the day before it adjourned.[34]

If policy historians have minimized Scenic Hudson's importance to NEPA, the attorneys who litigated the case have not. Albert K. Butzel, who was a key member of the team of litigators for the Scenic Hudson Preservation Conference, has asserted that the Scenic Hudson I decision "led directly to the National Environmental Policy Act, which was signed into law on January 1, 1970. This was manifest in the dual requirements that federal agencies evaluate the impacts of actions they were proposing or asked to approve in environmental impact statements and the correlative obligation to identify reasonable alternatives to those actions." Similarly, David Sive, attorney for the Sierra Club in the Storm King case, has argued that "the *Scenic Hudson I* opinion [was] in many respects the precursor of the National Environmental Policy Act." Butzel and Sive are two of the pioneers in the emergence of modern environmental law, and while they were not involved in the deliberations that resulted in the final shape of NEPA, their argument comes from the front lines of the courtroom. Perhaps most important, Judge James L. Oakes, in his dissenting opinion in Scenic Hudson II (1971), drew a direct link between Scenic Hudson I and NEPA: "In a very real sense this Act [NEPA] is a legislative response to and embodiment of the far-sighted and significant *Scenic Hudson* decision of this court."[35]

Perhaps none have been more insistent about the importance of Scenic Hudson I on the adoption of NEPA than John Cronin and Robert F.

Kennedy Jr. In *The Riverkeepers*, their passionate account of citizen activism in defending the Hudson River, the authors assert that the Scenic Hudson decision "required the FPC to perform a full environmental review of the Storm King project, the first full environmental impact statement ever. In 1969, Congress codified the Storm King decision in the most important piece of environmental legislation in history," the National Environmental Policy Act. Unfortunately, the authors provide no evidence to support this claim.[36]

In the absence of a full legislative record of congressional deliberations that resulted in NEPA, it is impossible to determine with certainty the significance of the battle over Storm King Mountain in the emergence of American environmental policy. The similarities between the act as adopted and the 1965 judicial ruling in Scenic Hudson I suggest a strong connection, though the legislative record is inconclusive. But there is no doubt that *Scenic Hudson Preservation Conference v. FPC* revolutionized environmental law.

2

POLITICS AND THE RIVER

Scenic Hudson's defense of Storm King Mountain was the opening battle over the future of the Hudson River Valley and, indeed, the future of American environmentalism. Storm King would spark a wide range of environmental concerns in succeeding years, and led many citizens to perceive that New York State was complicit in, or at least not doing enough to prevent, the pollution and development that were harming a cherished landscape. Fred Smith, a Rockefeller family adviser who chaired the advisory committee of the Hudson River Valley Commission, believed that the "widespread compulsion to do something constructive without delay about preserving and restoring the Hudson River environment" was the direct result of outrage over Con Ed's proposed pumped-storage power plant on Storm King Mountain.[1]

Protecting and restoring the ecology of the Hudson River would prove to be a long, difficult struggle, as the fate of the river and its environs hung in the balance. It also became a political struggle that involved the federal and state governments and environmental groups across the nation. New

York's governor, Nelson Aldrich Rockefeller, was inevitably drawn into what became the battle for the future of the Hudson River Valley, and in this he ran into the opposition of Stewart R. Udall, U.S. secretary of the interior, who thought that only federal intervention could help correct New York's shoddy record of dealing with pollution. Rockefeller was in some respects a visionary who saw a bright future for the river and its communities; in other ways he was fighting a rearguard action against Udall and fellow environmentalists.

In October 1964 Udall sent shock waves throughout the Hudson Valley when, during a visit to New York, he described the river as "an open sewer." Pollution flowed into the river from overwhelmed sewage treatment plants, factory pipes and dumping, urban runoff, farms, and scattered residences with on-site septic systems or that discharged human waste directly into the waterway. Calling for the nation to "rediscover our rivers," he spoke of the need for new policies and actions to "see if paradise can be regained." Udall specifically endorsed a plan prepared by two Columbia University professors, Percival Goodman and Alexander Kouzmanoff, who had completed a study—paid for by Richard L. Ottinger—titled "Breakthrough to the Hudson River." The study called for a new approach to planning for communities on the east bank of the Hudson, one that would reconnect residents with their river. It advocated the adoption of much stronger zoning regulations to control the development taking place along the river. Local governance in the valley was fragmented among villages, townships, and cities, which, in their competition for tax dollars, welcomed new construction that at times was detrimental to the well-being of the river and its residents. Goodman and Kouzmanoff advocated the channeling of residential development into new towns that would provide for work, residence, and recreation, and the rejuvenation of older cities. Udall's statement, and the *New York Times*'s presentation of the overall scope of the planning study, pointed to the need for immediate and effective action to control the pollution that was despoiling the river and the development that was ruining the adjacent landscape.[2]

One person who knew the river well and really didn't need Udall's prompting to act was Ottinger. On November 7, 1964, four days after his election to the House of Representatives, Ottinger announced his opposition to the Storm King plant. On January 18, 1965, the Democratic congressman from Westchester County made the Hudson River his cause. A devoted conservationist, Ottinger introduced a bill in Congress (H.R. 3012) to create a Hudson Highlands National Scenic Riverway. He envisioned the act as "part of a new conservation effort—an effort not only to protect and develop old resources but create new ones—not only to save our wilderness areas, but preserve the green spaces and scenic river valleys near our metropolitan areas." The region covered in the proposed law would extend from Yonkers to Beacon on the east bank and from the New Jersey state line to Newburgh on the west, and would include oversight of land extending for a mile east and west from the river's banks.[3]

The need for the act was obvious, Ottinger stated: communities along the Hudson "daily dump millions of pounds of raw sewage into the river in a continuing monument to bad planning over the past 100 years. Shellfish are already gone, oysters disappeared generations ago, the shad are diminishing and the whole striped bass fishing industry is threatened." While the bill emphasized the need for much stronger planning and zoning, it also empowered the secretary of the interior to "preserve areas of scenic, historic, and recreational value, to assist in the abatement of water pollution and the protection of pure water, and to rehabilitate blighted and decaying areas." The secretary of the interior was charged with the responsibility to "preserve, administer, and provide for the public use and enjoyment of the riverway." This included the "authority to enjoin individuals, corporations, partnerships and trusts; municipalities and agencies of the State and Federal government from condemnation, purchase or transfer of land or from timbering, excavation or construction on land." If the state or local governments were unwilling or unable to uphold the purposes of the act, the secretary was authorized to acquire conservation easements to protect the land in question and spend up to $20 million to purchase as much as five thousand acres for recreational use or to protect scenic areas. With a clear eye on Con Ed's proposed pumped-storage power plant at Storm King Mountain, the Ottinger bill would restrict the authority of the Federal Power Commission in licensing utility plants along the scenic riverway unless the secretary of the interior gave "express approval" of the project.[4]

The Ottinger bill was a powerful condemnation of New York State's stewardship of the Hudson. It was, in many respects, a legislative response to Udall's characterization of the river as a sewer. In subsequent testimony the congressman added, "Our potentially most beautiful rivers, like the Hudson, are open sewers, their banks littered with garbage and debris." He believed that only the federal government would ensure that the state and local governments take the steps necessary to improve water quality and the environment along the Hudson's banks. New York senators Jacob K. Javits and Robert F. Kennedy Jr. introduced similar legislation in that chamber. In March, Manhattan representative William F. Ryan announced plans to amend the Ottinger bill to extend the area it embraced to the southern tip of Manhattan Island and to include the New Jersey shore as well, and within months several similar bills were thrown into the legislative hopper.[5]

The Ottinger bill provoked the swift opposition of New York's powerful Republican governor, Nelson Rockefeller. On March 20, 1965, the governor announced the appointment of a temporary Hudson River Valley Commission and charged it "to develop plans and recommendations for the best protection and conservation of the resources of the Hudson River and its present and future use and enjoyment." In designating these responsibilities to the temporary commission, Rockefeller was trying to strike a balance between the groundswell of voices urging prompt and effective action in behalf of the river and land development regulations, especially planning and zoning, which are jealously guarded local prerogatives. Indeed, elected officials, especially in Rockland and Orange Counties, were wary of the commission and feared that it would interfere with local governance. As Rockefeller envisioned it, the commission would develop an "action program" to enhance the "recreational, industrial, historic, scenic, commercial, cultural, residential, and aesthetic" benefits of the river for present and future generations, but it would lead by example, by suasion, and would not have the power to enforce its rulings. Rockefeller appointed his brother, the widely admired conservationist Laurance, as chairman of the commission, and Conrad L. Wirth, formerly the director of the National Park Service, as its executive director. But as an unsigned, undated memorandum made clear, "the real renaissance of the river will result from cooperation by the municipalities that have—and should have—control over their own river fronts. The Federal Government cannot successfully eliminate zoning as a municipal prerogative any more than the State can." Another unsigned and undated document acknowledged that protecting the Hudson Valley "would be easier if there were a power which could decree land to be acquired or valley-wide zoning to be established," but conceded that "the practical and political realities of the matter are such that a supergovernment cannot and should not be created." As the federal study *Focus on the Hudson* (1966) noted, most local governments were "strongly 'Home Rule' motivated, with a determination to go it alone in controlling and using the land and water resources of the river."[6]

This was Rockefeller's dilemma: how to respond promptly and persuasively to a growing demand for action to protect the Hudson River Valley, yet to do so in a way that respected the powers of local governance. When he appointed the temporary commission, his brother Laurance apparently asked the white-shoe law firm Milbank Tweed Hadley & McCloy to recommend a framework for the commission he envisioned. The firm's task was "to consider a plan of organization for a new Hudson River Valley Commission which will be charged with administering and developing the scenic, historic, commercial, recreational and water resources of the Hudson River." The Milbank Tweed report acknowledged that "the Commission is intended to administer a comprehensive plan for the future use of the entire River" and as a result recommended "that it will be an authority with final control over all activities involving the River and its watershed area." That is, the Milbank Tweed attorneys believed that the commission should have real power, including the ability to veto proposed projects. If local governments, corporations, or individuals proposed projects it deemed harmful, it would be able "to enjoin any proposed use or building along the River which in the judgment of the Commission would be contrary to the purposes of the Compact or which would interfere with the implementation of established or pending plans." The commission Milbank Tweed envisioned would also have the power to purchase and control land, condemn land by eminent domain, sue, and finance its operations through the issuance of bonds, among other powers.[7]

The Milbank Tweed memorandum suggested a Hudson River Valley Commission very different from the agency Rockefeller had in mind. The governor surely hoped that the Hudson River Valley Commission would convince voters that the Ottinger bill was unnecessary, stave off federal intervention in what he considered New York's affairs, insulate him against environmentalists' outrage over his support of the Storm King power plant, and validate his family's reputation as the nation's leading conservationists, but of course without upsetting the status quo. If so, he was wrong. Scenic Hudson's chairman, Leo G. Rothschild, denounced the governor's plans for the Hudson River Valley Commission as "too little and too late." Although he applauded the commission as "a great moral victory for the determined conservationists who carried the fight to save the Hudson River Gorge from being converted into an industrial canal in the face of continued official disinterest," Rothschild instead supported a federal role in determining the future of the valley. The Ottinger bill, he asserted, would make it "more likely that the Interior Department will take over significant lands for river conservation purposes." Laurance Rockefeller came to his brother's defense, as he had done when the governor announced his support of Con Ed's power plant on Storm King Mountain. He expressed hope that the Ottinger bill would be "held in abeyance" to give the state the opportunity to plan the river's future. He also announced that the State Council of Parks, which he chaired, had made a preliminary study of the lower Hudson Valley and recommended the acquisition of twenty-five thousand acres for park use.[8]

As the battle over the future of the Hudson intensified, Senator R. Watson Pomeroy, chair of the state's Joint Legislative Committee on Natural Resources, introduced a bill to create a Lower Hudson River Valley Heritage Commission. Its purpose was "to preserve, protect, conserve, enhance, develop and promote the unique natural scenic beauty and to promote the study of its history, natural science and lore and to promote tourism and control the development of the Hudson River and its valley adjacent thereto." The Joint Legislative Committee, which opposed construction of Con Ed's power plant at Storm King Mountain, wanted the Heritage Commission to recommend areas valuable for their scenic beauty for acquisition by the state. The commission would have the power to designate "green belt areas" that would "preserve existing conditions or natural beauty and resources and to provide for or recommend restoration of blighted areas." The committee's report also called for a careful study of the historic resources of the Hudson River Valley and encouraged local governments, corporations, and individuals to reduce or eliminate discharges of pollution into the river. The commission would have the responsibility of approving any construction in an area designated as significant for its natural beauty or resources.[9]

Governor Rockefeller must have felt buffeted by bills introduced at the federal level by a liberal Democrat (Ottinger) and on the state level by a fellow Republican (Pomeroy). He frequently argued that 95 percent of the Hudson's course, from Lake Tear of the Clouds in the Adirondacks to the Atlantic, was entirely within New York, as was its major tributary, the Mohawk River. But as the *New York Times* reported, Rockefeller's solution, appointment of the temporary Hudson River Valley Commission, which was charged with planning and advising local governments but had no enforcement power, was a blatant attempt to "head off Federal intervention" in the river. Correspondence in the Laurance S. Rockefeller Papers confirms the *Times*'s interpretation. Several of the governor's close aides, including Henry L. Diamond and Fred Smith, perceived Ottinger's efforts as an affront to the governor and feared that Senator Kennedy, who along with Senator Javits had introduced the companion to the Hudson River National Scenic Riverway bill in the Senate, would be a "stooge" for the conservationists, who might well portray Rockefeller's appointment of the Hudson River Valley Commission as "a hurry-up, no federal action, rape-of-the-Hudson plot." At a staff meeting on November 3, 1965, those present instructed the governor's counsel to draft a statement for the governor's signature demonstrating that much of what Ottinger proposed in the Scenic Riverway bill was "completely 'Impossible.' "[10]

In the face of mounting criticism, on June 5, 1965, Rockefeller introduced his own plan for protecting the Hudson, a bill to establish a Hudson River Valley Scenic and Historic Corridor. In announcing this bill, the governor urged its prompt adoption by the legislature because "mounting public needs and pressures dictate that we should lose no time, and because of continuing threats on the part of the federal government to move into the state and take over, as their own, important elements of this remarkable area, in the mistaken belief that we do not desire or know how to protect and preserve it." The state legislature did indeed move quickly: the Senate approved the Historic Corridor bill unanimously on June 22, as did the Assembly, again unanimously, on June 28, the day Rockefeller signed it into law. This corridor, which would extend from the southern end of the Adirondack Forest Preserve to the Verrazano Narrows Bridge, was vastly larger than the area included in the Ottinger bill. As was true of the Ottinger bill, it would embrace an area extending a mile inland from the river's banks. In announcing this bill, Rockefeller called the Hudson Valley "an integral part of our heritage" and advocated legislative measures that would save "irreplaceable wilderness." He also charged the Hudson River Valley Commission to make a careful study of the corridor during the summer and "make detailed recommendations to me and the Legislature concerning practical ways to carry out the objects stated." The Rockefeller bill (chapter 560, Laws of New York, 1965) stated that the Hudson "links the greatest variety of scenic, historic and cultural resources to be found perhaps anywhere in the country" and asserted that the "orderly protection and use of this corridor is a matter of urgent and deeply felt concern to the people of this state." The act authorized the Hudson River Valley Commission to "make a detailed land use analysis, including a survey of the scenic, historic and cultural resources of the Hudson River Valley," and to report, by February 1, 1966, a practical program for protecting the river and its resources. The implementation of the corridor act would be advisory, as the Hudson River Valley Commission had no enforcement power.[11]

Within a week, Rockefeller announced the appointment of thirty-seven individuals—a mix of leaders in industry, conservation, and education circles, as well a few public officials and private citizens—as an advisory committee to the Hudson River Valley Commission. But the commission was obviously intended to thwart Ottinger and Udall. As an unsigned memorandum demonstrates, the alternative to the commission was "that the State would be saddled with one of the twenty or more proposals now before Congress" that would place the river "under federal jurisdiction." The river's future would be in the hands of Washington bureaucrats, not the "people directly interested in and familiar with the needs and values of the Valley." As Fred Smith wrote Laurance Rockefeller, this argument "will certainly irritate Ottinger and Udall," but he believed it was essential from the state's, and the governor's, perspective.[12]

The Hudson River Valley Commission was Rockefeller's response to the unique demands of the time. The commission had two principal responsibilities—to prepare a comprehensive plan for the valley, and to review projects by government, business, or private individuals that might adversely affect the river and adjacent lands. In carrying out each of these tasks the commission's ability was severely compromised. It could indeed create a regional plan, even a visionary one, and certainly Conrad Wirth's goal was laudable: apparently without thinking of the Tennessee Valley Authority as precedent, he told the commission that "this is the first time a complete, comprehensive plan has been attempted of a large geographic section of the United States," though he insisted that the plan should be a state project, with assistance provided by appropriate federal agencies. But even if the planners produced a document that was indeed visionary, the commission had to rely on local governments to implement it. The commission could review development projects to assess their impact on the scenic, cultural, or historic resources of the Hudson, but it did not have the authority to veto a project that it concluded would have negative consequences for the valley. As Rockefeller put it, the commission he created was "one that will have considerable influence but no power to dictate." In deliberations to create a permanent Hudson River Valley Commission, Bruce Howlett conceded that the permanent commission would have "advisory and coordinative powers," but that "no direct controls or final authority are vested in the Commission. To achieve its goals, it must rely on stature and prestige, and on existing governmental agencies to secure concrete effect to its objectives."[13]

The commissioners Rockefeller appointed did indeed confer status and prestige. In addition to his brother Laurance as chair, its members included Ambassador W. Averell Harriman, Marian Sulzberger Heiskell of the *New York Times*, Albany banker and civic leader Frank Wells Mc-Cabe, State Senator R. Watson Pomeroy, Vassar College president Alan Simpson, journalist Lowell Thomas, IBM chief executive officer Thomas Watson Jr., and the urbanist and planner William H. Whyte, among others. What the governor could not control was how much the commission's prestige would translate into acceptance of the comprehensive plan its staff was preparing or its review process of proposed development projects for their impact on the valley's scenic corridor.[14]

Pursuant to Rockefeller's appointment of the temporary commission, staff prepared drafts of a summary report, which, upon review and approval by the commissioners, was delivered to the governor and the legislature on February 1, 1966. The report began with the arresting sentence, "It is plain enough that the Valley is scarred." The Hudson was terribly polluted, its bluffs and mountains were being quarried, old riverfronts were in derelict condition, and the proliferation of billboards and sprawling suburbs was defacing the countryside. The report outlined a program

that the commissioners believed would protect the scenic and historic resources of the valley while accommodating commercial, industrial, and
residential growth. Providing for economic development was "vital" but
had to be "shaped so that it will enhance the beauty of this great Valley,
rather than destroy it."[15]

The report then presented its significant recommendations. First was
protection of scenic and recreation areas: the report advocated creation
of a $100 million Hudson River Fund ($50 million from the federal government, the remainder from state and private-sector sources) to acquire
150 sites totaling roughly one hundred thousand acres, with the highest
priority in the Palisades-Highlands part of the valley, closest to New York
City, where development pressures were greatest. An important corollary
was a program of conservation easement acquisition or donation to protect privately owned land. The commission recommended a program of
"cooperative zoning," similar to one adopted in the Lake George area
that became an important part of a broader scenic preservation effort
there, especially in maintaining farmland and protecting the grounds of
institutions. Providing residents access to the river's banks was important,
and the report called on the state and local governments to take steps to
provide much greater access, even to privately owned land, as well as the
development of commercial enterprises such as marinas. Walkways and
scenic roadsides were also part of the plan, which called for transforming
a thirty-two-mile stretch of the old Croton Aqueduct into a linear park,
as well as the control of billboards that were ruining the landscape and
better landscaping and development of roadways. The list goes on: an
automobile tour way connecting significant scenic, historic, and cultural
sites in the valley; a visual corridor that extended the authority of the
commission to all land visible from the river; establishment of a New York
State Historic Trust and creation of a state system of historic landmarks
and parks; consolidation of public land in the Adirondack and Catskill
parks; and cluster development instead of large-lot suburban sprawl. The
report also advocated a partnership between the federal government and
the states of New York and New Jersey in determining the future of the
Hudson River Valley. Governor Rockefeller praised the commission's report and the program it detailed "for the enhancement and preservation
of this historic valley."[16]

The temporary commission, its staff, and consultants undertook an impressive series of studies—on historic resources of the Hudson, archaeological sites, population, fish and wildlife, biological resources of the river, water resources, and industrial trends. Most important, its members realized that only a permanent commission could carry on its work of addressing the serious problems confronting the Hudson, and its final recommendation was for the establishment of such a body. Rockefeller pledged his support for legislation creating the federal-interstate compact the commission recommended, which he called "a very constructive and positive approach to insure permanent cooperative action between all levels of government." There was some opposition to a permanent commission. Gordon K. Cameron, the chairman of the Mid-Hudson Municipal Association, wrote State Senator Whitney North Seymour Jr. and urged him not to support the bill that would create the permanent commission. Cameron asserted that the commission's preliminary report was "totally out of balance in favor of scenery and recreation to what we feel is the detriment of any present or future commercial or industrial development of this historic river corridor" and that the bill under consideration was "a threat to the future of the people of this Valley."[17]

The state legislature nevertheless responded promptly to the governor's initiative and created a permanent commission through chapter 345, Laws of the State of New York, 1966. The preamble to the act described the Hudson as "one of America's proudest assets and most important scenic, historic and recreational riverways." Legislators charged the permanent commission "to encourage the preservation, enhancement and development of the scenic, historic and recreational and natural resources of the Hudson River valley, and to encourage the full development of the commercial, industrial, agricultural, residential and other resources which are vital to the continued progress" of the valley. The state act envisioned the compact being implemented by a commission of fifteen members, nine appointed by the governor of the state of New York, three by the governor of New Jersey, and three by the secretary of the interior. Its jurisdiction would cover all land within a mile of the river's banks and, if visible from the river, within two miles of its banks. The commission was specifically charged to complete a comprehensive plan for the river basin and to review plans for development to ensure that those projects would not have an adverse impact on the scenic, cultural, and historic resources of the Hudson. Unfortunately, the legislation gave the commission only fifteen days for a preliminary review and an additional thirty days for a final review of projects; but even if the commission concluded that a project under review would have an "unreasonably adverse effect" on the valley, it did not have the authority to stop it. In the memorandum accompanying his signing of the law, Rockefeller wrote: "This bill establishes a new opportunity to enhance and preserve the scenic and natural resources of the Hudson River valley and, at the same time, to encourage the full development of the vital commercial and industrial resources of the valley." That is, instead of being focused primarily on the preservation of the Hudson River basin's scenic and historic resources, the permanent commission was also charged with promoting economic development, a significant shift in focus from what conservationists advocated and, indeed, from the governor's Hudson River Corridor Act. The expectation was that the commission would have three years to prepare a comprehensive plan for the Hudson Valley and another two years for its implementation.[18]

Ottinger welcomed the creation of the Hudson River Valley Commission. He wrote Rockefeller that he sincerely hoped "we can get together on a joint federal-state program for the Hudson that will result in truly effective action." In a letter to Wirth he praised the "many novel and creative approaches in the report that I am sure will redound to the benefit of riverway residents throughout the country." But Ottinger was deeply concerned that the Hudson River Valley Commission Rockefeller proposed did not have the authority to do its job effectively. As he wrote Interior Secretary Udall, "The vital need now is for effective implementing legislation. The chief shortcoming of the [Hudson River Valley Commission] report is the lack of teeth in the powers it proposes to check future abuses by private interests and public agencies." He recognized, as did Udall, that the Hudson could not effectively be protected "by advisory recommendations of the proposed commission." He wanted the commission to have powers like those of the Delaware River Basin Commission, which could veto any uses it considered potentially detrimental to the river—and that veto was binding on all federal agencies.[19]

While Rockefeller was maneuvering to make the future of the Hudson River a state responsibility, Udall's Department of the Interior, through its Bureau of Outdoor Recreation, issued a report, *Focus on the Hudson:*

Evaluations of Proposals and Alternatives. The report predictably decried the pollution of the river and the incompatible development that was scarring its banks. It criticized the state as well as local governments because zoning "has not prevented conglomerate development along the river because it came too late and has never been completely enforced." As a result of inadequate land-use regulations, the report concluded, "substantial portions of the shoreline, including areas with high scenic and recreation values, were unwisely developed or exploited in the name of progress." The recommendations that *Focus on the Hudson* presented were far-reaching: establishment of a federal-interstate compact to create a permanent Hudson River Valley Commission, with equal representation of the federal government and the states of New York and New Jersey (not the ratio Rockefeller favored), with authority to review "all projects that would have a substantial impact on the basin and disapprove those not in accord with a comprehensive plan"; that restoration of the riverfront have highest priority, with special emphasis on public access and the creation of provisions for leisure activities; and that the upper Hudson be included in the wild rivers program then before Congress. The report then bluntly stated that the Storm King pumped-storage plant and the east bank Hudson River Expressway, which Rockefeller also championed, should not be built. Upon releasing the report Udall derided Rockefeller's Hudson River Valley Commission as weak and "inequitable." The governor must have been furious at the Department of the Interior's intervention in what he considered New York's affairs.[20]

Indeed, Rockefeller responded intemperately: he privately expressed concern that *Focus on the Hudson* "would limit commercial activity and attempt to control power projects" and expressed his belief that Udall was being pressured by Kennedy and Ottinger to resist his initiative. In a letter to Udall he rejected out of hand the recommendation that New York, New Jersey, and the federal government have equal representation on the compact commission. And he was adamant that the commission not have the power to "usurp essential local and State responsibilities." *Focus on the Hudson*, the governor stated, "would give the commission a veto over any project in the valley, and would give the commission the power to tax and the power to overturn local zoning laws, with all these powers to be exercised throughout the entire Hudson Valley basin." Rockefeller also defended the controversial Hudson River Expressway, which would have hugged the shoreline between Tarrytown and Croton and which, he asserted, would make the river accessible to residents. To Udall's criticism as reported in the *New York Times* the previous day, the governor derided *Focus on the Hudson* as consisting of "shallow, self-serving and partisan conclusions." Rockefeller then instructed the Hudson River Valley Commission to renew its efforts to develop a partnership with the federal government and New Jersey. While he did not state this explicitly in his letter to Udall, Rockefeller clearly meant a partnership on his terms, not one that gave equal weight to New Jersey and the federal government.[21]

As federal and state officials wrestled, often at cross purposes, to find the best way to end pollution and protect the Hudson, and particularly as he recognized that the Hudson River Valley Commission did not have the powers necessary to accomplish what he believed needed to be done, Ottinger turned to the idea of a federal-interstate compact. On March 10, 1966, he introduced a bill to create a Hudson River Basin Compact that would involve the two states and the federal government in determining the river's future (H.R. 13508). Based on the model of the Palisades Interstate Park Commission, the compact Ottinger envisioned would consist of three commissioners, two appointed respectively by the governors of New York and New Jersey, the third by the secretary of the interior. This bill established a three-year time frame in which the two state legislatures and the Congress would adopt identical legislation establishing the commission on a permanent basis. Rockefeller strenuously objected, once again insisting that New York have a majority of representatives on the commission, as did his brother Laurance, who also wanted New York to have a predominant role in the compact commission. Laurance did urge the governor to "take leadership in establishing an interstate-federal commission" on the Hudson River Valley, and expressed his belief that with the creation of the Hudson River Valley Commission "the state regained leadership in this situation." He urged his brother to "follow up strongly in this role." Unlike Ottinger's national scenic riverway bill, which was stalled in Congress, the compact bill quickly gained legislative approval and was signed into law by President Johnson. Ottinger's bill directed the secretary of the interior of cooperate with New York and New Jersey "on a program to develop, preserve, and restore the resources of the Hudson River and its shores." The law specifically called for the abatement of pollution, protection of the scenic beauty of the riverway, the preservation of historic and archaeological sites, and protection of the valley's wildlife. It also placed a stay on potentially adverse federal actions until the compact had been ratified by the states and Congress. According to the *New York Times*, the new law made Interior Secretary Udall "a virtual foster parent of the valley" while the two states and Congress worked on legislation to make the commission permanent.[22]

In explaining the legislation's intent, Ottinger insisted that the compact must "provide two absolutely essential elements—a comprehensive plan and effective means of enforcing that plan." In a letter of support for the bill, Udall likewise emphasized the importance of developing a comprehensive plan for the Hudson Valley and giving the agency responsible for developing and implementing it "all authority necessary to assure that the plan is not impaired and is carried out in the best manner possible." To do otherwise, he warned, "would be to condemn such an agency to the role of a passive onlooker." Other federal officials were less enthusiastic about the bill. Maurice R. Dunie, acting general counsel for the Department of Commerce, objected to a three-year "freeze" on highway projects, while Lee C. White, chairman of the Federal Power Commission, expressed his belief that giving the secretary of the interior veto power over the licensing of power plants in the Hudson Valley would undermine the commission's authority under the Federal Power Act.[23]

The main obstacle to an effective compact, Ottinger noted, was Rockefeller's resistance to a commission with real power. As he stated in the House of Representatives, both a comprehensive plan and an effective enforcement mechanism were "vital requirements lacking in legislation passed by New York State to authorize such a compact." The New York law envisioned a fifteen-member commission, with nine members appointed by the state's governor, effectively giving New York an ironclad majority of votes in the commission, which was surely unacceptable to New Jersey governor Richard Hughes as well as to Udall. Congressman John G. Dow, a Democrat who represented Rockland and Orange Counties, expressed regret that "the State of New York has chosen to go its own way for Hudson River preservation, through the medium of what is known as the Hudson River Valley Commission." Dow rued that as administered by the Hudson River Valley Commission, New York's law would have "few enforcement provisions." In supporting the Ottinger bill, the *New York Times* pointed out that it "would provide the stronger

legal safeguards required if the spoliation of the Hudson is to be halted."
The steps outlined in the final report of the temporary Hudson River Valley Commission would not be achieved "without the push of a strong
enforcement agency," which the Ottinger bill provided and would "thus
help preserve the river's grandeur against the depredations of the communities and industrial enterprises along its banks."[24]

The strong difference between Rockefeller's efforts and the Ottinger
bill (as well as a companion measure introduced in the Senate by Robert Kennedy) led to political name-calling rather than effective action.
Rockefeller sent a letter to President Johnson conveying a copy of his
Hudson River bill and asking for the president's "sympathetic attention."
He also denounced the Ottinger and Kennedy bills: if enacted, he wrote,
they "would in effect leave the valley in a state of suspended animation,"
which would be harmful to residents of the valley and all New Yorkers. When Rockefeller's letter became public, Ottinger was outraged. "We
thought we had taken the river out of politics," he stated. "By intervening
privately with the President this way, I think the Governor has damaged
immeasurably the cause of doing something for the river."[25]

The Hudson River Valley Commission began negotiations with the
federal government and New Jersey over the proposed compact. Alexander Aldrich, then the executive director of the commission, reported that
Rockefeller and Udall had met in early 1968 and "were close to agreement
on many points." Rockefeller's staff also met with Hughes's counsel "to
discuss the compact and particularly the draft" legislation submitted to
New Jersey. But even as negotiations continued, some Rockefeller appoin-
tees on the Hudson River Valley Commission expressed skepticism about
the compact. Charles T. Lanigan, for example, doubted "whether federal
participation in the compact would be in the best interests of the State."
The commission itself sent a letter to the governor stating that "Association with New Jersey and the Federal Government is of dubious value to
New York State or the Hudson Valley."[26]

Given Rockefeller's insistence on what Udall considered New York's
disproportionate representation on the compact commission, as well as
his resistance to a commission that would have real authority, the compact
was doomed, and the three-year window to create a permanent commission expired without the identical enabling legislation of the two states
and Congress that would have made it permanent. As the *Times* reported,

with the expiration of the compact the Hudson lost a safeguard. Russell Train, then under secretary of the interior, persuaded a sympathetic congressman to introduce a bill providing for a three-year renewal to the expired compact act. When that bill went nowhere, the *Times* published an editorial contending that under the compact "the Secretary's review power had a significant effect in preserving the environmental quality of the Hudson Riverway."[27]

The debate over the future of the Hudson River pitted conservationist and environmental concerns against home rule, federal intervention against state authority, and in retrospect it is obvious that Rockefeller's political concerns won out over efforts by Ottinger, Udall, and many others who hoped to clean up the river and protect its landscape. This is not to state that people cannot honestly disagree, especially when issues involve difficult choices, such as the relative values of scenic preservation or environmental concerns versus economic development. Surely Udall was as angry at Rockefeller's responses to his efforts as the governor was with his. The evidence in the documentary record, however, suggests, as Ottinger asserted, that it was Rockefeller who politicized the battle over the Hudson River Valley. Rockefeller appointed his brother and closest friend, Laurance, who was the largest individual benefactor of the national park system, to chair the temporary commission, and Wirth, a close associate of Laurance, to direct the commission. When Wirth left to take another Rockefeller position, as head of the New York State Historic Trust, the governor appointed his cousin and former aide Alexander Aldrich as executive director of the Hudson River Valley Commission on December 11, 1966. This patent nepotism must have made it obvious that the commission was a Rockefeller tool to fight Udall and the growing conservation and environmental community increasingly outraged over the state's stewardship of the Hudson River.[28]

Aldrich, predictably, became a staunch defender of the governor's interests. Aldrich, who had been defeated in the Republican primary when he sought a seat in the House of Representatives in the spring of 1966, wrote cousin Nelson that he needed a paying job. The job that he found most appealing was "a position with the Hudson River Valley Commission." The governor obliged, and as its executive director, Aldrich kept his cousin informed of important commission deliberations, and on several occasions he attempted to sway his fellow commissioners to do what the governor wanted. In August 1967 he advised the commission that Georgia-Pacific's proposed location of a gypsum plant in Buchanan, New York, was excellent and would create 250 to 300 jobs (the plant aroused considerable controversy, and Georgia-Pacific determined to look elsewhere in the valley for a suitable site). The following October Aldrich reported on the Storm King case, which the commission had not reviewed, and stated that the commission would take up the case after the FPC had made its decision and before the court's decision, which in all likelihood would have resulted in the commission's ratifying of the FPC's ruling (despite this, there is no evidence that the commission ever formally reviewed the Storm King case, and in his memoir Aldrich conceded that "we never came close to reviewing that proposal"). In June 1968, against Aldrich's recommendation, the commission scheduled a public hearing on the governor's proposed east bank Hudson River Expressway. The following month Aldrich urged the commission to "find favorably" for the governor's high-speed road, and the commission did indeed decide that the highway's benefits would "outweigh any adverse effects it might have." The commission made six suggestions for "improvements that could be made," but none were conditions for approval. Each of these decisions enraged many in the growing environmental community.[29]

Compromised as it was by politics, the Hudson River Valley Commission proved to be an ineffective steward of the valley's environment. It did not have the resources or power to challenge polluters—indeed, much of the cleanup of the waterway would eventually result from a $1 billion bond issue voters approved by a four-to-one margin in a referendum in November 1965, as well as federal funds to combat pollution. The state's bond issue created a fund to make grants to municipalities to pay 60 percent of the cost of constructing primary and secondary sewage treatment plants. When the bond issue passed, Rockefeller announced that New York would have unpolluted waters by 1972. Unfortunately, many municipalities could not afford the remaining 40 percent of the cost, and for some, issuing bonds to pay for treatment plants proved impossible because doing so would have exceeded their debt limits. Moreover, the state and federal aid would not cover the cost of installing sewer drains and pipes, which increased the cost, especially for poor rural communities. As a result, the *New York Times* reported, by 1970 fewer than a third of the major polluters of the Hudson had begun to build such treatment plants. Moreover, the $1 billion bond issue was itself sorely inadequate to clean up the state's riverways. Eliminating pollution in the Hudson, and the rest of the state's lakes and rivers, would be far more expensive, and take far longer, than Rockefeller estimated.[30]

The two principal responsibilities of the Hudson River Valley Commission were the preparation of a comprehensive plan for the valley and the review of all development projects to ensure that they did not have an adverse impact on the landscape. Measured by these responsibilities, the commission proved to be precisely the political cover Rockefeller intended when he appointed the temporary commission rather than becoming an effective advocate for the river's environment and its future. Perhaps because of the difficulties of crafting a comprehensive plan for the valley while respecting local prerogatives, perhaps because of the politics involved, the commission failed in its most important task. It never completed what its principal actors, from Rockefeller and the legislature to Conrad Wirth and other advocates for the commission, asserted was its primary charge, preparing a road map to ensure a better future for the Hudson River Valley. And as the planning process lagged, members of the commission, in the process of reviewing proposals for development along the Hudson, actually thought that each individual decision they were making would become a component of the plan eventually adopted. At its meeting of August 18, 1970, for example, commission counsel told the commissioners that they were "in a sense developing the [comprehensive] plan with each project we review. Although we do not have a plan for the Valley as yet, the present hearing approach may satisfy this reservation." This of course is the exact opposite of how planning is supposed to work: the approval process is supposed to implement the objectives of a plan, not serve as its building blocks. Thus in its most important charge, the Hudson River Valley Commission failed. It did not deliver a comprehensive plan that would guide the preservation of the scenic, historic, and cultural attributes of the Hudson or provide for controlled development along the river while also promoting, as Rockefeller hoped, the economic growth of the region.[31]

The second principal responsibility of the commission was the review of proposed projects within the river's viewshed. This was a really challenging task, especially given Rockefeller's insistence that industrial and commercial development could take place while preserving cherished environmental resources. In the vast majority of cases it reviewed, the commission routinely found that the project in question would not adversely affect the river or its environs. When the commission feared an adverse impact, it scheduled a public hearing in the community where the project was to be located. At the beginning of each public hearing, Aldrich and his successor, Carl J. Mays, invariably stated that the occasion was not an "adversary proceeding." As Aldrich remarked at a hearing in South Glens Falls, "The powers of the Commission are very limited. . . . We're not an enforcement agency. We don't have the authority to say to any project sponsor, 'You can't build here' or 'you can't demolish a certain building.' " All the commission could do was publicize what it anticipated would be the negative consequences of a development and hope that public opinion would influence the project sponsor to modify or abandon the plans. As the commission minutes noted following a public hearing of the proposed Castlecliff subdivision in the town of Stillwater, "it is sometimes necessary, because of a sponsor's reluctance to accept an alternative proposal, to go to a public hearing to gain a favorable public opinion that would engender the appropriate local action."[32]

The records of the Hudson River Valley Commission reveal how ineffective it was in resolving development that it feared was inappropriate. In South Glens Falls, the Sagamore Pulp Corporation proposed using a nine-to-fifteen-acre ravine as a landfill for the waste product from its manufacturing operation, which was making milk cartons. After the hearing the commission found that the project "would tend to impair the scenic and recreational and natural resources of the river." Five days later Aldrich successfully persuaded the commission to approve the project, subject to conditions that he expected would be imposed by the Board of Health. When Sagamore Pulp did not adhere to the revised plan, the commission asked the state attorney general, Louis Lefkowitz, to sue the company, and the Department of Environmental Conservation ordered the company to correct its violations of the state's sanitary code and fined it $3,000. But the damage to what some members of the commission considered a scenic ravine had already been done. The Department of Environmental Conservation's paltry fine would not make the ravine pristine again.[33]

The Chapel Hill homes project was a subdivision of eighty-one single-family homes on lots of one-third to one-half acre in Haverstraw.

Construction had begun prior to the commission's review, which resulted in a determination that the project would have an "adverse or serious impairment of natural, scenic, or historic resources." The commission then requested Lefkowitz to seek an injunction to stop the project and held a public hearing on July 5, 1968. At the hearing local officials challenged the Hudson River Valley Commission's authority, stating that the development met all the requirements of the town's law and had been reviewed by the planning board, other appropriate agencies in the town, and the town's counsel, which resulted in the granting of a permit to build. The town's solicitor, George Cobb, emphasized that Haverstraw had already granted approval for the project, and thus the commission really couldn't do anything to stop the development: "nothing constructive can be done here either in the name of the town of Haverstraw or of the Hudson River Valley Commission to change this subdivision as the approval has already been granted." At the commission's request Lefkowitz did initiate injunctive action, but the commission subsequently asked that he withdraw the filing "when it became apparent that home purchasers would suffer great hardship, and when it also became apparent that the finding would be that the project would not constitute an impairment of resources of the Hudson River Valley."[34]

The ineffectiveness of the commission's review process was also evident in a project in the town of Stillwater, on the west bank of the Hudson near Saratoga. In May 1970 the commission reviewed a subdivision plan already being developed by the Ketcham Construction Corporation. Ketcham had begun to erect twenty-eight prefabricated three-bedroom houses on a seventy-acre site and projected a total of 213 dwelling units in a neighborhood it called Castlecliff, which is southwest of the village center. At a public hearing on August 11, commission staff expressed deep reservations about the plan on environmental grounds and also because they considered it typically suburban and argued that the site should incorporate "wooded areas and right-of-ways" and that the developer should provide "an open space area running all through the site." A week later, when the commissioners discussed the Castlecliff subdivision, they justified the hearing "because of the sponsor's reluctance to accept an alternative proposal," but the Ketcham Construction Corporation went ahead and built the subdivision as planned. The Hudson River Valley Commission simply didn't have the power to stop the project.[35]

In other cases the commission successfully persuaded the Niagara Mohawk Power Company not to build overhead transmission lines that would cross the Hudson, and Orange and Rockland's electric utility to relocate proposed power lines so they would not disfigure a scenic mountain. The commission also was successful in negotiations with Niagara Mohawk when the utility proposed to construct a nuclear power plant in Easton, above the junction of the Mohawk and Hudson Rivers. The location was directly opposite the Saratoga National Historic Park, which led the New York State Historic Trust to oppose the plant because the structures would "mar greatly the inspiring historical significance of this Park." Even in this process, the conflicted mission of the commission was evident: Aldrich told the audience at a public hearing that the commission's responsibility was to promote "economic growth in the Hudson Valley" and emphasized the need for "inexpensive power generation located near the Capital District." At the subsequent meeting of the commission, Aldrich recommended a finding that the adverse effects of the proposal outweighed the benefits, and his fellow commissioners agreed. When the Atomic Energy Commission withdrew its support, Niagara Mohawk mothballed its plans for the nuclear plant, though it retained the land for a possible energy-producing facility in the future.[36]

What is most difficult to determine with certainty is the impact of advice the commission staff gave to developers before a project reached the commission for review. The surviving record, admittedly incomplete, suggests that when the staff reviewed preliminary plans and had concerns, it offered a range of alternatives to the developer that would have achieved a more beneficial result. Some project sponsors welcomed the advice, others ignored it, and still others—many, apparently—never bothered to submit a project for the commission's review. As one Rockefeller adviser noted, the commissioners "intercept only a small fraction of projects which may have a significant effect on the environment or municipal or state costs."[37]

Perhaps the most damning indictment of the Hudson River Valley Commission is that it was not what the river needed most—an energetic agency that had the resources and authority to address the severe pollution of the Hudson and to control development along its banks. Udall was absolutely correct when he described the river as "an open sewer," and Ottinger recognized that only federal intervention, or a federal-state compact, would be able to mitigate the pollution. Instead, as naturalist

Robert H. Boyle noted, Alexander Aldrich, who had been president of the group that successfully preserved Olana, Frederic E. Church's house and 250-acre estate south of the city of Hudson, believed that hiring a curator for the state historic site was the "most pressing problem facing the river." With more than a touch of sarcasm, Boyle wrote that when speaking to the annual meeting of the Hudson River Conservation Society, Aldrich urged members to write their representatives in Albany to budget the funds to hire a curator who could "look into Frederick [*sic*] Church's old checkbooks and papers upstairs at Olana Castle." As a state property, Olana did in fact deserve state funding, but Boyle seethed at the priority Aldrich gave it when pollution was a much greater problem. While other state agencies had more direct responsibility for controlling if not ending pollution, the Hudson River Valley Commission was a bully pulpit Aldrich chose not to use.[38]

This is not a great record of achievement for a commission that was supposed to plan and ensure a better future for the Hudson River Valley. Indeed, several of the commissioners, including Fergus Reid III, the last chairman of the panel, believed that it needed more teeth. It "must have greater power," Reid wrote in 1968. The "time is rapidly approaching when it [the commission] must assert itself more vigorously or begin to see the prestige and good will engendered thus far begin to shrink." He then identified the commission's political challenge as its "ability to thread its way along the narrow ground between the conservationists, Ottinger and the Federal Government on the one hand, and the more silent, but no less potent, local officials on the other." That tenuous balance, he warned, "may not last much longer." In responding to Reid, Rockefeller's counsel Robert Douglass praised the commission as doing "a great job" and remarked that it "should continue to make progress—but slowly." The commission, Douglass warned, should not be "overly ambitious" but should base its actions on what local officials and citizens throughout the Hudson River Valley wanted. Yet Reid recognized, and explained in the commission's 1969 annual report, that the "quality of the environment can no longer be treated as a by-product; it must become the fundamental commitment of society." He wanted to chair a commission that made environmental factors its primary mission.[39]

Toward the end of its brief life the Hudson River Valley Commission had lost its purpose, at least among power brokers in Albany. Its members hoped for new legislation that would expand its powers, but that was not forthcoming. Reid continued to emphasize the importance of the commission, but Rockefeller was content with the limited way in which it operated. In a July 8, 1970, press release, the governor praised the commission's work, which, he asserted, had "led to major changes in a number of proposals that might have impaired the Hudson Valley's natural resources or aesthetic character." Its advice to municipalities and developers "has brought about a broadened understanding of the many factors which must be considered if development is not to compromise the natural heritage of the Hudson Valley." Reid wrote Rockefeller in March 1971, when the legislature was considering a bill that would effectively eliminate the commission, that as an autonomous body, the commission has "the ability to cushion the executive and legislative branches of government from undue public criticism on controversial issues"— about as blatant a statement as possible about the political functions of the commission—and urged Rockefeller to "preserve the integrity of this most successful experiment in state government, namely government by persuasion rather than by fiat," which Reid believed was the commission's most important accomplishment.[40]

In 1971, when the state was facing a fiscal crisis, the commission, which had cost taxpayers approximately $1 million per year, saw its budget cut drastically. The legislature subsequently approved a bill to revamp the workings of the commission, which William H. Whyte described as "dismemberment" rather than "retrenchment and consolidation." Its planning function was transferred to a new agency, the Office of Planning Services, so its principal remaining responsibility was project review. Most of the commission's staff had been transferred to the Office of Planning Services, and as a result it had only eleven employees, only five of whom were capable of reviewing projects for development. As other staff resigned, the number of employees shrank even more. In April 1971 Mays informed the commission that it couldn't spend money and had to vacate its posh offices in Tarrytown. Commissioners were deeply unhappy about the reduced status of the agency: Whyte, for example, argued that the commission could not do its job with such a drastically reduced staff and suggested that "it would be better to abolish the Commission as an entity . . . rather than continue the illusory Commission operation." The commissioners as a body threatened to resign at the end of the year unless its role was strengthened. Rockefeller urged the commissioners to stay on and promised to meet with them at the beginning of 1972, but for all intents and purposes the commission's role had ended. Throughout 1971, Whyte observed, it was "dying a bit at a time." The demise of the Hudson River Valley Commission drew a mixed response from the board of directors of the *Clearwater*, the replica Hudson River sloop. "We are being sold out," the minutes read. "The staff and powers of H.R.V.C. should be greatly expanded, not tremendously diminished." The *Clearwater* directors noted that the commission "sadly neglected the river itself, water quality, and especially the biota," but nevertheless appreciated its focus on the Hudson, even if it was "not always effective or sincere. We cannot afford to lose this tiny plus," as there was no comparable forum for environmental concerns in the state.[41]

Rockefeller proved unwilling or unable to restore the commission to its former role. Perhaps the state's fiscal climate simply wouldn't allow it; perhaps the governor no longer felt he needed the commission; perhaps he had already perceived that his political future lay in Washington, D.C., not in Albany. Clearly, the commission was no longer a priority for the governor. At Laurance Rockefeller's urging, the commission was transferred from Planning Services to the Department of Parks and Recreation. It continued to exist, performing its project review responsibilities, until the legislature finally abolished it in 1980. At that time, the commission had received no funding for five years and was "actually defunct."[42]

The commission was never able to fulfill its mandate—to preserve the scenic, historic, and cultural resources of the Hudson River Valley. Created at the dawn of the modern environmental movement, supposedly in response to public outrage over a severely polluted riverway and the threatened destruction of its noble scenery, the commission was actually an effort to thwart the threat of federal intervention in the protection of the river's resources. Ultimately, at Rockefeller's insistence, the commission lacked the power to achieve what the governor promised, a clean river and intelligent development that gave the river back to its people. As Robert H. Boyle noted, the commission was "a bad joke" and "a puppet of Nelson Rockefeller."[43]

3

Pete Seeger and the *Clearwater*

On April 14, 1970, the Hudson River sloop *Clearwater* left its mooring at the South Street pier in Lower Manhattan and began a journey to the nation's capital, where the ship and its crew would participate in the first Earth Day. As the sloop sailed up the Potomac to testify to the importance of clean water and environmentalism, members of its crew confronted the enormity of the challenges ahead: they discovered that the Potomac was even more polluted than the Hudson. On Earth Day, April 22, 1970, the crew read a "State of the Hudson" report on the banks of the river, and Pete Seeger sang in a concert at the Sylvan Theater, on the grounds of the Washington Monument. Seeger and the crew gave a presentation in the Caucus Room of the Cannon House Office Building that included slides, song, dance, and choral presentations in the effort, as the *Washington Post* put it, "to hammer home the story of a dying river." The *Clearwater* crew then lobbied members of Congress in support of environmental legislation.[1]

In its first voyage from the Hudson to the capital, the *Clearwater* made a simple but powerful statement: that pollution was a scourge on the nation and that citizens mobilized for a cleaner environment were essential to the effort to safeguard our future and that of the earth. The sloop took on symbolic importance to the environmental movement then in its infancy. The *Clearwater* became, in effect, the unofficial flagship for environmental concerns nationwide. As Seeger explained to a *Post* reporter, the *Clearwater*'s cause, and environmentalism in general, had attracted "backers of every shade of political belief." In the years since that visit to the nation's capital, the sloop has been the most effective environmental educator in the Hudson River Valley.[2]

As the battle over Storm King Mountain was taking shape, Seeger had offered to join the fray. As a member of the Almanac Singers and the Weavers, Seeger had helped spark the revival of interest in folk music during the 1950s and 1960s. Toward the end of his life he had become a beloved troubadour of international stature, but even in the early 1960s Seeger was still a controversial figure. In the 1950s he had refused to answer direct questions about his association with the Communist Party in hearings before the House Un-American Activities Committee and was held in contempt of Congress. Seeger was widely denounced as a "red" and blacklisted from television and radio as well as most concert venues throughout the country. In the early 1960s, from where Seeger sat—in the modest log-and-stone house he had built on the southwestern face of Mount Beacon beginning in 1949, Con Ed's pumped-storage power plant on Storm King Mountain would be an eyesore. Worse, it would fundamentally change the Hudson Highlands he loved. Seeger and his spouse Toshi surely decided that they could not tolerate this intrusion on their viewshed, would not see a cherished natural landscape forever destroyed by a power plant. Instead of a pristine mountain, they would look out over a massive electricity-generating facility that would scar Storm King Mountain for all time.[3]

Seeger wanted to prevent that from happening, so he approached Scenic Hudson's board. He wanted to join, and in the spring of 1966 offered to hold a concert in the Hudson Valley to raise money for the cause and preach environmental awareness. At a meeting held at David Sive's

Manhattan law office, members of Scenic Hudson's executive and advisory committees expressed fear that Seeger's long association with leftist causes made it "too dangerous to have Mr. Seeger linked with Scenic Hudson for various reasons: namely, it might alienate some of our large contributors; it might make future hearings difficult if we are questioned by the FPC or Con Ed." Sive tried to counter this fear, suggesting that a "song festival with various other singers" would minimize any association with Seeger's left-wing past. One person, probably Carl Carmer, the conservative chairman of Scenic Hudson's board, was adamantly opposed. Seeger was too associated with left-wing politics, he argued, and would damage Scenic Hudson's standing among conservationists and the power structure in which the organization hoped to work. The committees and ultimately the board agreed: Seeger was not welcome.[4]

Undaunted, Seeger had another idea, one that surely emerged from his decades of folksinging and his long-standing attention to the working people of the country. This new idea also reflected his growing interest in sailing on the Hudson. After reading a book first published in 1908, *The Sloops of the Hudson*, by William E. Verplanck and Moses W. Collyer, Seeger became enchanted with the idea of restoring a historic sloop and returning it to the river. When he realized that no Hudson sloop had survived, Seeger and his friend Vic Schwarz decided to organize a group of people and build a replica of a nineteenth-century Hudson River sloop as a way of getting others to reconnect with the river. While it is tempting to think that the *Clearwater*, as the replica sloop would be called, emerged full-blown in Seeger's mind as a vehicle for a populist environmentalism, that was not the case. A one-and-a-half page typewritten document in the Marist College archives with the penciled notation "Pete's Plan 1966" outlines Seeger's original vision for the sloop. It begins with a brief history of the Hudson River sloop, from its heyday in the eighteenth and nineteenth centuries, when it was the principal means of shipping cargo on the river, through its demise at the hands of steamboats and railroads by the dawn of the twentieth. The document then sketches the plan to build a replica and states that Cyrus Hamlin, a naval architect in Kennebunkport, Maine, has been paid to make an initial design and determine the cost of building the sloop. What is especially significant about this initial vision statement is how different it is from the eventual mission of the *Clearwater*. There is no mention of the pollution in the river, no vision of the sloop becoming a floating classroom teaching environmental lessons, no sense that the sloop and its members might become a powerful force for environmental activism. Instead, Seeger envisioned the sloop organization as having a combined ownership of from four hundred to five hundred people who would make an initial donation "to cover building costs" as well as a yearly assessment for the ship's maintenance. "In return, each member would be entitled to one week's cruise during the season," determined on a first-come basis. The replica sloop would be a communally owned ship that provided its members the opportunity to experience the joy of sailing on the river.[5]

The evolution of the *Clearwater*'s mission occurred quickly. Hudson River Sloop Restoration's articles of incorporation identified it as a historical organization. Vic Schwarz, who together with Seeger founded Hudson River Sloop Restoration (HRSR), announced in late September 1966 that the replica sloop "will be like a Mystic Seaport restoration all wrapped up in one boat," a floating museum of Hudson River history. The *New York Times* described the idea for the sloop as "a living museum" that would visit cities and towns throughout the valley. Two years later, Alexander Saunders Jr., then president of the sloop's board of directors, announced that the organization had raised one-quarter of the funds needed to build the ship and that the construction plans, a fully rigged model, and educational materials on the history and significance of Hudson River sloops would be exhibited at the New York Boat Show. Saunders then reiterated Schwarz's vision, describing the sloop as "a floating Mystic Seaport" museum. "It will stop at each city and town along the Hudson with historical exhibits, serve as a stage for river concerts and provide the occassion [*sic*] for educational and recreational activities tied to the history of each port." Seeger himself later conceded that what became the *Clearwater* was initially "conceived not so much as an environmental vessel as an exercise in historical preservation." There was not yet a statement of what would become the *Clearwater*'s principal mission, environmental education and advocacy. Not until December 1971 did Hudson River Sloop Restoration amend its articles of incorporation to include an emphasis on environmental concerns (the new words are underscored in the original): "To acquaint people with matters relating to our cultural heritage *and the conditions of our waterways*; and to maintain and promote interest in the history, *ecology and condition* of the Hudson River and its tributaries." The amended articles also added ecological research to HRSR's mission and committed the organization to striving for "*the improvement of the present condition of such waterways.*"[6]

This evolution in Seeger's and the *Clearwater* board's vision for the replica sloop is about more than nomenclature. It points to fundamental differences of opinion about the sloop's mission. Seeger told journalist Lisa Yane that when the *Clearwater* was launched, "all hell broke loose." Yane reported that Seeger told her that one faction of the membership wanted to name the sloop *Heritage* and have its crew dress in period costumes, while another group favored an environmental role. As Seeger explained in an August 1970 interview, "Some people think the boat should be just a beautiful symbol of history; others want it to be the center of a confrontation on problems of ecology and environment." Finally, Seeger told Yane, Hudson River Sloop Restoration's members voted to name the ship *Clearwater* and determined that its mission, as Seeger put it, was "to clean up the Hudson and to make its shores accessible to everyone." Hal Cohen, one of Seeger's colleagues in launching the *Clearwater*, recalled that when they sailed into New York Harbor in 1969, the crew discussed the meaning of the sloop. "At that point," he recalled, "it became obvious that we couldn't be a historical restoration when we were sailing in a sewer." But only after several months of discussion did the board agree that the *Clearwater*'s mission would be environmentalism. Even when the organization determined to focus on environmental issues, board members remained divided about whether the highest priority should be environmental activism or the educational programs the sloop was conducting. Hudson River historian and fisherman Robert Boyle threatened to resign from the board in 1971 because he didn't believe that the *Clearwater* was aggressive enough in its focus on stopping pollution in the river.[7]

Thus what started out as "a wild dream of a few sailing nuts," in Seeger's words, became, sometime in 1968, what the *New York Times* described as "a symbol of hope for the polluted Hudson." Beginning in 1966, Seeger and friends gave a series of concerts throughout the Hudson Valley to raise money to pay for building the boat. Twenty years later, Seeger recalled that the first concert netted the fledgling group $167.50. At those fund-raising events he invariably sang "My Dirty Stream (The Hudson River Song)," which, while it decried the pollution in the river, projected his vision for the Hudson:

Figure 3. Pete Seeger performing in a fund-raising concert for the *Clearwater*. Photograph by Barbara Starner, undated. Courtesy of Hudson River Sloop Clearwater Inc.

Sailing down my dirty stream
Still I love it and I'll keep the dream
That some day, though maybe not this year
My Hudson River will once again run clear

Seeger first recorded the song on his 1964 album, *God Bless the Grass*, with an essay on the back cover on the importance of wilderness, by

Supreme Court Justice William O. Douglas. The album also included other proto-environmental pieces, "Cement Octopus," which decried freeway building in California, "The Faucets Are Dripping," on the amount of drinking water wastefully dripping away in New York City apartments and houses, and the title song, written by Malvina Reynolds, which celebrated the tenacity of grass as it worked its way through cement, a kind of validation of the natural world taking back over from the humanly created one. The final song on the album, "From Way Up Here," was recorded two years before NASA photographs, taken by Apollo astronauts, first pictured the earth against a background of black space. Seeger presciently emphasized the fragility of the planet, a theme he would talk and sing about over the next forty years.[8]

"My Dirty Stream" became an anthem for cleaning up the Hudson, and the *Clearwater* became Seeger's chosen vehicle for this environmental mission. As dollars and dimes and nickels collected at concerts began to mount up, the Lila Acheson Wallace Fund and the Rockefeller Brothers Fund each contributed $10,000 toward the cost of constructing the sloop. The keel was laid at the Harvey F. Gamage Shipbuilding Company's boatyard in South Bristol, Maine, in mid-October 1968. By this time christened *Clearwater*, the sloop was launched on May 17, 1969. Constructed at a cost of approximately $140,000, the ship measures 106 feet in length and extends 25 feet from beam to beam. The mast rises 106 feet above the deck and supports a mainsail, a topsail, and jib with a total sail area of more than four thousand square feet. After the *Clearwater* was launched, Saunders and Seeger informed volunteers that they had experienced delays in getting the sloop rigged and tested and that the sails would not be raised until mid-June. The plan called for Seeger and a crew of musicians, including Don McLean and Ramblin' Jack Elliott, to sail the *Clearwater* to New York, stopping along the way at New England ports to hold twenty-five fund-raising concerts. Those concerts, Seeger recalled, raised $27,000 to help pay the cost of constructing the sloop.[9]

The *Clearwater* sailed into New York Harbor on August 1, 1969. The sloop docked briefly at Bedloe's Island, home of the Statue of Liberty, where Mayor John V. Lindsay joined the crew. Lindsay briefly manned the tiller as *Clearwater* made its way to South Street, on the East River, where it docked that night. There Seeger and company spent several days holding folk concerts, jazz performances, and an arts and crafts fair. Speaking

Figure 4. The sloop *Clearwater* on the Hudson. Photograph by Charles Porter, undated. Courtesy of Charles Porter and Hudson River Sloop Clearwater Inc.

with a reporter for the *New York Times*, Seeger identified the *Clearwater*'s mission as a "soft sell job." "We want to bring tens of thousands of people to the water's edge so they can see that their waterway can be fun." Then, Seeger added, "It will be up to each person what he wants to do about pollution. Until people start to love their river, it's going to be a sewer." Those words encapsulate the *Clearwater*'s mature mission: an environmental ethos that seeks to reconnect people with their river and encourages them to demand an end to pollution so the river can once again become pristine. As Seeger explained during the *Clearwater*'s maiden voyage up the Hudson, "If towns all along the river start putting in waterfront parks instead of messes, if the people all get involved in the work of cleaning up the river, then we'll have something."[10]

After the New York City festivities, the *Clearwater* made its inaugural trip up the Hudson, attracting great crowds wherever it docked. The sloop is sailed by a salaried captain and two mates, and a crew, on average, of seven volunteers who spend a week aboard. Over the years the *Clearwater* has glided so gracefully on the river that it effectively masked the contentious times that Hudson River Sloop Restoration experienced in its first decade. Funds were always short during its formative period, not an unusual circumstance for a fledgling organization, and staff experienced times when their pay was not forthcoming. There were worries about "hangers on" who had finished their tours but stayed on the sloop. But perhaps most important were divisions in the board over Seeger's leadership and role as chairman. Donald Presutti, a vice president of the board from Newburgh, had joined Hudson River Sloop Restoration because he saw it as a means of realizing his "dream of a cleaner river and a reflection of our past history." At a meeting in mid-September 1970, Presutti introduced a motion to remove Seeger from the board. When that motion failed, Presutti resigned. He told the *New York Times* that he objected to the "hippie types" who were attracted to the *Clearwater* and that he no longer wanted to be associated with the image they were creating. In his letter of resignation Presutti added, "I feel the Hudson River Sloop Restoration cannot project the kind of image and accomplish the goals that I would care to be part of." Perhaps in response to these tensions, Seeger, who was elected honorary chairman of the board two months later, "gratefully declined to accept."[11]

Presutti's resignation points to the complexities Seeger's radical past brought to Hudson River Sloop Restoration, and so did other events. In the fall of 1978 village trustees in Cold Spring, on the east bank of the Hudson, voted to not allow the *Clearwater* to participate in a festival in Cold Spring Park the following May. They justified their decision by "citing the sloop's controversial backer and folksinging symbol, Pete Seeger." That same year, residents of a small river town decided that the *Clearwater* was "part of a Communist plot." One night, Seeger recalled, they cut all the mooring lines and threatened to "throw gasoline on deck and set it afire." And yet despite Presutti's protests, Seeger was the heart and soul of the *Clearwater*: He was a large donor and surely its most successful fund-raiser, and he and Toshi lent Hudson River Sloop Restoration significant amounts of money on at least two occasions. Toshi, with her formidable organizational skills, was also an invaluable member of the board. At a meeting on February 14, 1971, the *Clearwater*'s board wrestled with how best to define Seeger's relationship with the organization. Members reached a consensus that "without Seeger, there would be no Hudson River Sloop," but really didn't resolve the issue. Seeger, however, saw the *Clearwater* as bringing together young and old, rich and poor, conservative and liberal, in their common love for the river. He once told the story of a Kingston man who deeply resented the *Clearwater*'s countercultural image, and who had actually called the FBI and urged the bureau to investigate the organization. Yet when that man, at Seeger's invitation, sailed aboard the sloop and met its scruffy young volunteers firsthand, he became a generous donor and dedicated volunteer. The challenge was to replicate that transformative experience on a large scale, which would take time.[12]

In addition to funding shortfalls and Seeger's reputation, Hudson River Sloop Restoration also faced the growing pains typical to young organizations, especially ones guided largely by volunteers: when, and how, should it professionalize its operations? In an untitled memorandum, a long-range planning committee strongly advocated hiring an executive director with real power to carry out board policies. Indeed, it likened its ideal executive director to a city manager, a form of governance in many Hudson River Valley communities, who would bring professional expertise to the job. The memorandum specifically mentioned the difficulty of attracting someone like a David Brower, executive director of the Sierra Club, who could give the organization real credibility. The problem was not just affording the compensation for such a position. The memorandum added, "HRSR must prove that it has some broad, possibly national, appeal to people concerned about the environmental crisis. Before HRSR can attract more attention, it must have an environmental program."[13]

The board of Hudson River Sloop Restoration was also deeply divided. Surviving minutes do not reveal how fractured the *Clearwater*'s board was in 1970 and 1971, or what were the causes of those real tensions. An August 1971 report by Harry Dobson, then president of HRSR, reveals how troubling these divisions were, not just to members but to a significant funder. Dobson informed the board that the Lila Acheson Wallace Fund, which "had been most generous to the sloop in the past," would not contribute again until its directors see "substantial improvements" in the organization. "They are very much aware of the inner struggles of the past two years," Dobson stated, "and look for solid evidence of an on-going stability before committing funds." Dobson assured his fellow directors that Mrs. Wallace and her counsel, Barnabas McHenry, remained enthusiastic about the *Clearwater*, and while they did not want to dictate what must be done, they did "want to have an assurance that the strife of the past is 'eliminated, not just contained.'" Board engagement with the HRSR was also problematic: former president Hal Cohen resigned from the board in April 1975 "in protest over the number of board members who are not doing their fair share of the work required by the organization."[14]

Even the seemingly mundane task of manning the *Clearwater* proved vexatious. Allan Aunapu, the sloop's first captain, proved unpopular with several members of the board, including Fred Starner, who wanted to oust him. Starner wrote to fellow board member John Burns III that there was bad blood between Aunapu and Dominick Pirone, the organization's executive director, and urged that the captain be replaced on the grounds of "the desirability of having the staff comprized [sic] of people who can work together harmoniously." Starner hoped that the effort to get rid of Aunapu would "not spill over into the real issues, the conflict of ideologies, life styles, religions and the like between Allan and Dom (and many others on the board)"—a strategy that would allow fundamental differences to fester rather than resolve them. But Aunapu had Pete and Toshi

Seeger's strong support, so he remained until he chose to depart. Reed Haslam, another *Clearwater* sailor, also experienced problems with the HRSR board. Then-president John Burns simply fired him, at which point the board voted to give Haslam one month's pay and vacation pay as a severance package, as well as a strong letter of recommendation. Haslam wrote the board of directors to complain that "I and other persons have heard many rumors and vague statements and have attempted to find out the truth or complete reasons for this action," to no avail. When Burns insisted that Haslam tell people that he had resigned, the former sailor refused to do so, "as it was not the truth," whereupon Burns decided not to pay Haslam as promised. The seasonal nature of the job also made life difficult for the captain and the two mates: the *Clearwater* sailed from April through November, and was often on the water every day of the week. When Frank Fulchiero resigned as captain in May 1975, the executive committee ruefully noted that "HRSR has been remiss in not finding a way for captains to function efficiently without committing themselves to an inhumane work schedule." There were also frequent misunderstandings or miscommunications between board members and the *Clearwater*'s office staff and crew. One board member, Karen Leshin, urged that as much as possible, "all communication between staff and Board members, and among ourselves, be in writing," which she hoped would "change the style of communication, which produces problems repeatedly." Save for Presutti's resignation, none of this reached the press, but in its early years, HRSR seemingly careened from one crisis to another.[15]

Launching the *Clearwater* and determining its environmental mission were the high points of HRSR's early years. But problems abounded, and the most difficult of these was establishing an adequate financial basis for the organization. Apparently no one on the board expected that winter maintenance and storage costs would be as significant as they were, and so every year there was a dramatic appeal for contributions to offset those costs. In 1973 the *New York Times* reported that the cost of operating the *Clearwater* was approximately $100,000 a year. *Clearwater* itself became a financial challenge, as annual repairs and a significant reconstruction drained the organization's bank account. During the winter of 1975–76, the *Clearwater*, after only seven years of sailing on the Hudson, needed extensive work. A January 1976 report noted that "the degree to which CLEARWATER has deteriorated is appalling" and attributed the rot and decay of the wood to the Hudson's warm waters. The shipbuilder had used red oak rather than white oak for the hull, which proved far less suitable for a boat mainly plying the Hudson. The cost of replacing part of the hull and repairing other parts of the sloop far exceeded the organization's budget and was projected to reach as high as $80,000, more than half the cost of the original construction. As the report noted, "It is unusual for a seven year old vessel to have deteriorated to such an extent as CLEARWATER." Board president Angela Magill informed the public of these unanticipated expenses and noted that while HRSR had always operated on a shoestring budget, "that shoestring is shorter now than ever before." Because of the time required to make those essential repairs, the *Clearwater* would have an abbreviated sailing season in 1976. The sloop returned to New York barely in time to join the parade of tall ships in New York Harbor organized as part of the national bicentennial.[16]

Maynard Bray, the Maine shipbuilder who oversaw repairs to the sloop during the winter of 1976, informed the board that despite all the work undertaken, the *Clearwater* needed additional repairs. He warned the board, "To get CLEARWATER through to an age of twenty years is going to take much more concentration on her wellbeing than has been the case in years past. She must have continuous and effective maintenance." Bray wrote a maintenance manual for the crew but added, "All this will be ineffective if the crew and owners don't take the matter of routine maintenance seriously." During the winter of 1976–77, the *Clearwater* was in Mystic Seaport, Connecticut, for the additional repairs Bray recommended.[17]

Keeping the sloop on the river and the board working together were real challenges, as was keeping Hudson River Sloop Restoration afloat financially. There were other organizational difficulties as well. Seeger conceived the idea that every Hudson River town or city organize a sloop club, which would organize a festival when the *Clearwater* docked at their community and generate enthusiasm for the *Clearwater*'s mission as members who supported Hudson River Sloop Restoration. Seeger praised the Poughkeepsie club as especially effective and stated that it enjoyed the "wonderful cooperation" of the city manager and elected officials. The Beacon Sloop Club, which Seeger helped organize, was the prime mover in converting that city's garbage dump into a riverfront park. But the relationship between the sloop clubs and the understaffed central office was fraught with problems. The Poughkeepsie club was frustrated because local organizers of a summer 1971 festival did not get the support they expected from the parent organization. Nevertheless, the *New York Times* reported in 1975 that sloop clubs were "blossoming in Hudson River communities." Still, problems persisted: only a year later one board member noted that the sloop clubs "want and need more and better communication with and assistance from the Board and the Office." The sloop clubs organized as a congress and attempted to draft a new set of rules and regulations and hoped "to systematically raise the level and intensity of Clearwater membership participation in the organization's policy-making process." As executive director John Mylod conceded in the summer of 1990, the sloop clubs had proven less successful than anticipated. This he attributed to the board and administrative staff: "We haven't spent the kind of resources and organizing on the sloop clubs over the years that in retrospect we should have." The problem persisted: at the general meeting of September 27, 1984, someone mentioned the "difficulty in communication between some members and sloop affiliates, and the board of directors."[18]

Somehow, Hudson River Sloop Restoration, renamed Hudson River Sloop Clearwater Inc. in 1976, survived its tumultuous first decade. John Mylod began an eighteen-year tenure as executive director of the organization on September 1, 1976, but his first years on the job were certainly difficult. In the fall of 1979 new board leadership wanted to change the organization and fire its executive director. Things came to a head in May 1980, when board president Karen Leshin fired Mylod. The board then adopted a motion to replace Leshin and remove her from the board, whereupon Leshin's supporters on the board resigned. Mylod was rehired, and a large number of new members joined the board and brought with them the skills to make the organization run more efficiently. Only after the May 1980 confrontations did Clearwater Inc. become a truly effective organization, with Mylod leading a growing and thriving institution. As Seeger remarked in 1991, "John Mylod finally got us the stability we needed. Without him, it might still be chaos."[19]

Despite the initial lack of consensus about its mission, the *Clearwater* has indeed become a powerful symbol of and advocate for environmentalism. What Seeger envisioned, a populist environmentalism, was based on his belief that individual citizens matter. Every person had the ability to change his or her lifestyle to leave a better world behind. Individuals could choose to use fewer resources or simplify their diet; they could report corporations and municipalities and individual homes that were fouling waterways and the air; they could join in cleanups that transformed garbage dumps into parks that provided public access to the river. Seeger's vision was both global and intensely local. He linked the environmental crisis with larger challenges, of course, including racism and poverty. "I don't think we're going to be able to solve this environmental crisis," he stated, "unless we solve the social crisis." But his solution was local. As a child growing up in Nyack, New York, he swam in the Hudson River until the board of health closed nearby beaches, and from an early age he felt a deep attachment to the river. The Hudson once produced 1.5 million bushels of oysters and shellfish annually. Seeger recalled that he frequently bought shad directly from the fishermen's nets as recently as the 1950s. But pollution had destroyed the fisheries and had driven residents away from the Hudson's banks. Seeger decided to fight back, and he did so from his perch on Mount Beacon, by passing the hat at river festivals, or from the concert stage raising money for the *Clearwater*.[20]

In a 1981 interview, Seeger defined the most important challenge facing the world as "working within one's home community." In order to make the earth a better place, individuals had to embrace their local community. "The world is going to be saved," he stated, "by people who fight for their homes, whether they're fighting for the block where they live in the city or a stretch of mountain or river." He was heartened that all across the nation, citizens were "getting interested in their own communities and realizing that they're part of a long chain." On another occasion he told a reporter for the Sierra Club's magazine, "The key issues are those nearby, geographically and spiritually, and if the world is saved, it will likely be by people fighting for their homes," a struggle he likened to the American Revolution and the Vietnamese people overthrowing neocolonial oppression. Whether in print or on radio or film or in his folksy conversations from the concert stage, Seeger urged his audience to cherish their communities and work to make them better.[21]

What Seeger taught the thousands of the people who heard him was that the Hudson was their river, and they could reclaim it only if they worked at it, really hard. The polluters had far more money to influence legislators, locally, in state capitals, and in Washington, than did individual citizens, and had, through advertising, greater ability to shape popular opinion. The only effective recourse was an educated citizenry that acted to protect their homes and communities. And this proved contagious: Seeger's vision of the Hudson as a stream that ran clear became a vision for the Hudson far different from that of the men in suits who ran the Hudson River Valley Commission. It embraced people, and promoted a vision of communities reconnected with their river.[22]

The *Clearwater* became an effective platform for delivering Seeger's message, not just in the Hudson River Valley and Long Island Sound, its usual sailing haunts, but really throughout the Northeast. At the first Earth Day celebration in the nation's capital, the *New York Times* quoted Seeger as stating that the Hudson was "becoming an industrial sewer" and that the sloop was going to the nation's capital because "the problems of American rivers can't be solved by people like me who live on them. Only the Federal Government," he conceded in what was a rare departure from his faith in a populist environmentalism, "has the power to enact and enforce the laws that are needed."[23]

The *Clearwater* would occasionally venture beyond the Hudson in support of other environmental causes in subsequent years, especially in opposition to controversial nuclear power plants. In June 1978 the *Clearwater* sailed to New Hampshire to join a flotilla of boats protesting the 2,300-megawatt Seabrook nuclear plant, though in approving the sloop's presence at Seabrook the board resolved, "No illegal activities will be undertaken by any person or group representing the Hudson River Sloop CLEARWATER, Inc." The sloop also sailed to East Shoreham, New York, on the north shore of Long Island, to protest against the controversial nuclear power plant the Long Island Lighting Company had constructed there. These widely publicized forays into distant waters notwithstanding, most of the time the *Clearwater* stayed home. Its mission was environmental education and advocacy to restore a pristine Hudson River.[24]

The *Clearwater*'s educational program stands at the heart of the organization's mission, especially during the spring and fall, when the sloop normally devotes each weekday to a morning and an afternoon lesson on the river in its "Classroom of the Waves" program. Students and their teachers board the sloop toward the end of a curriculum devoted to the environment, some of it developed by Clearwater Inc. staff, so they are well prepared for the half-day's activities. About forty students are divided into five groups and spend approximately twenty minutes at each of five stations, studying fish, plankton, toxic chemicals and other pollutants in the water, navigation and steering the sloop, and the history of the river, its communities, people, and culture. The students, Greg Aunapu recalled, are "subtly instructed to respect nature and the balance of things." Aunapu emphasized that the hands-on learning students experience while aboard the *Clearwater* is very different from reading a textbook or looking at a computer screen. As education director Brian Forist explained, "We are planting seeds, hoping to change the way they see the world." The sail and the lessons, he stated, are "a way to bring what they've been learning into context." The participating school districts' financial support of this educational program helped the organization stay afloat in its early years. By 1993 approximately two hundred thousand people, mostly schoolchildren, had participated in the *Clearwater*'s onboard educational programs. Some programs take place on land. In May 1972, for example, approximately 250 students from ten Bronx high schools participated in a program at the Wave Hill Center for Environmental Studies. Historian and naturalist Robert Boyle urged the students to "get involved, and get interested in the river for the sake of it and yourselves." The students broke into smaller groups and engaged in discussions of the river, its fisheries, and the chemical and industrial pollution that was adversely affecting marine life. Seeger brought his banjo for the occasion and ended the "Hudson Fair" with song. In 1985 Clearwater Inc. launched its Hudson River Discovery Program, which over the next eight years provided instruction to more than one thousand teachers interested in developing environmental education curricula. Many of those teachers subsequently brought their classes to the river for onboard activities. In recent years Clearwater Inc. has hired additional educators to meet the increasing demand for its programs.[25]

One of the *Clearwater*'s most popular seasonal events was the annual pumpkin sail, which has been discontinued in recent years. The *Clearwater* docked at towns and villages in the upper Hudson Valley, where the crew and local volunteers loaded the deck with pumpkins and gourds. As the sloop sailed down the river, it stopped along the way and sold its cargo in the various river towns. Ostensibly a fund-raising event, the pumpkin sail usually broke even, as crew members gave pumpkins to children who could not afford to buy them. More important, the sail connected urban children with the bounty of the Hudson River Valley and thereby fostered an understanding of and attachment to the river in their lives. As Doug Cole, public affairs coordinator for the organization, told the *New York Times*, "Our main purpose is to make people more aware of the Hudson, and therefore get them to care more about it."[26]

Financing the sloop and its programs has been an essential responsibility of Clearwater Inc.'s board. This has meant not just encouraging memberships and raising money from individuals and foundations but also organizing special events such as concerts, riverfront cleanups, and the annual fund-raiser, the Great Hudson River Revival Festival. First held at Croton Point Park in Westchester County in June 1978, the festival quickly became the largest annual fund-raiser for the Clearwater organization. Seeger contacted friends, including Tom Paxton, Arlo Guthrie, Tom Chapin, and other well-known folksingers, along with local performers, dance groups representing cultures from around the world, and other entertainers, who performed on five outdoor stages. Artisans and craftsmen displayed their wares and taught workshops on everything from blacksmithing to small-boat building to making musical instruments. The following year Seeger expressed the hope that by including such a wide range of performers, "including a Japanese koto player, steel drummers from the West Indies, tap dancers and even a classical violinist," the festival would be embracing the cultural traditions of the human family. Subsequent festivals included performances by Theodore Bikel, Dizzy Gillespie, Don McLean, Emmylou Harris, Jay Ungar and Molly Mason, operatic mezzo-soprano Marilyn Horne, and the Hudson River Sloop Singers, among many others. The diverse programs included, in addition to music, dancing in a number of genres, storytelling, juggling, puppeteers, musical performers from South Africa and Palestine, regional American music, and rituals representing African American and Native American traditions. The festival had to move from Croton Point Park in 1988 when the adjacent county landfill was found to be leaking contaminated runoff into the park and was declared hazardous by the state. After the dump was sealed and planted with grass, the festival returned to the site in 1999.[27]

As the organization matured, Clearwater developed a research department to identify polluters. In this, Clearwater became, along with the Fishermen's Association, among the first of Hudson Valley environmental organizations to take on the corporations and municipalities that were fouling the river. In October 1971 new executive director Dom Pirone informed the board of directors that Hudson River Sloop Restoration "could be an effective agent for bringing certain polluters to the fore" and believed that undertaking this research could be a responsibility of the sloop clubs. The following December, board president John Burns publicly identified three major polluters in New Jersey—Diamond Shamrock Corporation, Textron, and Lever Brothers—that were dumping untreated waste into the Hudson or the Hackensack Rivers. At a public meeting held in Englewood, New Jersey, Burns stated that the announcement was "part of a continuing program by Hudson River Sloop Restoration, Inc. to investigate every geographical area impinging on the Hudson and to disclose to citizens just who the major polluters are in their areas." In 1972 the organization began publishing Clearwater Polluter Reports, which Burns described as a "tremendous success." These reports were produced by volunteers who tracked the discharge of waste through pipes. The pipe watchers scored a significant victory in March 1976 when a federal district court fined a Beacon tape manufacturer, Tuck Industries, $43,000 for illegally discharging pollutants into Fishkill Creek. Hudson River Sloop Restoration received $6,750 of the fine as the citizen group that brought the facts of the case to U.S. Attorneys. Hudson River Sloop Restoration adopted the monitoring of industrial waste as its "prime purpose" and took pride in its accomplishments as "one of the most effective anti–water pollution organizations around." The *New York Times* agreed, calling the *Clearwater* "a literal patrol boat, monitoring the river for evidence of pollution that would compel government agencies to do their regulatory jobs."[28]

Clearwater Inc. has evolved into an important environmental action organization. Since its understaffed and financially challenging early years, Clearwater has grown into an organization that, in 2012, had $2.6 million in assets and income that year of $3.243 million. Its staff, directors, and members have fought to achieve habitat (especially wetlands) restoration, to promote wise use of the river and its resources, to provide greater access to its shores, and to increase the public's appreciation of the river's "ecological and cultural heritage." Clearwater has also fought the filling in of more than two hundred acres of Hudson River shallows to build a high-speed expressway, Westway, and following the lead of

Joan K. Davidson of the J. M. Kaplan Fund, who has been a longtime defender of the Hudson, argued instead that the riverbank be developed as a park. The organization has sued the state Department of Environmental Conservation and the federal Environmental Protection Agency for their failure to enforce the terms of the Clean Water Act, has strenuously opposed the relicensing of the Indian Point nuclear power plants in testimony before the Atomic Safety Relicensing Board, and was a strong advocate for holding General Electric accountable for dumping thousands of tons of polychlorinated biphenyls (PCBs) into the river. The list of its causes could go on for pages—a green cities initiative, a river cities educational program that provides a range of activities for students of all ages in Newburgh and other communities, clean water initiatives in numerous communities. Two other landmark achievements were the opening of the Esopus Meadows Environmental Center in Ulster Park, New York, in 1993, and the location and construction of "homeport" facilities for the *Clearwater*, a winter home and repair yard for the sloop as well as a center for environmental education and river history, on Rondout Creek in Kingston. Clearwater expects to establish synergies with the nearby Hudson River Maritime Museum and contribute significantly to the revitalization of Kingston's riverfront.[29]

Clearwater also became involved in the preservation of Matthew Vassar's estate, Springside, on Academy Street in Poughkeepsie. This represented a significant departure from its environmental mission, and it is tempting to think that as an organization, Clearwater was returning to its original interest in historic preservation. More likely, Clearwater was responding to a developmental threat that would have placed a 191-unit condominium project on the remaining 27.7 acres of Springside, the largest undeveloped site in the city of Poughkeepsie and at the time its only National Historic Landmark. Springside is historically significant as the most intact surviving landscape designed by the mid-nineteenth-century "apostle of taste" Andrew Jackson Downing. Clearwater Inc. joined with Hudson River Heritage, Dutchess County Landmarks Association, and several private individuals in challenging the city's rezoning of the property, and eventually sued the city and the developer, Robert S. Ackerman, claiming that in reviewing the project the city had failed to adhere to the State Environmental Quality Review Act or prepare an environmental impact statement. After a protracted legal battle, John Mylod negotiated a settlement with the developer that confined new construction to areas outside the historic landscape and turned the Downing-designed part of the property over to a new private nonprofit organization, Springside Landscape Restoration, which has assumed responsibility for restoring, managing, and providing public access to the grounds.[30]

As the Clearwater organization found its feet, and its membership increased, the need for additional ships became apparent. Seeger reached into his pocket and paid for the construction of a thirty-two-foot ferry sloop he named the *Woody Guthrie*, which was built in Bearsville, New York, and launched at Kingston in 1978, at a cost of $75,000. This first of the "Clearwater children" could carry twenty passengers yet had a shallow-enough draft to be able to dock at river towns and cities where the water was not deep enough for the *Clearwater*. Although owned by Seeger, the *Woody Guthrie* was available for use by the Clearwater organization and sailing clubs. Operated by volunteers from the Beacon Sloop Club, the *Woody Guthrie* provided free, daily two-hour evening sails as it preached the *Clearwater*'s mission of environmentalism. But as was true of the *Clearwater*, the *Woody Guthrie*'s wood hull was unsuited to the Hudson's waters, and it had to be rebuilt "at substantial cost," according to the *New York Times*, in 2002 and 2003. When work on the hull was completed, the ferry sloop still needed $28,000 in additional repairs, which were undertaken the following year.[31]

Shortly after the *Woody Guthrie* was launched, a group of volunteer shipbuilders who organized as Ferry Sloops, a sister organization to Clearwater Inc., were hard at work constructing another ship. Their goal was to build a ferry sloop as "a vehicle for carrying out our mission of bringing people down to, and onto, the Hudson River so that they may sail its waters, learn its history, lore and ecology, and make a commitment to bringing back clean water." This daughter of the *Clearwater* had a concrete-and-steel hull. This was a construction process that began with layers of steel mesh stapled to a mold. Using trowels, workers then applied ferro-cement to the mesh to form a more durable, and much less expensive, hull than those of the wooden sloops. The hull cost only $15,000 to construct, the sloop in its entirety approximately $25,000. Named the *Sojourner Truth* after the Kingston-born former slave and champion of women's rights, the vessel began sailing on the Hudson in 1981. Originally moored in

Hastings-on-Hudson, the *Sojourner Truth* relocated to the John F. Kennedy Marina in Yonkers in 1992. The *Sojourner Truth* too has had its travails. In 1995 a fire, probably started by an arsonist, gutted much of the deck. Seven years later the sloop became unmoored and crashed on the rocks at Half Moon Bay, causing significant damage to the hull.[32]

Demand, especially for the *Clearwater*'s educational programs, quickly outpaced the ability of the organization to meet all requests. Beginning in 1983 the organization leased the ninety-five-foot schooner *Voyager* for the spring and fall educational programs, and hired additional environmental educators, but still could not accommodate all the schools that wanted to participate. Mylod noted the need for a second sloop in August 1985. Seeger expressed dismay in 1986 that thirty school systems that wanted to take advantage of the *Clearwater*'s "Classroom of the Waves" program were turned down because there simply wasn't enough time to accommodate them. The board, he told the *New York Times*, was "seriously thinking of building a second sloop of identical size and shape." The following year Clearwater Inc. had to turn down more than one hundred schools, which led the board to lease an eighty-one-foot sloop, the *Argia*. But even with three ships and the ferry sloops, the organization was not meeting the increasing demand for its educational programs.[33]

Members, community groups, public figures, scientists, and others also wanted to sail the *Clearwater*, but as was the case with schoolchildren, demand far exceeded available sailing time. In 1986, for example, the *Clearwater* could accommodate only 30 percent of member requests for opportunities to sail, perhaps as few as 10 percent in the Hudson between New York City and Poughkeepsie. The board worried that by turning away so many interested individuals and groups, the organization risked "the loss of good will, education potential or memberships." A case statement for a new sloop, prepared in 1987, expressed the board's and the staff's concern "that schools, communities and members are beginning to think that the Sloop and its programs no longer belong to them."[34]

The *Clearwater* defined much of the final half of Seeger's life. He continued to support everyday Americans, especially workers, and remained committed to civil rights for the nation's racial minorities, but increasingly he was associated with environmentalism. As the culture wars of the 1960s receded into memory, and more and more people came to agree with his outspoken opposition to the Vietnam War, Seeger did indeed become America's troubadour, the singer who engaged audiences and got them singing, who became a beloved figure, whether from a concert stage or the box at the Kennedy Center when he received national honors in 1994 (the same year he was awarded the National Endowment for the Arts National Medal of Arts), or as the subject of an admiring 2008 Public Broadcasting Service video, *The Power of Song*. At a concert outside Washington featuring Seeger and Arlo Guthrie in the early 1970s, most of the crowd clearly had come to hear Guthrie, as the event took place only three years after "Alice's Restaurant" became a generational anthem. But as the evening wore on, Seeger won over the audience, which responded enthusiastically to his sing-alongs and sang in full throat and cheered uproariously over his rendition of "Garbage." Seeger's joyful presence on stage, together with his environmental message and his folksy ways, captivated hundreds, perhaps thousands that evening, who at first may have been wondering who that scruffy old man with a banjo was. At the end of the concert, Seeger had a legion of new fans, and many of them supported his brand of populist environmentalism.

Seeger's vision for the *Clearwater*, his devotion to its mission, was surely a key to the broader public appreciation for his life's accomplishments. A cleaner Hudson was one great beneficiary of his life, and his audience embraced him for his commitment to this cause. Don McLean, whose song "American Pie" attracted a younger audience than Seeger's usual following to concerts supporting construction and ongoing maintenance of the *Clearwater*, was one of the original crew of the sloop as it sailed from Maine to New York in 1969. That year he released his first album, *Tapestry*, and the title song was a clarion call for environmentalism:

> Like a river of life flowing on since creation.
> Approaching the sea with each new generation.
> You're now just a stagnant and rancid disgrace
> That is rapidly drowning the whole human race.

The following year McLean published a small book, *Songs and Sketches of the First Clearwater Crew* (with sketches by Tom Allen). In the foreword Seeger wrote, "We strongly believe that the Hudson *can* be cleaned up, that the human race *can* survive, *if* we get together. All of us." McLean penned a poem in honor of Seeger for the small book:

he's a sailor
a bumbling, crafty, thoughtful, dreaming
chopstick drummer
a lover
a brightly colored creature
a root that knuckles through the soil
to reach you
a sculptured banjo body
   shedding human thoughts
on careless scraps of paper leaves
a voice of fiber bark . . .

Seeger would surely not have agreed with everything in McLean's verse, though he may have found that his young friend's characterization of him as bumbling and dreaming and a lover as pretty close to the mark. More important, Seeger's love for the Hudson River and its people initiated a remarkable transformation. The majestic *Clearwater*, and the festivals its volunteer supporters and staff have organized for almost fifty years, did indeed bring hundreds of thousands of residents back to the banks of the Hudson and made it possible for those people to reconnect with their river, to envision the possibilities of a cleaner Hudson. The *Clearwater* was never Seeger's boat—it belongs collectively to all members of Hudson River Sloop Clearwater—but its construction and maintenance over its first forty-five years owed so much to his vision and long-standing efforts to raise the money needed to get the sloop built and keep it on the water. The *Clearwater* continues to preach a populist environmentalism that he believed was essential to the future of the human race.[35]

The *Clearwater* was at its homeport on Rondout Creek during the winter of 2015, the third year of a three-year winter reconstruction of its hull that will cost almost $2 million. Work includes replacement of the centerboard trunk, bed logs, and the main hold, as well as major work aft, including the replacement of the transom. The goal is to replace all the wood below the waterline by the spring of 2016. The New York State Office of Parks,

Recreation, and Historic Preservation awarded the *Clearwater*, which was entered in the National Register of Historic Places in 2004, a matching grant of $497,303 to help pay for this work (NYSOPRHP also provided a substantial grant toward the cost of constructing the homeport), but in the still-difficult fund-raising environment in the aftermath of the Great Recession, Clearwater Inc. had to liquidate a considerable portion ($342,849) of its endowment to meet the terms of the matching grant and complete the work.[36]

Clearwater has always prided itself on being a truly grassroots environmental organization in the Hudson River Valley. But its substantial growth in recent years raises questions about the continuing validity of that claim. In 2012, for example, individual contributions, which surely include membership fees, represented only 14.71 percent of the organization's income. Together, corporate and foundation support almost equaled individual contributions, while income from government sources (20.64 percent) surpassed the grassroots support. How Clearwater spends its money is also important. In 2012 the organization devoted 10.87 percent of its operating expenses to development and 12.32 percent to environmental action (in the previous year, 12.9 percent was expended on development, only 9.23 percent on environmental action). In each year the largest single source of income, and expense, was special events, for which the cost in 2011 significantly exceeded income. Obviously, development is essential for any private nonprofit organization, but the trajectory in recent years may well threaten Clearwater's grassroots heritage. As the organization relies more and more on foundations and government grants, it may well face challenging decisions when its development goals and its mission of environmental activism collide.[37]

This concern notwithstanding, the sloop *Clearwater* remains a powerful symbol of environmentalism in the Hudson River Valley and beyond. Since its launching in 1969, approximately five hundred thousand people have sailed aboard the *Clearwater*, most of them schoolchildren, and perhaps twenty-five thousand children have participated in the organization's onshore Tideline programs. These are impressive numbers, and testify to the sloop's appeal. Equally important are the hundreds of thousands of visitors who have boarded and toured the sloop when it has docked at festivals in cities along the river. Some of the children who participated in the educational programs have returned to crew the *Clearwater* and have become passionate environmentalists. But it remains difficult to measure how effective these educational programs have been in fostering a key part of the *Clearwater*'s mission: "inspiring, educating, and activating the next generation of environmental leaders." To be sure, anecdotal evidence abounds—Robert F. Kennedy Jr.'s experience is that many of the children who sailed aboard the sloop became supporters of the Riverkeeper organization—but this is largely confined to a relatively small group of individuals with whom Clearwater Inc. and Riverkeeper have remained in contact. How those programs have affected the vast majority of schoolchildren in the years since they participated in Clearwater's educational programs is at this point impossible to determine. Nevertheless, Pete Seeger's original vision for the replica sloop has evolved into a powerful environmental statement that in so many ways has promoted an ethos of caring about the river among residents of the Hudson River Valley, and, as Kennedy put it, Seeger was a "pied piper" who brought people back to the banks of the river. In its graceful presence on the water, the *Clearwater* has undoubtedly captivated and inspired thousands, surely many of whom have embraced Seeger's vision of a cleaner Hudson.[38]

Seeger's death at age ninety-four on January 27, 2014, while expected, has been a blow to the Clearwater organization. Although he had largely withdrawn from the board over preceding decades, he remained the iconic symbol of the sloop and its environmental mission. He was also one of the most effective fund-raisers for the sloop. When friends organized a ninetieth birthday concert in New York's Madison Square Garden, Seeger agreed to the idea so long as its proceeds would benefit the *Clearwater*. He also continued to sing at the annual Great Hudson River Revival festival and encouraged friends to do so. Even during his final years, Seeger devoted his energies to the cause that had defined almost half his life, environmentalism in general and the Hudson River in particular.[39]

As an organization, Clearwater has struggled in the years since Seeger's death (and that of his spouse Toshi, a longtime and highly effective member of its board, who died in July 2013). Financial difficulties persisted, exacerbated by the enormous cost of replacing the *Clearwater*'s hull, which led to the cancellation of the 2016 Hudson River Revival concert. The concert annually raised approximately $160,000, but the 2015 event, plagued by heavy rain, netted only $31,000, even as it cost the organization $900,000 to rent Croton Point Park, build the stages, and pay the entertainers. The board decided to spend the money on restoring the sloop rather than holding the festival, which resulted in bitter division within the board and a widespread sense among members of the organization that the board was secretive and not communicating effectively with them. Peter Gross, the organization's third executive director in five years, resigned because of what his successor, Dave Conover, described as "significant differences" with the board over how to address the organization's finances. The board chose instead to organize a series of smaller concerts as fund-raising events. Not until the end of July 2016, when repairs to the *Clearwater*'s hull were completed, did the sloop once again began sailing on the Hudson. The late start to the sailing season cost the organization the income from spring educational programs.[40]

Despite the challenges the organization has faced since Seeger's death, Conover expressed optimism that fund-raising and membership recruitment efforts were succeeding. "I can't imagine the Hudson without the *Clearwater* sailing on it," he stated. "It's a really important part of Pete's environmental legacy." Seeger exemplified René Dubos's injunction to think globally but act locally. He was most immediately concerned with the local, the Hudson River, but he brought to audiences around the United States and the world his message of commitment to the environment and to strengthening local communities. How effective the *Clearwater*'s board and staff can be in building upon Seeger's vision, especially in establishing and maintaining a strong financial foundation for the organization, is the essential challenge going forward.[41]

4

THE FISHERMEN AND THE RIVERKEEPER

The Hudson River is an incredibly rich resource for marine life. When Henry Hudson first sailed up the river in 1609, one of his officers aboard the *Half Moon*, Robert Juet, recorded in his journal the abundance of the countryside as well as the sheer number and diversity of aquatic species. The Native Americans who approached Hudson's ship brought tobacco, wheat, and beads, but also a "great store of very good Oysters." The river, Juet observed, was full of fish, and when members of the crew tried their luck they returned with a "great store of very good fish." On one outing the catch included large salmon (as salmon are not native to the Hudson, naturalist Robert H. Boyle believes Juet must have misidentified striped bass), mullet at least a foot and a half long, and a ray so large that it took four men to hoist it aboard.[1]

Fishing has been a way of life along the Hudson since time immemorial, and certainly since the arrival of Dutch and English colonists in the seventeenth century those northern European settlers discovered what the native people had long known, that the river's waters provided a seemingly

Figure 5. "Fishing Station.—Sturgeon, Shad, Bass," from Benson J. Lossing, *The Hudson: From the Wilderness to the Sea* (Troy, N.Y., 1866), 145. Courtesy of Archives and Special Collections, James A. Cannavino Library, Marist College.

endless source of protein and delicious meals. During his travel down the Hudson in the late 1850s, Benson J. Lossing described how fishermen in the vicinity of Coxsackie used nets to capture the treasures of the river. Shad was the "most important fish," as it was "delicious as food, and caught in such immense numbers, as to make them cheap dishes for the poor man's table." Just above and below Poughkeepsie, fishermen caught astonishing numbers of sturgeon, two to eight feet in length and weighing from 100 to 450 pounds. They were so prominent a feature of the dining tables of the state capital that sturgeon were often called "Albany beef." "Bass and herring," Lossing added, "are also caught in abundance in almost every part of the river"[2]

Long one of the most important of Hudson Valley industries, fishing began a slow decline in the twentieth century as the river became more and more polluted. Untreated human and industrial waste had long been simply dumped into the rivers surrounding Manhattan Island. At night scavengers would empty the contents of privies and cesspools and shovel the human waste into the surrounding rivers. With the introduction of water from the Croton Aqueduct in 1842 and the building of a rudimentary sewer system beginning seven years later, more and more of New York's waste emptied into the Hudson. As New York City exploded in population and manufacturing throughout the nineteenth century, the amount of raw sewage entering the river increased exponentially. This must have been apparent to Lossing, who described Manhattan in great detail and also traveled by boat to the Jersey shore, Staten Island, and Long Island; but he did not mention the pollution that had already become a fact of life.[3]

New York City established the Metropolitan Board of Health in 1866, and the state created its Board of Health in 1880. As the amount of pollution in waterways increased, the State Board of Health began investigating the condition of the Croton River and its tributaries. In 1889 and again in 1891 the board reported that pollution had become so severe as to threaten the principal source of the city's water supply. While health officials did not comment on the impact of pollution on aquatic life, surely it was significant.[4]

In that age of laissez-faire capitalism, pollution only increased. In 1939 the Hudson Valley Survey Commission recommended that "progress in cleaning up the pollution of the Hudson River should be continued and brought to completion at the earliest possible moment." Whereas the State Board of Health was concerned principally about the effects of pollution on drinking water in communities along the Hudson, the Survey Commission also worried about the degree to which pollution was "a deterrent to reasonable development" and its impact on recreational uses of the river, especially swimming. The Board of Health reported that swimming was most frequent "at points near the large cities or municipalities which are not equipped with sewage treatment facilities, where the dangers of pollution are greatest." This was the decade during which Nyack had closed the popular beaches where Pete Seeger had enjoyed swimming in the river as a child. While the board was pleased with the progress of constructing sewage treatment plants in recent years, it recognized that much more needed to be done. Again, the report paid no attention to aquatic life.[5]

In the years after World War II, pollution intensified. The General Motors plant in Tarrytown dumped paint directly into the river (historian Raymond Mohl, who grew up in Tarrytown, told me that as a teenager he could look at the river and see what color GM was painting its cars each day). The Diesel and Electric Shops of the New York Central Railroad and its successor, Penn Central, dumped huge amounts of oil every day at Harmon, on the east bank. The Anaconda Wire and Cable Company had turned the riverfront at Hastings-on-Hudson into what John Cronin and Robert F. Kennedy Jr. have described as "a toxic Armageddon." The list could go on for pages. For those walking along the west shore railroad tracks north of Newburgh the air was redolent of untreated sewage emptying into the river from the majestic late nineteenth-century houses lining the hilltop above. Up and down the river, municipalities and industries were continuing the practice Theodore Roosevelt had decried in 1913, turning our rivers and streams into dumping grounds, polluting the air, and exterminating fish as well as animals.[6]

As sewage and other pollutants and toxics continued to flow into the Hudson at increasing rates, the effect on the river's commercial fisheries was devastating. Shad caught in the river tasted of oil, and buyers at the Fulton Fish Market would pay rock-bottom prices for Hudson River catches of striped bass and then sell them, at a significant markup, as having come from the Chesapeake Bay. The Hudson's commercial fishermen were dwindling in number, and their livelihood was in jeopardy. Sportsmen who loved fishing for striped bass would spend millions of dollars for equipment and lodging on Long Island, coastal New Jersey, and along the New England coast, but rarely ventured into the Hudson itself, such were the fears of pollution. In many ways, the Hudson's fisheries were in dire straits in the years before the passage of major environmental legislation of the 1970s, and the proposed pumped-storage power plant at Storm King Mountain, in the heart of the striped bass spawning ground, posed a cataclysmic threat to the industry.[7]

How to stop the pollution despoiling the Hudson River, how to protect the livelihood of its fishermen, became the personal mission of Robert H. Boyle. During the early 1960s, Boyle moved to metropolitan New York to work as a writer for *Sports Illustrated*. He lived in a house in Cold Spring, on the east bank of the Hudson, and as a devoted fisherman gravitated to the river. At Verplanck Point Boyle met two commercial fishermen, Ace Lent and Charlie White, and as the men's friendship grew, Lent and White shared their knowledge of the river and its oral traditions with Boyle. The sportswriter's circle of friends soon came to include the commercial fishermen who plied the waters of Haverstraw Bay and the Tappan Zee, and eventually extended north on the river to Albany. Based on the knowledge he was gaining from the fishermen, and from his own experiences on the river and its tributaries, Boyle became infuriated at the amount of pollution being dumped into the Hudson. He took up the pen and used his position at *Sports Illustrated* to call the wider public's attention to what was happening to the river.[8]

Boyle's first article on the Hudson was published in the August 17, 1964, issue of *Sports Illustrated*. Much of the article is descriptive of the remarkable richness of the aquatic life in the river, though it elegantly describes the valley's scenery, especially the Catskills and the Highlands. It also expresses alarm at the extent of pollution, especially in the Albany Pool and at New York City. At the Albany Pool, Boyle wrote, "The Hudson is so awesomely foul here that it is a source of wonder to sanitary engineers." For ten miles below Albany the river was essentially dead, "a fishless stretch of water." The health of the river recovered as it flowed south, but at New York, he reported, millions of gallons of raw sewage were dumped into the river every day. Boyle expressed optimism that the Interstate Sanitary Commission was identifying major industrial polluters but conceded that its staff of five inspectors was too small for the enormous job of protecting the river.[9]

A second Boyle article published the following November was written with "personal and purposeful wrath." In it Boyle denounced the polluters and developers who were despoiling the American landscape. Everywhere he looked, Boyle asserted, "much of what is lovely, rich and real about the U.S. is scheduled for wholesale destruction or defacement." America the beautiful, he wrote, "is becoming America the ugly, the wasted, the blasted and the blighted." The villains were road builders, engineers, corporations, and public officials enamored with a false gospel of progress that was resulting in the "desecration of the landscape." Boyle called instead for an ambitious program of park creation and open space acquisition, the preservation of ecologically sensitive areas, and a citizenry committed to defending their neighborhoods. Only strong and concerted action could prevent America from going "down the drain." In a sidebar piece, Secretary of the Interior Stewart Udall described Boyle as outraged and expressed the hope that "his sense of outrage is contagious." Everyone, he stated, "is lessened by every act that defaces or diminishes the American earth."[10]

Boyle then wrote an even more searing indictment of governmental officials, especially those in the state's Conservation Department who should have been protecting the public interest in the Hudson River but instead were ignoring evidence they should have been using to challenge major industries that were having an adverse impact on its ecology. Boyle had heard from a fellow fisherman, Arthur Glowka, and marine biologist Dominick Pirone that there were enormous fish kills at Con Ed's Indian Point reactor number 1. Pirone told Boyle that he had seen thousands of dead or dying fish at a discharge pipe at Indian Point. The fish were attracted by the warm water returning to the river. Pirone and Glowka had seen photographs of striped bass piled as high as twelve feet in a nearby dump, and had learned that Con Ed kept two trucks on hand to move the dead fish to the landfill. When Glowka went to the Conservation Department office in Poughkeepsie to study the entire set of photographs, he was told that they didn't exist. Boyle followed up, and within a year he located the man who took them, George Yellot, a bank officer and deputy game warden in Peekskill. When Boyle explained the purpose of his visit, Yellot told him that an official from the Conservation Department had visited him and asked for the photographs, which he handed over. Another Conservation Department official came by a couple of weeks later and asked for the duplicates, which again Yellot surrendered. But as he and Boyle talked, Yellot reached into a drawer and handed Boyle a third set. The Conservation Department never asked for triplicates.[11]

Boyle was enraged, both because of the enormity of the fish kill and because he realized that the Conservation Department was complicit in a cover-up. In April 1965 he published "A Stink of Dead Stripers," which included one of the photographs Yellot had given him. The article highlighted the failure of a public agency to protect the public interest. As Boyle put it, "Officials at the New York State Conservation Department not only have denied that such pictures existed, they have hushed the fact that the pictures were held by the department itself." He specifically mentioned the regional supervisor and the regional fish manager at the Conservation Department's Poughkeepsie office, who had refused Pirone and Glowka's request to see the photographs and the files relating to Indian Point. Boyle added that when citizens concerned about the fish kills at Indian Point and the potential impact of the Storm King plant on spawning grounds for striped bass sought to present information in the Storm

Figure 6. Art Glowka and Robert H. Boyle. Photograph by John P. Christin, 1966. Courtesy of Riverkeeper.

King proceedings, the Federal Power Commission refused to reopen the hearings and allowed the flagrantly erroneous (and apparently willfully false) testimony of Con Ed's consultant, Alfred Perlmutter, to stand as the only discussion of the topic in the hearing record. A state agency and a federal agency charged with protecting the public were instead protecting a private utility company at the public's expense.[12]

If Pete Seeger promoted a kind of populist environmentalism, Cronin and Kennedy have described Boyle and the fishermen as exemplifying a "blue-collar environmentalism." Boyle realized that traditional conservation, especially the protection of wilderness areas far from home, was doing little to protect the places where people—especially working people—actually lived. Because of pollution, adult residents of Verplanck Point and Crotonville and other Hudson River communities, who as children had learned to swim in the river, who had picnicked with their families along its banks, who had fished its waters throughout their lives, could not pass on those simple pleasures to their children. As John Cronin looked back on his childhood in Yonkers, he recalled that the river "was not a destination but another point in the circle of our lives. It was a part of our neighborhood and family." What had been the residents' birthright, a clean river and its bounty, was taken away by poor public policy, public officials more committed to protecting industry than to doing their jobs, and by municipal and corporate polluters.[13]

Boyle fought back by organizing the Hudson River Fishermen's Association in February 1966. The group's purpose was to "encourage the rational use of the aquatic resources of the Hudson River and its tributaries . . . gather, study and disseminate information about the ecology of the Hudson watershed, particularly in regard to the life histories and needs of fishes; endeavor to protect the spawning and nursery grounds of desirable sports and commercial fishes; and assist in efforts to abate pollution." Collectively the members of the Fishermen's Association committed themselves to bringing about "the ecological betterment of the watershed." It was a small organization at first: founding members included Pirone and Glowka, as well as a handful of other professionals, individuals who grew up along the river, and the commercial fishermen Boyle had befriended. As their first issue the fishermen decided to take on the oil that Penn Central was spewing into the river at its Harmon Diesel and Electric Shops. The Harmon operation had been dumping "countless thousands of gallons" of oil directly into the river, Boyle asserted. As a fisherman, he encountered vast stretches of the river coated with a sheen of oil, and also saw the consequences of the illegal discharge on aquatic life. Other members of the Fishermen's Association were as angry as Boyle. They called officials at the Army Corps of Engineers to report what amounted to hundreds of violations. The Army Corps and the Federal Water Pollution Control Administration stonewalled the fishermen, occasionally promising to investigate but never doing so. Finally, in June 1968, the Hudson River Fishermen's Association and Congressman Richard Ottinger filed suit against Penn Central and the Army Corps of Engineers. Ottinger and David Sive, an attorney for the Sierra Club, represented the association. With the evidence the fishermen has assembled, Penn Central eventually settled, in November 1969, on four of the suit's claims and was fined $4,000—a pittance compared to the cost of cleaning up the oil it had been discharging into the river for decades.[14]

In researching his book *The Hudson River: A Natural and Unnatural History*, Boyle had come upon two laws enacted near the end of the nineteenth century, the federal Rivers and Harbors Act of 1899 and the New

York Harbor Act of 1888, which had banned the release of pollutants into the nation's (and the state's) waterways, though these laws specifically exempted raw sewage. Each law included a provision awarding a bounty to the person or organization that reported a violation. Boyle had attorneys at Time-Life investigate, and they found that the two laws were still on the books, though the bounty provision had never been applied. The Fishermen's Association's suit against Penn Central became the test case for the bounty provision, and although the U.S. Attorneys who were part of the suit against Penn Central were reluctant to do so, the fishermen received $2,000, half the fine levied against the railroad, for reporting the violation.[15]

The Fishermen's Association would continue its efforts to protect the Hudson through its "Bag a Polluter" program. This was the idea of Art Glowka, and it called on citizens up and down the river to fill out prepaid postcards identifying polluters, the date and time of the violation, and any adverse effects they could observe. As an incentive to citizens, the postcards also contained a notice that a provision of the Rivers and Harbors Act made it possible for individuals who reported a polluter to receive as much as $1,250 from any fines subsequently levied against polluters. The postcards would be sent to the Fishermen's Association office in Ossining, where volunteers would inform the Army Corps of Engineers of the incident, investigate the pollution, and demand that the violations cease. The "Bag a Polluter" program resulted in the association taking action against the Hudson Wire Company, which Boyle characterized as "one of the most noxious polluters of the river in the Ossining area." It was discharging acids into the Kill Brook, a tributary of the Hudson. When the Fishermen's Association identified the company's violations and generated publicity about its discharges, Hudson Wire announced that it would halt its pollution.[16]

When necessary, the Fishermen's Association would also pursue litigation, often jointly with other environmental organizations. Albert K. Butzel, a veteran attorney from the Storm King litigation, became one of the Fishermen's Association's advocates. He initiated several lawsuits, perhaps most impressively in opposition to Westway, a superhighway proposed to replace the decrepit West Side Highway (part of which had collapsed in 1973) to bring cars into Lower Manhattan. Westway would have required the filling in of 242 acres of the Hudson shallows in an area critically important to the river's striped bass population. The state's environmental commissioner, Peter A. A. Berle, denied a clear air permit because of the amount of air pollution cars using Westway would produce. Berle was fired, and his replacement, Robert Flacke, eventually issued the permit. Westway also needed approval from the Army Corps of Engineers because of the need to fill in those 242 acres of the river. Butzel and the expert witnesses the Fishermen's Association brought to the case demonstrated that construction of the highway would devastate the river's striped bass. Especially important was testimony of the biologist R. Ian Fletcher, which demonstrated that proponents of the highway had greatly underestimated the impact of construction on the river's fisheries and that the Corps' consultants had intentionally presented their data in a way that was intended to confuse rather than enlighten citizens, regulators, and elected officials. Despite strong Westway support from elected officials—from the White House to New York's governor and U.S. senators to the city's mayor, Edward Koch—as well as developers and construction unions, Butzel and the Fishermen's Association, along with other intervenors, prevailed. Much of the money earmarked for the highway went instead to improving the city's mass-transit system. Within a few years the Fishermen's Association had filed dozens of lawsuits against industries and municipalities that were polluting the Hudson.[17]

Cases the Fishermen's Association joined included, with Scenic Hudson, a successful suit against Con Ed's plan to use the stone removed to make way for the proposed underground powerhouse at Storm King as fill to create a park along the river. The association became party to the Defend Our River Committee in a suit challenging the Army Corps of Engineers' issuance of a permit to Eberhard M. Thierman, a property owner in Grandview-on-Hudson, to fill a shallow area of the river to enlarge his lot (the District Court ruled that the Army Corps had not conducted a public hearing on the permit or prepared an environmental impact statement). The fishermen joined the Cortlandt Conservation Association in a legal challenge that prevented the expansion of the Croton municipal dump into the river, and, with Lakeland High School students, the fishermen successfully petitioned in federal court to force the New York State National Guard to remove the fill it had dumped in the Camp Smith marsh. As Thomas A. Whyatt explained to the mayor of Peekskill, which was considering using fill to create the site for a project in Peekskill Bay that would include housing, commercial space, and a park, the Fishermen's Association was determined to protect the Hudson River shallows, which "are essential to the continued health and life-giving properties of the river—providing spawning and nursery areas for the Hudson's rich abundances of fish resources." These shallow areas, he pointed out, are "among the most fertile environments in the world."[18]

Boyle eventually suggested that the Hudson River needed a full-time watchman, or "riverkeeper." As he explained in his book, he envisioned the appointment of a naturalist or conservationist who would be "out on the river the length of the year, nailing polluters on the spot, telling highwaymen they cannot build the road here but over there, talking to schoolchildren, telling anglers where the stripers or sturgeon are running—in essence, giving a sense of time, place, and purpose to people who live in or visit the valley." Boyle's idea for a riverkeeper was modeled after the career of William James Lunn, who for almost fifty years was employed by the Houghton Club to exercise stewardship of the Test, perhaps the finest trout stream in England. Lunn was everywhere, cutting weeds, raising trout in hatcheries and restocking the river, ensuring there were aquatic insects aplenty for the Test's trout, in effect personifying the river. Boyle hoped that the riverkeeper would be a "no-nonsense naturalist, with the idiosyncrasies, migrations, and workings of the Hudson engrained in his mind." Boyle concluded this discussion by asserting, "We need someone like this on the Hudson and on every major river in the country."[19]

Four years after Boyle published this idea, the Fishermen's Association and the Hudson River Conservation Society announced the appointment of Tom Whyatt as the first riverkeeper in 1973. Whyatt, a graduate of Harvard University and the University of Minnesota School of Law, had worked at the Boyce Thompson Institute in Yorkers, an important organization for research on the Hudson. In announcing Whyatt's appointment, the Fishermen's Association and the Conservation Society explained that as riverkeeper, he was charged to "investigate complaints about pollution and scenic destruction, present and potential, in the Hudson Valley from Manhattan to the Adirondacks." Echoing Boyle's articulation of his riverkeeper idea, the Fishermen's Association and the Conservation Society stated that "Whyatt's assignment is to help save this great river and to give a sense of time, place and purpose to people who live in or visit the Hudson Valley." The conservation groups expressed hope that the appointment of the first riverkeeper would be an event of "national significance" and that it would become a model adopted by other rivers "because unfortunately neither the state nor federal governments truly care much about conserving such important national resources as marine fisheries and historic sites."[20]

One of Whyatt's first acts as riverkeeper was to start a "People's Pipewatch" program. In an effort akin to Glowka's "Bag a Polluter" program, Whyatt organized a small group called the River Rats in 1983 to train their eyes on pollutants being discharged into the Hudson or its tributaries. Those River Rats reported approximately twenty individual companies that were discharging into the river in violation of the Clean Water Act. Riverkeeper Whyatt demanded that those companies immediately cease their illegal activities. Whyatt also opposed Irvington's intention to expand its waterfront park by filling in Hudson River shallows, which he believed were essential to the river's ecology and fisheries. Perhaps most important, Whyatt became an environmental educator, speaking to hundreds of service clubs, schools, garden clubs, and the like, preaching the gospel of the ecological and historical importance of the Hudson River Valley. Unfortunately, the modest funding provided by the Fishermen's Association and the Conservation Society, later joined by Clearwater, could not continue to support the position, and Whyatt subsequently went on to become environmental director of Clearwater and served as executive director of the Open Space Institute and as executive director of the Westchester Land Trust. The position of riverkeeper fell into abeyance until Boyle, with $25,000 the Fishermen had received as part of the Hudson River Peace Treaty, decided that the best use of the money would be to revive the Riverkeeper program. He approached John Cronin, one of the original River Rats and for several years a commercial fisherman on the river, and suggested that he take on the task. Cronin spoke with Whyatt, who enthusiastically supported the idea, and Riverkeeper began its second career as an environmental force on the Hudson in 1982.[21]

In 1982 the Fishermen's Association contracted with Andre Mele, a Kingston boatbuilder, to construct a twenty-five-foot patrol boat. Launched on May 14, 1983, with Cronin on the Hudson in that small craft, the Riverkeeper organization quickly became a critically important advocate for the Hudson. Shortly after the *New York Times* published an article about his appointment as riverkeeper, Cronin heard from both

NBC and CBS News, which wanted to chronicle the building of the boat and his first day on the river. With an NBC crew onboard, Cronin followed up on a tip from a state trooper that oceangoing oil tankers were anchoring opposite Hyde Park, taking in Hudson River water to clean their holds, and then filling up with river water for transport to Aruba. On that first day on the river, Cronin found an Exxon tanker doing exactly what the state trooper described to him. With megaphone in hand, and news cameras rolling, he hailed the skipper of the tanker, the *Palm Beach*. Over the course of months Cronin and volunteers took samples of the pollution discharged from various tankers, and, in a press release, the Fishermen's Association charged Exxon with dumping toxic petrochemicals in the Hudson and then stealing its water. The story line garnered national and even international attention. Exxon denied any wrongdoing and stated that empty tankers visiting the area near Hyde Park and Port Ewen were a rare event. But Frank Parslow, a resident of Port Ewen who was a commercial fisherman, had recorded the names and dates of more than a dozen tankers, all affiliated with Exxon, doing exactly what Cronin had asserted—despoiling the river and then taking its water to sell on a distant island. Parslow shared this information with Cronin. Faced with irrefutable evidence, Exxon settled, paying $1.5 million to New York State and $500,000 to the Fishermen's Association. The state used the money to establish the Hudson River Improvement Fund, the association to maintain the Riverkeeper program and help fund local improvements that would benefit the river. The fishermen had taken on one of the largest corporations in the world—and won![22]

In 1986 the Fishermen's Association became Riverkeeper Inc., which became an even more powerful voice for clean water and the Hudson's fisheries. After the Exxon case, Riverkeeper took on the enormous amount of pollution spewing into the Hudson from dozens of factories and municipal sewage treatment plants and even funeral homes at Quassaic Creek, the stream that separates the city of Newburgh and the town of New Windsor. While stretches of the creek, shrouded by deciduous trees, still sparkled, for much of its short run from Chadwick Lake to the river the Quassaic was terribly polluted. Robert F. Kennedy Jr., had joined Riverkeeper as a staff attorney at this time and made the creek a personal cause. Together with volunteers he tracked down the polluters fouling the creek pipe by pipe. They demonstrated that the effluents released into the Quassaic, and ultimately the Hudson, far exceeded the permits many of the companies had received from a compliant Department of Environmental Conservation to pour waste into the waterway. The evidence amassed by the Fishermen's Association was so powerful that each of the twenty polluters settled before going to court. The Department of Environmental Conservation received $350,000 in penalties, the U.S. Attorney received $50,000, and Riverkeeper $150,000, along with $50,000 in fees. Riverkeeper devoted its share of the penalty to establish a fund to help restore the creek.[23]

In succeeding years Riverkeeper successfully sued Orange County, New York, for filling in a fifty-acre wetland; took on the U.S. Military Academy at West Point for dumping untreated sewage in the Hudson; forced the state Department of Transportation to cease its illegal dumping and filling in of wetlands; and sued the state Department of Correctional Services for its release of untreated sewage. Cronin and Ian Fletcher also negotiated with Con Ed and effectively forced the utility to install modified Ristolph screens, at a cost of $25 million, to reduce fish kills. Cronin and Kennedy have recounted these and other battles in their important book, *The Riverkeepers*, and interested readers can follow their stories there.[24]

With Cronin as riverkeeper from 1983 until 2000, the organization has been a powerful force in defense of the Hudson River since its origins with the Fishermen's Association, especially in its litigation and advocacy. The job didn't end with Quassaic Creek or Westway, as Riverkeeper became part of a much broader environmental movement that strives to hold polluters accountable for their actions and public officials for their inaction in defending the Hudson. Paul Gallay, the Hudson riverkeeper since 2010, expressed his frustration at the lack of support from essential public agencies when he asserted in 2015 that "the state's commitment to clean water has become nearly non-existent. Cuts to New York's environmental staff have been draconian, contributing to a shameful 64 percent decline in water enforcement since 2006." Gallay was particularly incensed that the state, for all its seemingly positive statements about the importance of protecting the environment, was in fact doing very little. Indeed, Gallay charged the state with being woefully behind in investment in water quality infrastructure.[25]

In 1987 Pace Law professors Nicholas Robinson and Richard Ottinger, together with Kennedy and Cronin, established the Pace Environmental

Litigation Clinic, which, with student litigators supervised by Kennedy, by this time the chief prosecuting attorney at Riverkeeper, has taken on a number of important environmental cases involving some of the river's worst polluters. Riverkeeper has been the most determined opponent of the relicensing of the Indian Point nuclear power plants, not because it is opposed to nuclear power but because the once-through cooling system used at Indian Point entrains and destroys millions of fish, eggs, and larvae each year. Together with Scenic Hudson and Clearwater, Riverkeeper has been forceful in holding General Electric accountable for dredging the PCBs it illegally dumped in the upper Hudson, and it strongly, and successfully, supported a ban on fracking. In September 2010 Riverkeeper published *Fractured Communities*, a series of case studies of the environmental impacts of fracking on drinking water, air quality, and contaminated soil. The report concluded that fracking "results in significant adverse environmental impacts." At least in part as a result of Riverkeeper's efforts, on December 17, 2014, New York governor Andrew Cuomo banned fracking in New York State.[26]

True to its origins with the hardscrabble Fishermen's Association, Riverkeeper has also taken on powerful corporations, as well as the state and city of New York. One important victory in 1987 required New York City to acquire a significant amount of land (it subsequently purchased twelve hundred acres of woodland on Belleayre Mountain) to protect the purity of the waters that feed its reservoirs in the Catskills, which provide 1.5 billion gallons of drinking water to the city each day. New York City's water from the Catskill reservoirs is unfiltered, and to avoid the estimated $6 billion it would have cost to build filtration plants, the city acquired this buffering land, adopted a plan of responsible development, and established a program to help upstate communities develop sustainable economies. The New York City Watershed Agreement set a national precedent for watershed protection and has been emulated in a number of places. But Riverkeeper subsequently found that the city's Department of Environmental Protection had eviscerated its Watershed Police force, whose members were "unable to perform their critical function: protecting the City's water supply from pollution, vandalism and terrorism." Deep cuts in personnel, poor wages, and antiquated equipment, together with bureaucratic resistance to pursuing and punishing violators, all accounted for the sorry state of the Watershed Police. At one point in the early 1990s the department had exactly one pollution enforcement officer. By 1996 that number had risen to five, who were responsible for patrolling the entire two-thousand-square-mile watershed, an impossible task. "The blame," Robert Kennedy Jr. wrote in a searing report, "lies squarely on the shoulders of an administration that has systematically underpaid, undermanned, overworked, undersupplied, undersupervised and under-trained its bedraggled and demoralized officers"—all at the expense of the public good.[27]

Riverkeeper has become a watchdog organization protecting New York City's water supply and a staunch defender of the Clean Water Act, ever ready to resort to litigation to protect the environment. As was true of its advocacy for the city's drinking water, together with then–attorney general Andrew Cuomo, Riverkeeper took on Exxon Mobil again, this time for discharging between seventeen and thirty million gallons of oil into the soil and groundwater at Greenpoint, New York, the worst oil spill in the state's history. Much of the oil leached into Newtown Creek, a tributary of the Hudson. Riverkeeper and the state reached a settlement with the petroleum giant in 2010 that requires it to clean up the spill and establish an Environmental Benefit Project, with $19.5 million in funding, at the time the largest environmental fine in the state's history, to finance antipollution efforts, restore the damaged environment along the creek, and create open space in Greenpoint.[28]

Riverkeeper also took on major polluters based on its investigation of the Gowanus Canal in Brooklyn. In the mid-nineteenth century, Gowanus Creek had been transformed into a short, 1.8-mile canal to improve shipping, and soon it was lined with foundries, gas manufacturing plants, coal yards, and other industries that simply dumped their untreated waste into the waterway. By the mid-twentieth century the canal was a fetid, incredibly polluted body, fouled by coal tar, heavy metals, pesticides, volatile organic compounds, sewage, and PCBs that flowed into New York Harbor. Using the Clean Water Act, Riverkeeper filed notices of intent to sue against major polluters, which were subsequently assessed fines of $482,000. The canal was designated a Superfund site in March 2010. After complex negotiations between the U.S. Environmental Protection Agency and New York City's Department of Environmental Protection, the canal was slated for a cleanup that will cost more than $500 million.[29]

*

Figure 7. Launch day for the Fishermen's Association's first patrol boat.
Courtesy of Riverkeeper.

Clean water—for fish to swim in, for citizens to drink and swim or boat in—has since the organization of the Fishermen's Association been the principal cause of Riverkeeper. The organization is a dogged defender of the river's fisheries. It commissioned a report, *The Status of Fish Populations and the Ecology of the Hudson* (the Pisces Report, April 2008), which demonstrated that "the fish community has been changing rapidly since 1985 and is showing clear signs of increased instability." Ominously, the Pisces Report provided evidence that ten of the river's thirteen most important fish species had declined in abundance since the 1980s, especially shad (the shad fishery was closed in 2010), river herring, and sturgeon, which was listed as an endangered species in 2014. Hudson River fish were in a long-term decline, and populations of several species had crashed. The Pisces Report attributed the alarming decline in the fishery to overfishing, habitat destruction, and rising water temperatures, but asserted that the biggest culprit was the power plants that line the river's banks. Riverkeeper has called for a comprehensive program to protect and restore the Hudson's fisheries.[30]

In its ongoing effort to protect our human right to clean water, Riverkeeper has recruited a small army of volunteers to take samples to assess water quality at seventy-four locations in the river and at eighty-four sites along 165 miles of the river's tributaries. The samples are sent to Cornell University, an academic partner of Riverkeeper, for analysis. John Lipscomb, captain of the patrol boat, also collects data, especially on fecal pollution. In addition, Riverkeeper collaborates in its sampling efforts with partner organizations, including the New York City Water Trail Association. The data collected points to a sobering conclusion: in 2013, Riverkeeper reported that "a quarter of all water samples taken by Riverkeeper since 2006 exceed federal guidelines because of overflows from leaky sewers and aging water treatment plants." Riverkeeper has used the data that the citizen-scientists have amassed to convict polluters and make its case for stronger enforcement of the Clean Water Act in the courtroom or at the state capital and in Washington, D.C. Other academic institutions that support Riverkeeper are the Lamont-Doherty Earth Observatory at Columbia University, the State University of New York at Cobleskill, and Queens College. Together with volunteers, academic scientists, and their students, the staff and litigators at Riverkeeper have amassed an impressive record of identifying and prosecuting those who have grossly violated the Hudson River. For example, those citizen-scientists provided the data that enabled Riverkeeper to convict polluters of Catskill Creek, a picturesque stream that flows from the Catskill Mountains to the Hudson and that was a significant inspiration for Thomas Cole, arguably the most important figure in the emergence of an American tradition in landscape painting, the Hudson River School.[31]

Riverkeeper has published the results of its testing program annually. It focuses on determining fecal contamination by monitoring the presence of enterococcus, using an EPA-approved standard for measuring disease-causing pathogens, as well as other measures of the river's health, including water temperature, dissolved oxygen, salinity, turbidity, and chlorophyll. The most recent report, *How's the Water? 2015*, based on more than six thousand water samples collected in the river and its tributaries and analyzed by Riverkeeper's partner scientists, demonstrated that 23 percent of samples tested in the river and 48 percent taken at access points in New York City failed to meet the Clean Water Act's standards for safe swimming. Riverkeeper argued that sewage treatment plants in the Hudson Valley and New York City, the source of most of the fecal

Figure 8. Riverkeeper's patrol boat, the *R. Ian Fletcher*. Photograph by Leah Rae. Courtesy of Riverkeeper.

contamination, needed upgrading at a projected cost of $5.9 billion. To ensure clean water for all citizens, Riverkeeper has advocated improved monitoring of water quality, significant increases in funding for wastewater infrastructure, and greater funding to support the Clean Water Act, as the state Department of Environmental Conservation's Division of Water and its enforcement efforts has suffered significant budgetary constraints and loss of staff in recent years. Riverkeeper also supports continued research and the development of new, better tools for measuring water quality.[32]

While Riverkeeper's accomplishments in improving water quality have been impressive, its greatest challenge in the immediate future is combined sewer outflows. In most older Hudson River cities with combined sewage and stormwater systems, as exist elsewhere in the Northeast and Midwest, rainwater that flows into storm drains passes through the treatment plants. During periods of heavy rainfall or snowmelt, water from the storm drains overwhelms the capacity of the treatment plants and allows untreated sewage as well as polluted stormwater to flow directly into waterways. New York City's fourteen sewage treatment plants release an estimated twenty-seven billion gallons of untreated sewage and polluted stormwater into the Hudson, its tributaries, and New York Harbor each year. In 2008 Basil Seggos, then a staff member at Riverkeeper and now commissioner of the Department of Environmental Conservation, proposed a green infrastructure program to capture and use the stormwater before it entered the sewage system. Much of water could be then used to promote more vegetation, which would result in a true greening of the city. This was also a theme of Riverkeeper's 2008 report *Sustainable Raindrops*. In 2010 New York City announced a Green Infrastructure plan that would spend millions of dollars to control sewage and stormwater overflow. Two years later the city committed to spent $2.6 billion on sewage treatment infrastructure to substantially reduce pollution in the Hudson River estuary and New York Harbor. Riverkeeper's next hire will be a person who, together with citizen scientists and partner organizations, will test the water and monitor compliance with this program.[33]

Even as it has become an important environmental organization, collaborating with universities, sponsoring world-class research, and publishing its own papers on issues that threaten the Hudson, Riverkeeper has also cultivated a strong constituency of members who care deeply about the river. Scenic Hudson had started a volunteer cleanup program, but when it discontinued that effort, Riverkeeper adopted it. In its first "Sweep," on June 2, 2012, some 450 volunteers working at thirty locations collected five hundred bags of trash weighing an estimated seven tons. The following year more than 1,400 volunteers collected thirty-eight tons of trash, and in 2014 some 2,900 volunteers worked at eighty-two locations along the river. In its fifth year, 2016, Sweep's 2,200 volunteers worked at 109 locations and collected 1,635 bags of trash (estimated at 48,800 pounds). Volunteers also removed 423 tires from the river and its tributaries. Paul Gallay believes that the annual Sweep is important in strengthening Riverkeeper's bonds to communities and also enhances civic engagement by attracting activists and volunteers determined to protect the environmental quality of places where they live.[34]

Riverkeeper has also expressed concern about the pace of new construction on the Hudson's banks. In 2008 it described the pattern of recent development along the river as "a gold rush to develop the waterfront." If left unchecked, Riverkeeper warned, "developers will gobble up every remaining parcel of undeveloped land." It cited a Scenic Hudson report that seventeen thousand new housing units were planned for the riverfront between Yonkers and Albany. The following year Riverkeeper expressed the fear that "walls of high priced condominiums" would block public access to the river and that runoff from impervious surfaces—rooftops, roads, parking lots, and sidewalks—would carry pollution into the river. Although speaking out against developers might at first seem to be a new direction for Riverkeeper, it is squarely within its fifty-year tradition of defending water quality in the Hudson and promoting public access to the river. The organization cannot overrule local planning and zoning boards, but it has raised an important concern among its members, many of whom are community activists who may well speak with local officials in opposition to developments that threaten the quality of life in their communities. This is not mission expansion but a next step toward fulfilling its mission.[35]

Riverkeeper also opposed a new Tappan Zee Bridge, a piece of Governor Andrew Cuomo's ambitious infrastructure investment program. It has argued that the cost of repairing and improving the existing bridge would be a fraction of what the new one will cost. It has also expressed concern that sinking the pier foundations for the new bridge, and removing those of the old one, could harm the shallows of the Tappan Zee, which are important to the river's fisheries. But the bridge is going up today, though Riverkeeper did succeed in preventing the governor from raiding an environmental bond fund for $460 million designated for clean water to help pay for the bridge's construction. The long-term effects of the bridge project on the river's fisheries will not be known for years. Taxpayers, of course, will feel the cost long before then. Riverkeeper and Scenic Hudson successfully fought for $11.5 million in mitigation and restoration funding for damages caused by the bridge's construction.[36]

Riverkeeper doesn't have the enormous endowment that Scenic Hudson accumulated over the years, and relies on its members' annual contributions to fund much of its efforts. It also relies on hundreds of volunteers to support its work. In addition to the water sampling program and the annual Sweep, these citizen activists come together to survey fishermen about PCBs; engage in tree plantings, cleanups of parks, shorelines, and other areas; work to accomplish invasive species removal; and numerous other activities. In 2014 alone, volunteers logged 10,962 hours of service. In addition to promoting a cleaner environment, these volunteer efforts are important because they give residents a sense of ownership of the river.[37]

Riverkeeper's path from its origins with the fishermen to an aggressive modern environmental group has not been without its challenges. Perhaps the greatest of these occurred in 2000, when Kennedy hired William Wegner as a staff scientist. Robert Boyle investigated Wegner's career and discovered that he had been convicted as part of a ring that was smuggling cockatoo eggs from Australia to the United States, hatching the birds, and then selling them. Wegner was indicted, convicted, and received a five-year sentence and was fined $10,000. Kennedy justified the hire, stating that Wegner was an excellent scientist and comparing his crimes to Kennedy's own youthful arrest for drug use, stating that Wegner deserved a second chance. Boyle was incensed that Riverkeeper's staff included a man convicted of environmental crimes. "You don't hire a child molester to run a nursery school," he told a *New York Times* reporter. Boyle was especially concerned that having Wegner on the staff would hurt Riverkeeper in litigation. "Can you imagine what Mayor Rudolph Giuliani, a former hardball United States attorney who has taken some hard knocks from Bobby over the [city's] watershed, would do if he discovered that

Wegner was working for us? It boggles the mind." Boyle, Riverkeeper's founder and longtime president, resigned from the organization's board when Kennedy refused to fire Wegner, as did seven other members of the board.[38]

In his argument that the Hudson needed a riverkeeper, Boyle stated that every major waterway in the United States should have just such a watchdog. The success of the Hudson's Riverkeeper program inspired environmentalists, at first in the United States and eventually around the world, to create their own riverkeepers. Today, the Waterkeeper Alliance, which organized in 1992, reports that there are more than three hundred Waterkeeper organizations in the United States and in thirty-four other countries. What began as Boyle's fond hope to protect the Hudson River has become a global force for clean water.[39]

The *New York Times* reported on January 7, 2017, that Riverkeeper, the State of New York, and Entergy, the corporation that owns Indian Point nuclear plants numbers 2 and 3, had agreed that the plants would close in 2020 and 2021. The formal agreement was signed on January 9. Riverkeeper will assume the responsibility for monitoring safety and progress toward closing these facilities. As part of the settlement, Entergy will create a $15 million fund to pay for river restoration and remediation, including wetlands protection, control of invasive species, and habitat surveys. This has been a long, hard-fought battle for Riverkeeper, and it promises to end the worst of the fish kills that have plagued the Hudson River for decades. It also should end the very real concerns of millions of residents who live nearby, even as much as fifty or more miles away, as there has never been a satisfactory evacuation plan for the metropolitan New York area in case of a nuclear accident. The energy produced by Indian Point will be replaced by clean energy, principally wind and solar, so its closing will not increase the amount of carbon and other pollutants that a replacement by conventional power plants would have caused. This agreement would not have been possible without the long-standing efforts of Riverkeeper, as well as the support of Governor Andrew Cuomo and other elected officials in Albany.[40]

From its beginnings with the Fishermen's Association, Riverkeeper has made a cleaner Hudson River its most important priority, and it did so well before the federal and state governments fully embraced the public's right to clean water. Riverkeeper has stayed true to its origins: as Paul Gallay has explained, its operating philosophy to protect clean water remains "Support the grassroots. Be data driven. Don't flinch when the going gets tough." Its emphasis on identifying the sources of pollution, and its reliance on citizen activists to accumulate the data studied by its partner scientists, have made environmentalism profoundly personal for many of its volunteers. As Pete Seeger often reminded his audiences, the Hudson is our river, and Riverkeeper's members have taken that to heart.[41]

5

THE CONTINUING BATTLE AGAINST
POWER PLANTS

On September 27, 1969, Rod Vandivert submitted a special report, "Utilities and the Hudson River," to the annual meeting of the New York State Conservation Council. He did so not as executive director of the Scenic Hudson Preservation Conference but as a member of the Suffolk County Fish and Game Association. In the report, Vandivert warned of the dramatic expansion of electrical generating capacity under way or being planned for the Hudson River Valley. "The Hudson River," he wrote, "may very well become host to the greatest concentration of utility plants on any estuary in the nation." The list he presented included Indian Point units 2, 3, 4, 5, and 6 (the last three have not been built), as well as other conventional or nuclear plants on the west bank of the river then in the planning stages. Vandivert's special concern in the report was how dramatically thermal pollution from the concentration of plants in a five- or six-mile stretch of the river would dramatically impact the ecology of the Hudson. He also expressed frustration that the utilities, led by Consolidated Edison (Con Ed), were effectively trying to minimize if not completely eliminate any public role in the decision-making process.[1]

Power plants, whether conventional (coal, oil, or, increasingly, natural gas) or nuclear, generate intense heat. Thus they are often located adjacent to rivers and large lakes, and draw huge amounts of water to cool their cores—in the case of large nuclear plants, millions of gallons of water every day. As the Scenic Hudson case and Riverkeeper's battle against the relicensing of the Indian Point nuclear reactors have demonstrated, the withdrawal of such large amounts of water has had a devastating effect on fish populations, while the water is usually returned to the river or lake at an increased temperature of as much as fifteen degrees Fahrenheit, with significant effects on the aquatic ecosystem. The planning and construction of new power plants along the Hudson became flash points for environmentalists in the 1970s and have continued to be so since then.

Four years after Vandivert's warning, the Power Authority of the State of New York (PASNY) began searching for sites on which to construct new electricity-generating plants. Stone and Webster, an engineering firm, was hired by the Metropolitan Transportation Authority to study thirty-one locations for potential development, all but one of them in the Hudson River Valley. The following February, PASNY announced its intent to construct, along or near the west bank of the Hudson in southern Greene County, a 1,200-megawatt "pressurized-water nuclear reactor steam supply system" power plant, designed by Stone and Webster and constructed by the Babcock & Wilcox Company—the firm that built the Three Mile Island nuclear plant in Dauphin County, Pennsylvania, on the Susquehanna River southeast of Harrisburg. The authority had narrowed the potential sites to two locations, one in Cementon, about four miles south of the village of Catskill, and the other just west of the village of Athens, ten miles to the north. PASNY also proposed construction of a pumped-storage power plant at Prattsville, in the Catskills in western Greene County, to take advantage of the power produced by the nuclear facility in excess of normal demand.[2]

In presenting its plan, the Power Authority emphasized that the electricity generated was essential to the expansion of New York City's subway system and the operation of its commuter railroads, which hardly endeared the proposal to upstate residents. Worse, the Cementon location, which PASNY decided upon fifteen months later (with Athens as the required alternative), was at the sweeping bend of the Hudson River in the viewshed of Olana, the majestic house and estate of nineteenth-century landscape painter Frederic E. Church. Just south of the city of Hudson on the east bank, Olana had recently become a New York State historic site. With a domed reactor building 205 feet in height and a cooling tower projected to reach 450 feet or more, with a diameter of 250 feet at the top, and a large vapor plume that would be especially visible during the winter months, a Cementon plant would have been a blight on the landscape, not just for the view southwest from Olana but also when seen from the Catskill escarpment, a popular state park eight miles to the west, and elsewhere throughout the mid-Hudson Valley. The vapor plume from the plant would, at times, be even more intrusive than the cooling tower. Given the widespread concern about the second and third nuclear plants at Indian Point, the ongoing battle over Storm King Mountain, and increasing concerns about the safety and viability of nuclear power, it is unsurprising that local elected officials and a significant group of citizens and organizations challenged the siting and design of the proposed plant.[3]

PASNY is a public authority established by an act of the state legislature, Chapter 722, Laws of New York, 1931. Public authorities were relatively new in the United States at the time: the first significant such organization, the Port of New York Authority (1921), which was modeled after the Metropolitan Board of Works in London (1851), was created to meet the commercial and transportation needs of two states and several hundred municipalities. Public authorities have substantial powers, including the ability to issue tax-exempt bonds and exercise eminent domain, and are structured in ways that usually shield them from public accountability. In its early years PASNY built hydroelectric power plants, mainly along the Niagara and Saint Lawrence Rivers, far from metropolitan centers. Its funding came from the sale of bonds and, after the power plants were operational, of electricity. In 1968, however, Governor Nelson A. Rockefeller signed a law expanding PASNY's generating capabilities to include nuclear and pumped-storage power plants. The proposed nuclear plant in southern Greene County would have been PASNY's second foray into nuclear-powered electricity generation, after the James A. FitzPatrick plant adjacent to Lake Ontario in Oswego County, which became operational in July 1975.[4]

The mid-1970s was a time when demand for electricity was increasing significantly and projections for needed generating capacity soared. Arthur Hauspurg, president of Con Ed, the utility that provides electricity for New York City and Westchester County, estimated in 1976 that demand for power was increasing by 2.9 percent annually. He also stated that the "long-range forecast for electric growth in our service territory indicates the need for about 600,000 kilowatts of new generating capacity a year in the 1990's," or approximately "five million kilowatts of new generation during the decade." Decisions about what kind of power plant to build, and where, were also affected by the recent oil embargo, which had sent prices for oil and gasoline to unprecedented heights. Thus those planning the next generation of power plants focused on nuclear and coal. For nuclear that meant locations next to a significant body of water that could be used for cooling, which in New York State narrowed the choice of locations to areas adjacent to the Hudson River and Lakes Ontario and Erie. Still another complication, as landscape architect Carl H. Petrich has pointed out, was that the best potential sites for any new electricity generation facilities, nuclear or otherwise, had already been occupied by an older generation of power plants.[5]

Surely as a result of the controversy sparked by Con Ed's plan to build a pumped-storage plant at Storm King Mountain, PASNY moved carefully. In deciding upon the 284-acre Cementon tract as the location for its proposed power plant, PASNY planners undoubtedly hoped that building and operating the plant would not be controversial in a largely rural area that was struggling economically. They also expected that Cementon would not generate the strong opposition to a nuclear plant that had quickly developed among residents of Athens. Moreover, PASNY planners surely anticipated that the area's legacy of industrial uses, especially the three large cement plants that gave the locale its name, would minimize the kind of criticism that Con Ed had experienced over the preceding decade and the legal battles with Scenic Hudson that were ongoing. If so, PASNY's planners were unprepared for the opposition that quickly emerged following the announcement of the Cementon location. As artist Alan Gussow noted in testimony he prepared for presentation to the U.S. Nuclear Regulatory Commission (NRC), at Cementon "the presence of massive man-made forms detracts significantly from what is surely one of the most scenic reaches of the river." Gussow added that even with the visual intrusions of its industrial past, the landscape at Cementon was significant: there, he testified, "we have the expanse of river and the backdrop of the Catskill Mountain range, presenting us with a landscape which has been recognized for over one hundred years as the quintessential scenic, pastoral vista, one that has a very special place it seems to me in the American sensibility."[6]

The alternative site, just west of Athens, was not on the banks of the Hudson River but approximately a mile and a half inland. Athens was, and is today, a small village, directly opposite the city of Hudson, with a mix of colonial and nineteenth-century buildings and some twentieth-century intrusions on the historic streetscape. The proposed plant would have been partly concealed by a ridgeline, but its cooling tower and vapor plume would have been visible almost everywhere within the village as well as from the river and important locations on both banks. As Gussow noted in his testimony for consideration by the NRC, if the power plant were constructed on the site, "It would intrude in every season, standing out like an exclamation mark or enormous pyramid, the overriding visual feature of the view from this choice location. The tower would dwarf everything else; I think it would be aesthetically damaging beyond words."[7]

Once again the battle lines were drawn, with those supporting development—really the reindustrialization of the mid-Hudson River Valley—against those who cherished its landscape as a special place. The power authority began the long process of gaining approvals from the New York State Board on Electric Generation Siting and the Environment and the federal NRC, even as Greene County opponents organized as Citizens to Preserve the Hudson Valley. By the beginning of 1974 the citizens group had obtained five thousand signatures on petitions that denounced the proposed plant as a defilement of the landscape of their beloved valley.[8]

When PASNY announced the two sites in Greene County on June 20, 1973, the county legislature voted unanimously for a moratorium on the construction of any power plants within the county. The following year the county legislature expressed its unanimous opposition to the proposed nuclear plant at Cementon, and two years later it authorized hiring outside experts to help in the preparation of testimony before the NRC, among other acts. NRC staff determined that 80 percent of the residents of Greene County opposed the nuclear plant and that 60 percent also opposed a coal-fired one. Elected officials in villages and towns within Greene County heeded their constituents and also expressed opposition. Herbert C. Scott, of the Athens town board, expressed a widely held sentiment among upstate residents when he inquired, "If they need a plant to provide power for New York City, why not build in New York?" Robert Bruner, the mayor of Athens, shared many of his constituents' concerns about the safety of a nuclear plant just west of the village. "People are afraid of an atomic plant," he told a reporter for the *New York Times*. "Who's going to buy a home here?" The Greene County Planning Commission joined other public agencies in opposing the plant. In addition to expressing concerns about safety, opponents questioned the impact of the proposed nuclear plant on the scenery of the Hudson Valley and on its fisheries, as the water intakes at Con Ed's Indian Point nuclear plants had devastated the fish population in the vicinity of Buchanan.[9]

An analysis of the economic impact of the proposed Cementon plant by Elizabeth Peelle concluded that it would not produce net long-term benefits for the area. To be sure, during construction contractors would have employed an estimated twenty-one hundred workers, who would have been paid $294 million during the six years it would take to build the facility. However, most of the construction workers would have come from outside the immediate area, which would have placed great stress on an already tight local housing market, and as a result of increasing rents, many longtime residents, especially the elderly, could have been displaced. Those workers who commuted from the Albany area, approximately forty miles north, would have spent their income elsewhere and would not have benefited the local economy. Moreover, if the Cementon plant were built, it is likely that the Lehigh Portland Cement Company plant, very close to the site, would have closed, which would have resulted in the loss of more than 200 jobs. As the nuclear plant would have required an estimated workforce of 215 when operational, total employment would have been a net wash. It seems likely that the nuclear plant would have employed significantly more engineers and white-collar workers than the cement plant, at a higher pay scale, but this would have left many blue-collar workers without jobs they had counted on. In addition, if built, the power plant would have had a devastating impact on the finances of the Town of Catskill (in which Cementon is located) and its school district: Portland Cement paid a total of approximately $212,000 in taxes to the town and the school district each year, whereas PASNY, as a state agency, would not have been required to pay taxes. To be sure, PASNY promised to make payments in lieu of taxes of $10,400 annually, but this was only about

5 percent of what the Lehigh Cement Company paid. Greene County's analysis of the fiscal impact of the proposed plant demonstrated that it would have required additional public services necessitating higher local taxes. Getting materials and equipment to the site would also have required significant infrastructure spending to realign or relocate existing roadways. And there was concern that if the Cementon plant were built, it would have an adverse impact on the tourism industry. To the overwhelming majority of residents and elected officials in Greene County, Cementon was a losing proposition, with few if any local benefits.[10]

On July 25, 1975, PASNY filed applications to federal and state agencies for approval to build the Greene County Nuclear Power Plant at Cementon. The approval process, notoriously slow, began internally at the NRC, which contracted with the U.S. Department of Energy's Oak Ridge National Laboratory to prepare the required environmental impact statement. Based on the assessment of experts at Oak Ridge, the NRC issued a draft environmental statement in March 1976 that recommended approval of the license application. Hearings on the application, held jointly by the Atomic Safety and Licensing Board of the NRC and the state Board on Electric Generation Siting and the Environment, began in May 1977. Most of the massive amount of documentation provided by PASNY and its experts concerned technical details of construction and operation, the increasing demand for electrical power, especially in the New York City metropolitan area, cost-benefit analysis, economic benefits of construction, and environmental impact, which those experts concluded would be minimal.[11]

Documentation on the proposed plant's impact on the landscape of the Hudson River Valley received scant attention in the draft EIS. Testimony by PASNY's consultants, Donald N. Stone, Robert W. Graves, and Bruce E. Podwal, is telling in how limited their analysis of aesthetic considerations actually was. In their testimony these individuals limited their remarks to three concerns. First was the question of the plant's potentially negative effect on the value of riverfront properties on the east side of the river, which they attempted to refute by noting that the construction of the cement plants in the early 1960s had not adversely affected such values. Second was the visual impact of the cooling tower and vapor plume. Here the experts stated that the "visual integration" of the buildings and the cooling tower "is heightened by the choice of a single, off-white color for both concrete and metal-clad surfaces," which, they argued, "contributes to an overall impression of the facility as a harmonious industrial design." They concluded this section of their remarks by noting that "when viewed from most visually sensitive and intensive land use areas, the plant would appear as a unified mass of simple geometric forms." Third, these experts dismissed the contention that the proposed plant would mar the view of the Catskill Mountains, especially from Columbia County. They pointed to six photographs with the cooling tower superimposed to argue that the proposed facility "will not obstruct from view the Catskill Mountain range which stretches across the horizon."[12]

This testimony was striking both in its unquestioning assumption that a "harmonious industrial design" of "simple geometric forms" was appropriate at the Cementon location, and its failure to address the impact of the proposed plant on the viewshed from Olana. Similarly, in the environmental review accompanying its licensing application, PASNY argued that "the proposed plant is surrounded by three adjacent cement mills which have been visible from the same location for many years," an assertion that, while true, ignores the massive difference in scale the cooling tower and visible plume would introduce into the landscape.[13]

During the period of public comment that followed publication of the NRC's draft environmental statement, opponents of the nuclear facility, led by J. Winthrop Aldrich and the Hudson River Conservation Society, pointed out that the draft being considered made no assessment of the plant's visual impact on the Hudson River Valley landscape. Loretta Simon, a trustee of the village of Athens, was a housewife and the mother of a small child as well as an artist and art teacher when she spoke at a public meeting held at Columbia-Greene Community College. She challenged PASNY's plan because it provided no assessment of how the plant would fundamentally change the landscape. She became a key activist in Greene County, and identified scores of historic buildings and viewpoints within the five-mile radius of Cementon and Athens that were essential to Aldrich and the Conservation Society in their legal challenge to the licensing. Her work in promoting greater awareness among residents of the negative consequences that would result if the Cementon plant were built led Greene County to hire Simon as an environmental analyst. Because these concerns raised important points that were not considered in the draft environmental statement, in December 1977 the hearings were expanded to include three intervenor groups concerned about the plant's impact on aesthetics and scenery. As the Oak Ridge team was evaluating public comments and preparing the final environmental statement, Carl H. Petrich joined the laboratory staff in April 1977. A Duke University graduate who had a master's degree in landscape architecture from the University of Michigan, Petrich assumed primary responsibility for assessing the visual impact of the proposed plant. Eventually, he became the principal author of that crucial section of the final environmental statement.[14]

Aesthetic impact, so inadequately addressed by PASNY's experts, became the key determinant of the NRC's evaluation of the permit application for the Cementon plant. This was an essential component of the review process, as the National Environmental Policy Act of 1969 mandated that the federal government "preserve important historic, cultural, and natural aspects of our national heritage, and maintain, wherever possible, an environment which supports diversity and variety of individual choice."[15]

In his work on the Cementon environmental impact statement, Petrich developed a sophisticated methodology for assessing visual impact. Because at this time the NRC was reviewing Cementon and its alternative location, Athens, as potential sites, Petrich first assessed the scenic quality of each from a number of points in the landscape from which the proposed plant would be visible. Using a model for measuring landscape preferences developed by landscape architect E. H. Zube and his colleagues at the University of Massachusetts, Petrich evaluated each site in terms of its landscape qualities—topography, existing land use, and the like—to determine the value of the scenic attributes of each site. He then turned to his technical colleagues at Oak Ridge for help in developing computer models that would demonstrate the highly variable impact of the vapor plume at various times of the day and seasons of the year. Petrich also designed and conducted a visual preference survey to assess "how people feel about their environment and possible changes to it." The survey consisted of a two-page questionnaire and forty photographs—eight groups of three, and sixteen others. An artist carefully superimposed scaled images of the cooling tower and a typical vapor plume on sixteen of the photographs, which also included the existing cement plants. This enabled those participating in the survey to understand how the nuclear plant would change their familiar landscape. Each of the eight groups of three photographs consisted of the actual scene, the same photograph with cooling tower and plume superimposed, and the same photograph with the existing cement plants. Those residents surveyed evaluated the twenty-four photographs of the plant site on a 1–5 scale, with 1 being the least favorable response, 5 the most favorable.[16]

Petrich's survey produced 154 valid responses. It had, be believes, "a balanced distribution of respondents by age, sex, income, occupation, duration of residence in the region, and present residence." Based on the responses, Petrich concluded that most residents were strongly opposed to the introduction of the cooling tower and plume in the landscape; that respondents were presumably familiar with and had adjusted to the presence of the cement plants and found them much less objectionable than the proposed nuclear plant; that they cherished this part of the Hudson River Valley as having a high scenic quality and a large number of historical and cultural sites; and that they believed that locating the nuclear plant at the Athens site would have "less visual impact" than one at Cementon.[17]

Petrich also devoted considerable attention to the history and culture of the Hudson River Valley, especially the writings of Washington Irving and James Fenimore Cooper and the art of the Hudson River School of landscape painting. As he wrote in a draft that became the basis for his analysis of the visual impact of the power plant, "America's first great literary and painting efforts derived from the tensions and hopes of this era, of this place. The foundation of America's culture as well as commerce simultaneously grew here." He relied on Frederic Church's painting *The Hudson Valley in Winter from Olana* (c. 1866–1872), which the noted historian of American art John K. Howat has described as being "as close to perfection as anything done by American artists painting in the field." This painting, which depicts the view from Olana southwest toward the Cementon site, proved hugely influential in establishing the significance of the viewshed the power plant would violate. Indeed, according to Aldrich of the Conservation Society (and later the longtime deputy commissioner for historic preservation in the New York State Office of Parks, Recreation and Historic Preservation), "that painting changed history." Olana, Church's thirty-seven-room house atop Sienghenbergh (or Long) Hill and the surrounding estate of 250 acres, was carefully sited by the artist to take advantage of the spectacular views of the Hudson and the Catskills that its location commanded. Jervis McEntee, an important Hudson River School painter and Church's former pupil, visited Olana in 1872, as the mansion was nearing completion, and described it as "certainly a beautiful house" that "commands one of the finest views of river & mountain in the country." When the fate of Olana hung in precarious balance only a decade before the Cementon controversy, Yale architectural historian Vincent Scully described Church's three-dimensional creation at Olana—house and outbuildings, landscape, and collections—as "his last and most enduring work, the ultimate justification for his art." The Friends of Olana and the New York State Office of Parks and Recreation, which maintains Olana as a historic site, rightly feared that the proposed Cementon plant would fatally compromise the view that Church, and the tens of thousands of visitors who came to Olana each year, found enthralling. The Friends became intervenors in the Nuclear Regulatory Commission proceedings.[18]

Petrich also contacted noted historians of American painting Theodore Stebbins, David Huntington, Barbara Novak, and John Wilmerding. Novak, who taught American art at Barnard College, wrote Petrich that if she were asked to pick "one area of landscape that the nation as a whole and the federal government specifically should designate as a national landmark, as a step toward the preservation of our American past and culture, I would choose this area." Wilmerding, then curator of American painting and sculpture at the National Gallery of Art, was even more emphatic:

> The Olana landscape is unique in being a total synthesis of distinctive scenic beauty *and* important artist's original house, studio, collection, and grounds. In other words, we ought to preserve not merely a beautiful view in its own right, but one integrally fused with an extant embodiment of the very artist's vision which helped to define for Americans a century ago the significance of our national panorama. What I am urging is saving both the view *of* as well as the view *from* something. To disrupt one, in my opinion, irrevocably damages the other. What is supremely important here, I believe, is that you preserve an American landscape not just to be *seen*, but to be *understood*.

Petrich later recalled that Huntington "pointed me in the direction of the deeper meaning of what the views from Olana and Olana itself meant at that time in American history." The voices for the viewshed, for the environment, were compelling and became more and more important as Petrich and his colleagues at Oak Ridge National Laboratory were drafting the final environmental statement.[19]

Even as Petrich and his colleagues were preparing their report, opponents of the proposed Cementon plant continued their efforts. In addition to the Hudson River Conservation Society, Greene County, the Friends of Olana, and the Columbia County Historical Society, their ranks included the Scenic Hudson Preservation Conference, the Hudson River Sloop Clearwater, the Catskill Center for Conservation and Development, the Mid-Hudson Nuclear Opponents, and, belatedly, the state Office of Parks, Recreation and Historic Preservation, the custodian of Olana. The Conservation Society and other intervenors hired Energy Systems Research Group as experts to help prepare testimony to refute PASNY's claims before the joint federal-state hearings and Robert C. Stover as their attorney (he worked pro bono) to emphasize the importance of the scenic attributes of the landscape. Greene County hired Albert K. Butzel, one of the key litigants on behalf of Scenic Hudson in the Storm King proceedings. Energy Systems Group's principal on the Cementon case, Stephen S. Bernow, a physicist educated at Columbia University, challenged the cost-benefit analysis PASNY had introduced in testimony before the joint hearings and presented data that questioned the need for the proposed plant. John Mavretich of Mid-Hudson Nuclear Opponents challenged PASNY's application in terms of need and fuel substitution. As James P. Rod and Mary Lou Lamping informed their colleagues on the Clearwater board of directors, they were certain that these issues would be critical to defeating Cementon. "We believe," they wrote, that "this will be an enormous step toward preventing construction of any of the remaining seven proposed power plants on the River, for essentially the same arguments of a provable 'no need' can be shown for all of them." Moreover, the testimony that Energy Systems Research Group was providing in the case against Cementon "can be applicable to licensing proceedings in most other states as well."[20]

Other experts also prepared testimony on aesthetic impact, including Alan Gussow; David Huntington, an authority on the artist Frederic

Church and whose remarks focused on the impact of the Cementon plant on the Olana viewshed; Richard Benas, then an environmental analyst for the state Department of Environmental Conservation; James Biddle, president of the National Trust for Historic Preservation; and Harvey K. Flad, a young geographer at Vassar College, who under contract with the Hudson River Conservation Society and Greene County prepared a remarkably extensive and thoughtful analysis—almost a small book—on the impact of the plant when seen from a host of locations in the mid-Hudson River Valley.[21]

Flad's testimony was especially important because he supplemented Petrich's visual impact analysis with a thorough grounding in the history of cultural landscapes. He was appreciative of the various agricultural uses of the land and how they had changed over time, as well as the more modest buildings, especially vernacular structures, that were largely overlooked in Petrich's analysis. Flad also paid careful attention to the region's

Figure HF-7
:EMENTON SITE - View from
:ermantown shoreline near
:old storage plant with
:CNPP superimposed.

Figure 9. Photograph by Michael Fredericks Jr., with superimposed drawing by A. Symmetrics and Associates of the proposed Greene County Nuclear Power Plant, Cementon site, as viewed from Germantown. Courtesy of Harvey Flad.

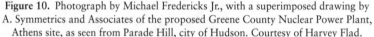

Figure liF-3

ATHENS SITE - View from Parade
Hill, City of Hudson, with
GCNPP superimposed.

Figure 10. Photograph by Michael Fredericks Jr., with a superimposed drawing by
A. Symmetrics and Associates of the proposed Greene County Nuclear Power Plant,
Athens site, as seen from Parade Hill, city of Hudson. Courtesy of Harvey Flad.

significant contributions to the history of landscape design and town planning. He argued, for example, that the town of Hudson was platted in the
late eighteenth century to maximize views of the river. The proprietors
had reserved land for a parade ground on what became known as Promenade Hill, with extensive views of the Hudson.

Flad also introduced as part of his testimony photo-simulations showing the visual impact of the power plant. The Poughkeepsie architectural
firm A. Symmetrics and Associates carefully superimposed drawings of
the plant on photographs taken by Michael Fredericks Jr. These images,
Flad recalled, made "a huge impression" at the hearing and were "key to
the GCNPP decision." In his testimony Flad also pointed out the important demographic dimensions of this area of the Hudson Valley. In effect,
he introduced to the proceedings the importance of community character and argued persuasively that the Cementon plant would diminish the
landscape and culture of this important stretch of the valley. Based on

Flad's work, community character became a new standard for evaluating the impact of proposed projects. A member of the staff of the New York State Public Service Commission judged Flad's testimony to be "the most substantive and professionally developed work which we have ever received from an intervenor."[22]

According to Petrich, as the final environmental statement was taking shape, his immediate supervisor, realizing that the assessment was breaking new ground in emphasizing visual impact, alerted the highest levels of leadership at Oak Ridge, who reviewed and ultimately supported Petrich's analysis and recommendations. When the NRC informed Oak Ridge that it would not publish the final environmental statement, with its recommendation that the license be denied, the leaders of Oak Ridge replied that they would publish it anyway, and would explain why the NRC had not. This forced NRC's hand: failing to produce a thorough though negative environmental assessment would have enabled critics to portray the commission as being in the thrall of the very industry it was supposed to regulate and not an effective representative of the public good. Thus the NRC reluctantly issued the document in February 1979.[23]

The "Final Environmental Statement by the U.S. Nuclear Regulatory Commission for Greene County Nuclear Power Plant Proposed by Power Authority of the Sate of New York" is a monument to the increasing importance of environmentalism in American regulatory law. Petrich effectively refuted the claims by PASNY experts that the proposed Cementon plant would have little impact on the landscape and scenery of the Hudson Valley. Those experts had testified that the cement plants did not significantly impair the view from Olana, and neither would the proposed nuclear plant, whereas the final environmental statement concluded that the nuclear facility was "so much larger than the cement plants that its cooling tower would be easily seen" and its vapor plume would be so large as to attract the viewer's eye to the nuclear plant. Petrich and his colleagues at Oak Ridge also emphasized the importance of the majestic bend in the river with the Catskills in the distance, asserting that "this view is one of extremely high scenic quality . . . and that further development on the scale of the proposed power plant would degrade the view beyond a critical threshold level. The result would be a very serious deleterious impact on a view nationally important for its scenic beauty and historical meaning." The Cementon plant would also impair the view from the

Catskill escarpment, Petrich and the Oak Ridge team determined, noting that "the addition of the power plant would draw attention to this area and stamp this rural, pastoral view with the connotative label of heavy industry." The final environmental statement concluded its assessment of scenic impact by asserting that the "construction and operation of the power plant would seriously affect an area of high scenic quality for the Hudson Valley, one of unique rural and small village atmosphere." The Cementon plant would have "an unacceptable adverse impact on a National Historic Landmark, Olana," that no change in design or materials could mitigate.[24]

Clearly, the case for Cementon was crumbling, and PASNY officials realized this. For the first time in its history, or that of its predecessor, the Atomic Energy Commission, the NRC staff recommended that the commissioners deny a license to construct the proposed nuclear power plant, based principally on aesthetics (the socioeconomic impact of the plant was also a factor, but it appears to have been much less significant). The final environmental statement identified and evaluated "aesthetic values that were fundamental to the citizens of the United States, not just New York," Richard Benas later recalled, and its analysis of the proposed plant's visual impact really defined the discipline. The final environmental statement also examined alternatives to the Cementon site. Staff studied the thirty potential locations in the Hudson River Valley proposed in Stone and Webster's *Plant Site Study* of October 1973. Based on this report, as well as visits to the potential locations it had identified outside the New York metropolitan area, the final environmental statement judged six of those sites, including one at Athens, as "superior."[25]

Although Clearwater had urged Aldrich and the Conservation Society to abandon aesthetics as a trivial argument and to focus instead on larger issues, it was not the possibility of electricity conservation (need) or alternatives to nuclear power (fuel substitution) that would derail PASNY's Cementon application. It was aesthetics, the impact the power plant would have on the landscape of the Hudson River Valley, though PASNY officials apparently never fully understood this. A month after the NRC released the final environmental statement, PASNY chairman Frederick R. Clark suggested to his board of directors that the authority halt its planning for the nuclear facility at Cementon, largely because the cost, originally estimated at $1.3 billion, had soared to $3.1 billion. The joint NRC-state hearings had been scheduled to resume in March 1979, but PASNY requested a suspension of the scheduled dates. Then, on March 28, 1979, a malfunction in the cooling system in the nuclear power plant at Three Mile Island resulted in the worst nuclear disaster in American history. That Three Mile Island was built by the contracting firm hired to construct Cementon, Babcock & Wilcox, and that some engineers claimed that the firm's reactors had a "generic deficiency," put PASNY in an indefensible position: on April 5 its board of directors announced that the authority would sell its nuclear assets at Cementon and would instead build a coal-fired plant ten miles to the north, at Athens. On January 18, 1980, PASNY withdrew its application from the state Board on Electric Generation Siting and the Environment, and on January 30 that board closed its proceedings on the Cementon plant.[26]

In sending a copy of the "Order Closing Proceeding" to Harvey Flad, attorney Robert C. Stover described the order as "the death sentence of the Greene County Nuclear Plant." PASNY, which Robert H. Boyle characterized as "a bullying body that cares not a whit for the environment," had been defeated by environmentalists, and, through the final environmental statement, the utility industry suffered a major setback. Defeating the Cementon plant was, J. Winthrop Aldrich wrote, "a major victory for all who cherish the American landscape—especially the renowned scenery and culturally significant environment of the Hudson River." However, because the NRC commissioners did not ultimately rule on the application, the case did not enshrine aesthetics or scenic values in federal regulatory law. In the aftermath of the Cementon case, Rick Benas prepared a policy directive, "Assessing and Mitigating Visual Impacts," for the Department of Environmental Conservation. Based on his own work as well as that of Petrich and Flad, this report became an important tool in enforcing New York's State Environmental Quality Review Act (SEQRA). Benas's directive has since been adopted by a number of other states. The importance of visual impact analysis is perhaps the greatest legacy of the Cementon battle.[27]

Cementon remained a battleground, however. In 1985 the Alsen Coal Company proposed to build a massive terminal there. Coal would be brought to the site by railroad, at the rate of several one-hundred-car trains each day, and unloaded to massive, fifty-five-foot-high piles, from which it would be transferred to oceangoing vessels for transport to Europe.

Scenic Hudson and other environmental groups, including Hudson River GREEN, Clearwater, Hudson River Heritage, and the Columbia County Farm Bureau, filed a lawsuit challenging DEC's issuance of a permit to Alsen based on the inadequacy of the environmental impact statement. The case dragged on until 1990, when DEC ruled that Alsen had failed to meet permit conditions and that the permits the DEC had previously issued were invalid.[28]

The battle against the proposed nuclear plant at Cementon was a major victory for those who cherished the Hudson River Valley, and for environmentalists the final environmental statement was a breakthrough in its emphasis on scenic and cultural values. But the demand for electrical power continued to increase in New York State as it did nationwide, and utilities looked to the valley as the most advantageous site for future plants to meet rising demand. Orange & Rockland's Bowline plants 1 and 2, near Haverstraw, began operating in 1972 and 1974, while Central Hudson Gas & Electric's Roseton 1 and 2 units, north of Newburgh, commenced production of electricity in 1974. These were fossil fuel plants. Con Ed's nuclear units 2 and 3 at Indian Point became operational respectively in 1973 and 1976 (unit 3 was sold to PASNY during Con Ed's near bankruptcy). In 1976 Con Ed announced that it was considering the location of a massive nuclear or coal-fired plant at Lloyd-Esopus, near New Paltz, and a similar plant near Red Hook, about two miles from the east bank of the river. New York State Electric and Gas Corporation also announced plans for a 2.4-megawatt facility, either nuclear or coal-powered, in Stuyvesant, Columbia County.[29]

As was true of Indian Point 3 and Cementon, the *New York Times* reported, "the proposal for a nuclear power plant at Esopus-Lloyd evoked immediate objections from environmental groups that have consistently fought the expansion of what they regard as unsightly, unneeded and dangerous atomic energy plants in the scenic Hudson Valley." Peter D. G. Brown, a professor at the State University of New York at New Paltz and chair of Mid-Hudson Nuclear Opponents, stated that these projects, if approved and built, "would give the Mid-Hudson Valley one of the largest concentrations of nuclear power anywhere in the world, with devastating ecological and national-security implications for years to come." An unnamed Hudson River Valley Commission official told Robert H. Boyle that "a total of twenty-four sites were being surveyed along the Hudson for possible nuclear plants." Less than a decade after Rod Vandivert's warning about the potential concentration of power plants along the river, the Hudson Valley was in imminent danger of becoming a nuclear alley or avenue of electricity.[30]

The New York State Energy Research and Development Authority (NYSERDA), successor agency to the state's Atomic and Space Development Authority, is known today for its emphasis on energy conservation and renewables. But in November 1975 it published a conceptual master plan for the development of a massive nuclear power facility on a thirty-two-hundred-acre site spanning the towns of Lloyd and Esopus, on the west bank of the Hudson near New Paltz. The project envisioned in the conceptual master plan was enormous, and consisted of as many as four 1,000-megawatt nuclear reactors, each with a cooling tower that reached five hundred feet in the air. Some of the land would be an environmental buffer, part a nature preserve, which Audubon New York had begun assembling on the property prior to this announcement of the site's suitability for use as an electricity generating facility.[31]

NYSERDA's conceptual master plan is a curious document, largely prepared by twelve technical consulting firms over a three-year period at a cost to taxpayers of more than $1 million. It is curious in that the authority, despite the word "development" in its title, did not have statutory authority to construct nuclear plants. Instead, the master plan was an invitation to utilities to take advantage of the work that NYSERDA's consultants had already completed to form the basis for what the utilities could expect to be a quick approval of an environmental impact statement and licensing application. This was the case in the siting of two plants in Cayuga and Orleans Counties, adjacent to Lake Ontario, where private utilities constructed electricity-generating facilities. In short, the authority had shunted to taxpayers much of the cost of due diligence that a private utility would have to assume if it were looking for a nuclear site.[32]

NYSERDA's plan described the Esopus-Lloyd site, just south of the John Burroughs Nature Sanctuary, as consisting of ridge-and-valley topography, mostly covered with second-growth trees but with significant wetlands, especially along Black Creek, an environmentally significant and beautiful watercourse that flows into the Hudson River, and sixty-acre Chodikee Lake. The report claimed that it was presenting "a sound

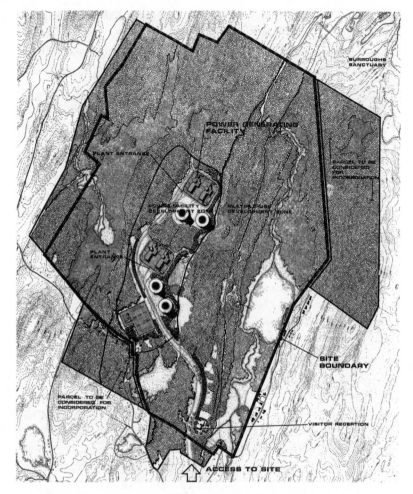

Figure 11. New York State Energy Research and Development Authority, environmental management plan, *Lloyd Site Master Development Plan: Concept Phase Report* (Nov. 1975), showing the proposed nuclear reactors for the Lloyd-Esopus site in Ulster County. Courtesy of Peter D. G. Brown.

environmental base and a flexible development program" for the site. Consultants studied four potential types of energy generation: coal-fired plants with cooling towers; coal-fired plants with spray pond; nuclear plants with cooling towers; and nuclear plants with spray pond. Their analysis led the consultants to recommend construction of four nuclear plants with cooling towers. These four reactors and ancillary buildings would require the use of only 233 acres of the site and would be capable of producing 4,000 megawatts of electricity. The planners explained that their interdisciplinary approach to the study led to a multiuse program for the site: in addition to electricity generation, the plan called for the creation of a nature preserve, an interpretative center for visitors that would host energy conservation and education programs, and a small agricultural research program, with perhaps some facilities for active recreation. The consultants conceded that the cooling towers would be visible from points in Minnewaska State Park and Mohonk, both atop the Shawangunk Ridge, but asserted that because they were eight and twelve miles away, the visual impact would not be significant. And, as the plants would be located in a low-lying area, the ridges to the east and west would effectively block the view of the complex.[33]

Even before publication of the master plan, many residents of Lloyd were concerned about the possibility of a nuclear plant in their midst. Local activists persuaded town officials to conduct a referendum on the issue, which was held on June 1, 1974. Although construction of a nuclear plant by a private utility would bring significant tax revenues to the town, citizens voted overwhelmingly (71 percent) against such a facility. Publication of NYSERDA's conceptual master plan the following year provoked an immediate response. On January 11, 1975, two months after its publication, SUNY New Paltz professors Peter Brown and Stephen J. Egemeier organized a forum, moderated by Congressman Hamilton Fish and held at the New Paltz High School, to dispute the "very flimsy investigation" NYSERDA's plan presented. The report of that forum was quickly published by Mid-Hudson Nuclear Opponents as *Nuclear Power in the Hudson Valley: Its Impact on You*. The published forum consisted of six papers (five by scientists, one by a social scientist, most of whom were teaching at colleges and universities in the mid-Hudson Valley). Each examined the potential consequences of the proposed nuclear plant in terms of its economic and social impact, its effects on the biology and hydrology of the region, other environmental impacts, and potential consequences for public health. The publication also included statements from the principal environmental organizations in the Hudson Valley, including Scenic Hudson, the Hudson River Fishermen's Association, and the Mid-Hudson Group Sierra Club, as well as local groups and private citizens. Perhaps because the proposed nuclear plant was far enough inland that it would not be visible from the river, speakers at the New Paltz forum did not address aesthetic issues. At the end of February 1977, Mid-Hudson Nuclear Opponents called a press conference in Poughkeepsie and issued a "Declaration of Nuclear Resistance" that, among other things, urged property owners to refuse to sell their land to utilities or to grant them the right to use it.[34]

A year after NYSERDA published its conceptual master plan, even as Mid-Hudson Nuclear Opponents was organizing in opposition to an as-yet unnamed developer of a nuclear facility, Consolidated Edison announced that it had chosen the Lloyd-Esopus site and another near Red Hook, in northern Dutchess County, as potential locations for a new nuclear or coal-fired electricity generating facility. Arthur Hauspurg of Con Ed claimed that the proposed plant was essential to meet the demand for the utility's power output through the dawn of the next century. Lloyd-Esopus was apparently the primary site, Red Hook the alternative.[35]

NYSERDA's consultants were no more adept at evaluating visual impact than were PASNY's in the Cementon case. They largely asserted but did not demonstrate convincingly that visual impact would not be a factor if the project were built. But as he had done at Cementon, Harvey Flad undertook a thorough assessment of the visual impact of the proposed project and its effect on community character. He prepared a study of the "visual pollution" that would result were the nuclear plant to be constructed and asserted that aesthetic impacts "have not been studied in detail for the environmental impact statement" submitted by Con Ed. The proposed nuclear plant at Lloyd, and especially its cooling towers, would have "a detrimental aesthetic impact upon the mid-Hudson valley region." The cooling towers and the vapor plume would be omnipresent and visible from important historic sites in Hyde Park and throughout Dutchess and Columbia Counties. The transmission towers also "would create a very strong visual imprint upon the rural region," introducing a stark contrast with the landscape and marking the intrusion of urban and industrial modernity into a region characterized by small towns and farms.[36]

The Mid-Hudson Nuclear Opponents, which Brown chaired, soon attracted approximately twenty-five hundred dues-paying members, including Congressman Fish. The group initiated a series of lawsuits against Con Ed in the hope of derailing the nuclear plant and promoted renewable energy instead. Its members pushed for referenda in Ulster County towns, which voted overwhelmingly against nuclear power, and successfully delayed approval of a license to commence construction. And then the disaster at Three Mile Island ended the era of construction of nuclear power plants in the United States.[37]

After the debacles at Cementon and Lloyd-Esopus and the near meltdown at Three Mile Island, no nuclear power plants would be built in the Hudson Valley through the end of the twentieth century. But the alternative site PASNY had proposed for Cementon, west of Athens, eventually would become the location of a natural gas-fired generating facility. This was one of the locations that Petrich and the Oak Ridge staff had identified as "superior" for a nuclear facility in the 1979 final environmental statement devoted to Cementon. In September 1997, the U.S. Generating Company (USGen), a subsidiary of the Pacific Gas & Electric Corporation, submitted an "Article X Pre-Application Report" to the state Department of Public Service. A non-utility electricity generating company that sold power on the open market, USGen proposed to construct a 1,080-megawatt plant west of the village of Athens. The site was attractive for development as a power plant because of its proximity to a natural gas pipeline as well as existing high-voltage transmissions lines, and access to highways, rail transportation, and the Hudson River. An estimated five million gallons of water would be withdrawn from the river each day to cool the power-generating facility and, via its discharge, add to the thermal pollution of the waterway.[38]

The economic impact of the proposed power plant on Greene County and the village of Athens would be minimal. Representatives of USGen informed researchers at the Center for Governmental Research (CGR) that while construction would employ approximately six hundred workers, once the plant was operational it would employ only thirty workers with a total payroll of about $2.25 million. It would, the CGR report concluded, have only a modest impact on the local economy. Given the low tax structure of the county and the municipality, CGR researchers concluded that the tax benefits would be small and concentrated in the village and its school district. They also found that the generating plant would occupy only fourteen acres of the two-hundred-acre site, but would probably make the remaining land—the most attractive development location in the entire county—less appealing for other uses. Alternatives, such as a pharmaceutical plant or even a large furniture woodworking factory, would deliver greater long-term benefits to the community. The researchers' conclusions were hardly a ringing endorsement of the project.[39]

Once again environmentalists and what the *New York Times* characterized as "ferocious local opposition" challenged the licensing of the proposed plant. This was, after all, a scenic stretch of the river, and within Olana's viewshed, so critical in the Cementon deliberations. Flad's analysis of the visual impact of a nuclear plant on the site is indicative of the location's scenic and historical importance. While he conceded that the view northwest from Olana was not as dramatic as that toward Cementon, Flad nevertheless argued that it was significant and should be preserved. While much of the directional view was at that time blocked by trees that had grown since Church's death in 1900, Flad pointed out that there was interest in removing this secondary growth "to more fully represent the landscaping in Church's day," and if this were undertaken, he predicted that the visual impact of the cooling towers would be "severe indeed." Significant vistas from Hudson, especially that from Promenade Hill Park, "would be strongly impacted" were the proposed nuclear plant constructed at Athens. And, Flad argued, the nuclear facility and the vapor plume would have a major impact on the historic village of Athens itself. "Wherever one stands in the Historic District of Athens," Flad wrote, "one would be subjected to views of the tower or the plume, looming over the everyday existence of the inhabitants of this village." Views from Claverack and Ghent, as well as from designated scenic roadways, including the Taconic Parkway, would also be affected by the presence of the power plant.[40]

Obviously, smokestacks associated with a natural gas generating power plant would be much smaller in scale than the cooling tower of a nuclear reactor. By relying on natural gas rather than coal, the Athens plant would emit far less smoke and particulate matter into the atmosphere through its stacks. The impact of the Athens generating facility would be significantly less than that of a nuclear or a conventional coal-fired plant. While this was a challenge to environmentalists, so was the boundary of the "Scenic Areas of Statewide Significance" at Athens, which was drawn close to the river and excluded the village and the site that the power plant would occupy to its west. Effectively, the state had determined that this was not a significant landscape worth protecting. Nevertheless, environmentalists

Figure 12. USGen's Athens Generating Plant, Athens, N.Y., as seen from Olana. Photograph by Peter Aaron, 2017. © Peter Aaron / OTTO.

expressed grave concern about the proposed development. The Olana Partnership, successor organization to the Friends of Olana, was adamant in arguing for the importance of the viewshed, and Scenic Hudson played a leading role in opposing the plant through formal comments on the permits, publicity, and eventually a lawsuit challenging the New York Department of State's finding that the siting of the plant would be consistent with the state's coastal management policies. What made opponents all the more determined was that the Athens plant was going through the regulatory approval process at the same time that the St. Lawrence Cement Company was proposing to construct a major new facility just east of Olana, in Greenport, Columbia County. To opponents it seemed that the reindustrialization of the Hudson Valley would roll back the progress that had been made over the previous generation in restoring the river's ecology and protecting the quality of life along its banks.[41]

So began yet another battle that pitted environmentalism against economic development, those who cherished the scenic values and quality of life along the Hudson versus those who embraced new industries that, they hoped, would result in a more prosperous future. The Athens case differed in significant ways from the Cementon and Lloyd-Esopus cases: as a conventional power plant, there would be no review by the NRC. Issuance of a permit was a state regulatory decision, and Governor George Pataki strongly supported the plant's construction.[42]

Hearings on the Athens plant began on March 25, 1999. The Pataki administration announced its final environmental approval of the proposed plant on June 2, 2000, the siting board approved the project on June 13, 2000, and the Army Corps of Engineers issued a permit on May 25, 2001. Site construction began the following day.[43]

Before the litigation resulted in a decision, Ned Sullivan, the president of Scenic Hudson, met with Pataki and persuaded him to require a closed-loop cooling technology that would reduce the amount of water drawn from the river from approximately five million gallons a day to 185,000. Scenic Hudson and other environmental groups had fought for decades to persuade the utilities and regulators to adopt this technology, and the Pataki administration agreed that it should be a condition of the licensing approval. This was a major victory for Scenic Hudson, and the river. The settlement of Scenic Hudson's lawsuit also required USGen to make several significant concessions in its plan for the facility, including changes in design that would mitigate other adverse effects of the plant's presence by lowering the profile of the power house and changing the color and reflectability of the paint. In addition, as part of the settlement, USGen agreed to establish a $2.5 million trust fund to mitigate the scenic impact of the power plant. This fund, administered by the Hudson River Foundation, paid for trail projects in Greene and Columbia Counties and supported the efforts of the Columbia Land Conservancy. It also helped pay for the restoration of the carriage roads at Olana, and financed repairs to significant historic or civic buildings, among other uses.[44]

In announcing the settlement, Scenic Hudson did not use the word "compromise," but that is what Sullivan had achieved. The National Oceanic and Atmospheric Administration, which had mandated preparation of New York's *Scenic Areas of Statewide Significance*, had issued a written opinion to the Department of State that challenged some of the most important contentions of Scenic Hudson's lawsuit, specifically noting that the state was not required to analyze alternatives to a proposed project in determining whether the application was in compliance with the Coastal Zone Management Act. Sullivan, and Scenic Hudson's board and staff, were trying to do the best they could with what they realized was probably a losing hand. What they achieved was considerable. Yes, the smokestacks are visible from Olana, which has made significant efforts in recent years to return the landscape to the condition it was during Church's lifetime, and the removal of second-growth trees has indeed restored vistas to the west and northwest, bringing the Athens plant into the viewshed. But the insistence on closed-loop cooling technology dramatically reduced the environmental impact of the power plant, as did changes in the design. The compromise enraged some environmentalists, who would have held out for total victory, and others who resented that Scenic Hudson, as the most effective organization in the valley, had a seat at the negotiating table while they were not party to the conversations. But in retrospect it appears that Scenic Hudson negotiated about as effectively as possible and achieved the best outcome it could under the circumstances.[45]

The issue of power along the Hudson became a major environmental concern when Con Ed announced its intention to build a pumped-storage plant at Storm King Mountain in 1962. It has remained a compelling drama into the twenty-first century, and undoubtedly will continue to be so in the years to come. The fundamental issues haven't changed—humanity versus nature, industrialism verses scenic, historical, and cultural values—even as electricity demand has increased. As we as a society consider the question of carbon footprints, renewables, and sustainability, we would be wise to reflect on what Robert H. Boyle wrote about the Hudson in 1969: "It is not a river that God made for power companies or pulp mill owners. The Hudson is a living, natural system."[46]

6

SCENIC HUDSON'S EXPANDING MISSION

When Russell Train announced the "Hudson River Peace Treaty" on December 19, 1980, which ended Scenic Hudson's seventeen-year battle against Con Ed's proposed pumped-storage power plant at Storm King Mountain, the organization might simply have claimed victory and disbanded. Indeed, after the so-called Scenic Hudson II decision (1971), which upheld the Federal Power Commission's licensing of the power plant, Scenic Hudson foundered. Two prominent supporters, Stephen and Smokey Duggan, had left in 1970 to establish the Natural Resources Defense Council. Money to pay attorneys and run the organization was a constant challenge: Rod Vandivert, the talented and energetic executive director, was reduced to consultant status and went to work for the Hudson River Valley Council, a small environmental group that was opposing the Metropolitan Transportation Authority's plan to transform Stewart Air Force Base, near Newburgh, into greater New York's fourth major commercial airport. Frances (Franny) Reese almost singlehandedly kept Scenic Hudson intact throughout the 1970s, the years when the Fishermen's

Association litigation was more effective in challenging Con Ed than was Scenic Hudson, and when ecology was supplanting the scenic, historical, and cultural foundations of the Scenic Hudson I decision (1965).[1]

Instead of declaring victory, Scenic Hudson's board decided to continue its work of defending the Hudson. Indeed, well before the "peace treaty," it had been engaged in other environmental issues. Often in collaboration with the Fishermen's Association and the Hudson River Conservation Society, it was party to a series of lawsuits challenging the filling in of Hudson River shallows. During the 1970s, Scenic Hudson prepared nominations that placed a significant number of buildings in the Hudson Highlands on the National Register of Historic Places, joined the opposition to the commercial jetport at Stewart, and responded to requests from several communities that sought its aid in fighting unwanted development. Even as the fate of Storm King Mountain hung in the balance, Scenic Hudson voiced opposition to a high-rise apartment building on the riverfront in Hastings, as well as an apartment complex in the Hudson Highlands and plans for a subdivision of single-family homes along Idlewild Brook, in Cornwall. It also contributed $1,500 to support the efforts of opponents of the proposed nuclear plant at Cementon, and opposed an Army Corps of Engineers plan to skim millions of gallons of water from the Hudson to supply customers in New York City and Nassau County.[2]

Between 1973, a time when the organization must have been in despair, and 1983, Scenic Hudson achieved several remarkable successes. These included establishing the Scenic Hudson Land Trust, which became a force with the substantial bequest from DeWitt and Lila Acheson Wallace; beginning a program to address riverfront development; and fighting successfully to preserve thirty-five hundred acres, in four marshes, as National Estuarine Research Reserves. Not all of this had been accomplished by December 1980, but it does indicate how quickly Scenic Hudson had broadened its vision. Under the aegis of its effective and indomitable leaders, Franny Reese and Klara Sauer, Scenic Hudson adopted an ambitious mission that led to a proactive engagement in preserving the distinctive landscape, history, and culture of the Hudson Valley. Through initiatives that have preserved farmland and places of distinctive scenic or historical significance, as well as its efforts to develop riverside parks in cities and secure greater public access to the river, Scenic Hudson has become the most important conservation organization in the Hudson River Valley and surely one of the most consequential in the United States.[3]

The years since World War II saw the collapse of much of the industry that had grown up on the banks of the Hudson in the nineteenth and early twentieth centuries. Deindustrialization left many older cities struggling economically, but it also—together with the environmental legislation of the 1970s and the construction of sewage treatment plants—led to a dramatic improvement in the river's water quality and made the valley a much more desirable place to live. Residents of New York City began buying second homes, especially in Dutchess and Columbia Counties, and by the turn of the new century, tourism, a $5 billion industry in 2014, had supplanted manufacturing as the economic engine of the middle and upper Hudson River Valley.[4]

But as the *New York Times* reported in 2000, proposals for power plants (including the one at Athens), microchip fabrication facilities, and a massive cement factory portended the reindustrialization of the Hudson Valley. New York's governor at the time, George Pataki, welcomed these projects, claiming that they would not negatively affect the quality of life or the environment. "We are pro-business, pro-industry," he stated, adding, "We are also pro-environment." Pataki was indeed a strong environmentalist as governor: during his administration the state acquired significant land for park development or expansion. Some residents welcomed the promise of economic development for the jobs it would create and the prosperity it would bring, while others saw the reindustrialization of the valley as a fundamental threat to a cherished place. The same year in which the *New York Times* described the massive projects proposed for the valley, the National Trust for Historic Preservation, at the urging of Scenic Hudson, joined residents who opposed these developments, naming the Hudson Valley as one of eleven most endangered places in the nation. Richard Moe, president of the National Trust, explained that the sheer scale of these recent proposals, together with suburban sprawl, "could amount to a reindustrialization of the Hudson Valley and undo a lot of the progress that has been made."[5]

The most controversial of these proposals was for the construction of a massive cement plant in Greenport, just south of the city of Hudson. Hudson, which began as a whaling port, had evolved into an industrial city in the nineteenth century, and cement making was one of its important industries, though the plants there had closed in the years since World War II. In 1999, however, St. Lawrence Cement, a subsidiary of the Swiss-Canadian multinational Holcim Ltd., proposed to replace its aging cement facility in the town of Catskill (one of the Cementon plants) with a vastly larger "state of the art" plant on a 1,222-acre limestone quarry and more than five hundred adjacent acres it owned across the river in Columbia County. The dimensions of the project were stunning: a cement manufacturing facility at the quarry that would produce 2.2 million metric tons of cement annually; a vastly enlarged dock just south of Hudson, which would have required dredging and filling in a part of the river adjacent to the site; and a two-and-a-half-mile-long enclosed conveyor to carry the cement from the plant to barges at the dock. The manufacturing facility would be enormous—twenty buildings more than two hundred feet in height, including, as Department of Environmental Conservation (DEC) commissioner Erin M. Crotty put it, "a raw mill system, kiln feed blending silo, preheater/precalciner tower, rotary kiln, clinker cooler, finish mill system and associated balance-of-plant systems and facilities," as well as a 406-foot smokestack. Most of the buildings and the stack would be visible from important scenic locations in the Hudson Valley, but especially from Olana. The plume from the smokestack would have been significant, at times extending about six miles. Marc S. Gerstman, attorney for Scenic Hudson and the coalition of opponents of the plant, described St. Lawrence Cement's project as the largest, greatest threat to the valley since Con Ed's proposal to build the pumped-storage power plant at Storm King Mountain in 1962. Scenic Hudson didn't publicly announce opposition to the proposed plant until 1991—it was a relative latecomer to the cause—but eventually recognized that, if built, the plant would become "the dominant and discordant feature in one of our country's most famous viewsheds—the landscape surrounding Frederic Church's Olana."[6]

Predictably, announcement of this plan sparked outrage among many residents and environmentalists, as well as from New England states that would be downwind of the plant. At a public briefing on the project, a representative of St. Lawrence Cement attempted to calm local residents by asserting that they need not worry about air quality because the four-hundred-foot stack ensured that prevailing winds would carry the pollutants far away. On a normal day, this representative stated, all the pollution would be in Maine in six hours, which enraged elected officials and citizens throughout New England. Scenic Hudson president Ned Sullivan, a former environmental commissioner for Maine, immediately called his former boss, Governor Angus King, who asked him to prepare a letter protesting the plant that he would send to Governor Pataki. Sullivan also secured letters of protest from top officials in other New England states. A local group headed by Sam Pratt, Friends of Hudson, was the first to oppose the plant, and its efforts would be key. Organized by Pratt and Peter Jung, Friends quickly grew from perhaps 25 individuals to more than 4,000 dues-paying members. Those members attended a countless number of public meetings to express their opposition to the plant, inundated elective officials and regulators with letters, cards, and phone calls, and insisted that their voices be heard. Stop the Plant signs soon appeared in yards and along roadsides throughout Columbia County. Pratt was able to unite diverse constituencies—residents of Hudson, farmers, and second-home owners in Columbia County—in opposition to the plant. He also prepared a schematic drawing demonstrating how dramatically the proposed cement plant would dwarf the Statue of Liberty, the St. Charles Hotel in Hudson, and Olana.[7]

The Olana Partnership, the private-sector group that supports the state in its stewardship of Frederic Church's house and extensive grounds, a unique state historic site and a National Historic Landmark, was also outspoken in opposition to the cement plant. Scenic Hudson joined more than twenty local and regional groups that collectively were known as the Hudson Valley Preservation Coalition. Friends of Hudson, the Olana Partnership, and the coalition worked independently but in concert to defeat the plant. Steadfast in their resistance over almost seven years, these opponents of St. Lawrence Cement surely influenced the administrative ruling that ultimately prevented construction of the plant.[8]

St. Lawrence Cement argued that its proposed plant would be beneficial for the local economy and would not have an adverse impact on the environment or quality of life. It conceded that the smokestack would emit more than five hundred million pounds of pollutants each year, though experts hired by Friends of Hudson, the industrial engineering firm Camp, Dresser & McKee, believed that the volume of pollutants would be much higher. It was principally on the health consequences of the plant that Friends based its opposition. Dr. Jeff Monkash, a physician and formerly chief of medicine at Columbia Memorial Hospital, testified at a June 21, 2001, hearing that by a vote of 35–1 the hospital's doctors issued a statement charging that St. Lawrence Cement's proposed plant was "a serious risk to our county's health, our community's health, which will result in increased death rates for people with advanced heart and lung disease, increased cancer rates and the worsening of asthma in children." At the same hearing Dr. Norman Posner likened St. Lawrence Cement officials to "merchants of death masquerading as our saviors." Friends of Hudson volunteers investigated St. Lawrence Cement's significant violations of environmental laws at its other facilities in the United States—which had resulted in numerous fines from the EPA—as well as in Europe and South Africa. They also investigated the plant's potential impact on wetlands and biota, as well as other potentially adverse consequences, and fought a public relations battle against what they considered the company's grossly misleading advertisements and mailings touting the plant's beneficial impacts on the county and the region.[9]

St. Lawrence Cement anticipated that it would not have to undergo a rigorous environmental review under the State Environmental Quality Review Act, as the quarry at Greenport had been in operation for decades prior to the legislative adoption of SEQRA and had been grandfathered by DEC staff. Opponents expressed concern over several issues: air quality in a region already not in compliance with federal standards, and especially public health, given the toxics and particulate matter emanating from the smokestack; the visual impact of the plant complex; noise from blasting at the quarry; the amount of truck traffic on rural roads necessary to bring raw materials to the quarry site; and, ultimately, the impact of the plant on community character and quality of life. Opponents also expressed concern over the size and scale of the dock operations and questioned the much-touted economic benefits the plant would bring to the region (according to St. Lawrence Cement most of the workers would be transferred from Cementon; the Greenport project would add one new job).[10]

Soon after St. Lawrence Cement announced its plans for the Greenport mine, DEC staff determined that the project might have a negative impact on the environment and required the company to submit a draft environmental impact statement (EIS). St. Lawrence Cement submitted a preliminary EIS in March 2000 and, following revisions based on comments by DEC staff, submitted a final draft EIS on May 2, 2001. The document, sixteen hundred pages long, describes the proposed plant's operations and its impact on the economy, environment, and character of nearby communities. Then followed a lengthy legislative hearing, held at Columbia-Greene Community College on June 21, 2001, in which residents and other interested parties could comment on the document. More than 1,000 people attended the hearing, and 121 individuals spoke, only 15 of them in support of the plant. Letters and petitions submitted to the administrative law judges overwhelmingly opposed the plant.[11]

Earlier in the day of the legislative hearing, Administrative Law Judges Helene Goldberger and Maria Villa convened a preliminary issues conference with attorneys representing the various stakeholders. Among the group present, attorneys from LeBoeuf, Lamb, Greene & MacRae represented St. Lawrence Cement; Jeffrey Baker represented Friends of Hudson; Marc Gerstman was there on behalf of Scenic Hudson and other groups in the Hudson Valley Preservation Coalition; John Caffry was present for the Olana Partnership; and Albert K. Butzel represented the Natural Resources Defense Council. At the meeting, staff distributed draft permits DEC had prepared, and participants agreed to make a visit to the site the following day to examine on the ground what impact the proposed facility might have. At the request of the Olana Partnership and the coalition, the administrative law judges scheduled a second field trip for August 16, 2001, to examine the project's visual impact. On that day balloons were flown to indicate the height of the smokestack and buildings at the plant, while representatives of St. Lawrence Cement and the various organizations opposed to the project visited Olana and the waterfront park in Hudson then under construction immediately north of the dock area, as well as other points in the city. They also visited various other scenic places from which the cement plant would be visible, including points in Claverack, and several scenic roadways in the vicinity. The balloons demonstrated to on-the-fence residents just how massive the proposed facility would be, and many became supporters of Friends of Hudson. Participants also crossed the river to the Athens waterfront to study how the proposed plant would impact the view from there. The initial ruling issued by DEC described this itinerary but did not reveal what participants learned or whether the tour might have changed their thinking. Sam Pratt recalls that to participants on the tour it was obvious that the visualizations St. Lawrence Cement had presented in its application were "selective at best, misleading at worst." The plant's impact would be much more significant than the company had claimed.[12]

Based on the June 2001 hearing and documents submitted by St. Lawrence Cement and DEC staff, as well as by opponents of the plant, Administrative Law Judges Goldberger and Villa determined, on December 7, 2001, that there were indeed critical issues subject to adjudication. This was a setback for St. Lawrence Cement, as DEC staff had argued that by incorporating stipulations or conditions in the draft permits, legal proceedings were unnecessary. Richard Benas, an environmental analyst at DEC, for example, testified that "the Applicant [St. Lawrence Cement] has minimized impacts to the maximum extent practicable" and "has offered substantial offsets and decommissioning," the latter largely a scaling back (but not complete elimination of) its operations at Cementon, which would have somewhat improved the viewshed southwest from Olana. Among the questions deemed worthy of adjudication were St. Lawrence Cement's air-dispersion modeling, smokestack emissions, noise, riverine habitat mitigation plan, visual impact, and economic impact. Following this determination, attorneys filed briefs and responses to clarify their corporate or organizational positions and challenge claims made by the other side. St. Lawrence Cement reiterated its argument that the proposed plant was necessary and would not adversely affect the environment, whereas opponents expressed their concern over the plant's threat to public health, challenged its supposed economic benefits, and questioned the need for the plant as well as its impact on historic resources, especially Olana. Harvey Flad once again testified about the impact of the proposed construction on the community character and landscape of the Hudson River Valley. Scenic Hudson proposed an alternative economic vision for the region, one based not on an enormous cement plant or other large industries but on its "world-class natural, cultural and historic assets."[13]

Amid all the legal maneuvering, DEC commissioner Crotty ruled, in September 2004, that because of the vastly increased scale of operations, the St. Lawrence Cement plant was not grandfathered and was subject to adjudication. In response to opponents, St. Lawrence Cement announced its intent to relocate the plant to the low ground of the quarry, which would reduce its visible bulk as well as the height of the smokestack (though this raised the question of how much more pollution would be visited on nearby residents).[14]

Attorneys Baker, Caffry, and Gerstman argued that in addition to the threat of pollution, the St. Lawrence Cement plant would be in violation of policies 23, 24, and 25 of the state's federally mandated Coastal Management Program (CMP). This was an issue first raised by Laura Skutch, a member of the group that opposed the Athens Generating Plant, and her research was instrumental in convincing the groups opposing the St. Lawrence Cement plant that they could use the CMP regulations in their legal challenge. The CMP policies established the requirement to "protect, enhance, and restore structures, districts, areas or sites that are of significance in the history, architecture, archaeology or culture of the State, its communities, or the Nation"; "prevent impairment of Scenic Resources of Statewide Significance"; and "protect, restore or enhance natural and man-made resources which are not identified as being of Statewide significance, but which contribute to the overall scenic quality of the coastal area." The Catskill-Olana and the Columbia-Greene North Scenic Areas of Statewide Significance (SASS) would have been severely impacted by the proposed cement plant.[15]

St. Lawrence Cement needed to obtain seventeen permits to construct the facility it envisioned for Greenport. Permitters ranged from federal agencies, such as the Army Corps of Engineers (for permission to dredge and fill in part of the Hudson River at its dock facility) and the Environmental Protection Agency, to state agencies, including the DEC, the Department of State (which administers the Local Waterfront Revitalization Programs), and the Office of General Services, to Columbia County and the municipalities of Greenport, Hudson, and Catskill. DEC staff were generally supportive of the plant, though Commissioner Crotty raised serious doubts about the project. On October 22, 2004, St. Lawrence Cement filed an application for one of those required permits with the state Department of State, seeking certification that the plant was consistent with New York's Coastal Management Program and its waterfront revitalization program. In a lengthy ruling dated April 19, 2005, Secretary of State Randy A. Daniels determined that the application was inconsistent with those programs and denied the permit. Daniels's ruling focused in part on the economic benefits of the proposed plant, which he rejected as inconsequential. He then argued that "most communities along the Hudson River are reconnecting with the river through a mix of residential, commercial and recreational development that maximizes public access to the river." The plus side of deindustrialization—together with Environmental Protection Fund programs that in recent years had allocated more than $25 million to river communities for projects "to enhance their economic vitality, increase tax revenues, add jobs, revitalize downtowns, and provide public recreational opportunities to the waterfront"—was transforming once-gritty industrial landscapes into parks and glittering new developments. The proposed St. Lawrence Cement plant, Daniels ruled, was antithetical to the Coastal Management Program's goal of enhancing "existing and anticipated uses" and would not contribute to recent efforts undertaken by the city of Hudson to revitalize its waterfront. Indeed, he wrote, the increased industrial activity at the dock site "would be out of scale and character with the surrounding pedestrian-oriented parks, small-scale historic architecture and the City's Historic District, recreational boating activities, commercial retail, and tourism-oriented uses on the City's waterfront."[16]

In addition, Daniels followed the lead of Baker, Caffry, and Gerstman in rejecting the permit application based on policies 23, 24, and 25 of the state's Coastal Management Plan. The evidence St. Lawrence Cement submitted, Daniels concluded, demonstrated that the proposed plant and its plume, "visible about 39% of daylight hours," and the dock "would affect historic resources and visual quality of the area." Among these were historical districts in Hudson and Athens, as well as numerous individual structures listed or deemed eligible for inclusion in the National Register of Historic Places. But perhaps most important was the impact the plant would have on New York's Scenic Areas of Statewide Significance, especially the Catskill-Olana SASS, which "inspired the first indigenous American painting movement," the Hudson River School. What made the Catskill-Olana SASS unique, Daniels wrote, is "its unusual landscape variety and unity of major landscape components among striking contrasts." The secretary of state paid especial attention to Olana, which he described as "a designed landscape of extraordinary importance that recognizes its connection to the landscape beyond its borders," its viewshed, which Frederic Church painted frequently. Daniels rightly noted that the artist had incorporated the "superlative views of the Hudson Valley in the design of both the mansion and the grounds," which "establishes an intrinsic connection between the property and the land outside its borders." The proposed plant, he ruled, "would present a significant adverse change to the scale, proportions, compositions and enjoyment of nearby historic resources, and would not protect, restore or enhance the scenic riverfront resources." St. Lawrence Cement's application was inconsistent with the state's Coastal Management Program.[17]

Four days after Daniels's ruling, on April 23, 2005, St. Lawrence Cement announced that it would not appeal and would instead withdraw its application for permits to construct the facility. This was a tremendous victory for the Friends of Hudson, the Olana Partnership, Scenic Hudson, and other members of the Hudson Valley Preservation Coalition. The decision affirmed the importance of community character as well as the landscape and historic resources of the Hudson River Valley. In her history of the St. Lawrence Cement controversy, Miriam D. Silverman compared the significance of Daniels's decision to Scenic Hudson's battle against the pumped-storage power plant at Storm King Mountain and described it as "a groundbreaking step in the legal protection of quality of life." It was more than that: the rulings by Crotty and Daniels surely resulted at least in part from the efforts of Friends of Hudson and other opponents of the plant—citizen volunteers who for seven years fought, against overwhelming odds, a powerful multinational corporation, to protect their community and region.[18]

Secretary of State Daniels's denial of a permit for the St. Lawrence Cement plant was a bold step in the protection of the Hudson River Valley. For Scenic Hudson the battle represented something more: affirmation of its strategy of collaborating with other environmental and local citizen groups—and over the years there would be many other such groups—in pursuing common goals, and also using its considerable financial resources and expertise to protect the landscape, scenery, and communities along the river. Much as Pete Seeger saw *Clearwater*'s mission as reconnecting residents with the river, Scenic Hudson has pursued the same goal through conservation, land preservation, advocacy, and park building. This is evident in the broadening of Scenic Hudson's vision since the Storm King case.

The groundwork for this broader mission dates to 1980, when the Center for the Hudson River Valley merged with the Scenic Hudson Preservation Conference. As Scenic Hudson was the larger, more widely known of the two, the combined organization took the name Scenic Hudson Inc.

Since then, Scenic Hudson has embarked on a number of strategies that its staff and board members believe are essential to the future of the valley. Franny Reese, who chaired Scenic Hudson's board of directors from 1976 until 1984, strongly promoted this pivot in the organization's mission, as did longtime executive director Klara Sauer. Sullivan, who was hired as president in 1999, was charged by Scenic Hudson's board to double the size of the staff and increase the operating capacity and regional impact of the organization. To be sure, as the St. Lawrence Cement and Athens Generating cases demonstrate, Scenic Hudson would continue to oppose developmental threats to the valley, but it also became a champion of efforts that would improve the quality of life for residents. It has been aggressive in promoting land conservation, farmland preservation, land-use planning, and the protection and improvement of environmental quality, including pollution controls and cleaning up PCBs in the riverbed. It has backed the development of riverfront parks, along with environmental education and awareness. Analysis of each of these efforts reveals the success Scenic Hudson has achieved in the more than thirty years since the peace treaty with Con Ed.[19]

Land conservation is surely the most significant of these successes. Scenic Hudson emerged from the 1980 peace treaty financially stable, but the roughly $200,000 it received as part of the settlement was hardly commensurate with the enormous challenge of buying significant, and expensive, threatened properties. This began to change in 1983, when the Hudson River Conservation Society merged with Scenic Hudson and became its land trust division (incorporated as the Scenic Hudson Land Trust in 1990). That same year, through the effort of Barnabas McHenry, their adviser and counsel, DeWitt and Lila Acheson Wallace established Scenic Hudson's Wallace Fund for the Hudson Highlands. This was one part of an enormous gift ($1.7 billion) to thirteen institutions, including the Metropolitan Museum of Art, Lincoln Center, the Wildlife Conservation Society, the Open Space Institute, and Macalester College, among others. The Fund for the Hudson Highlands came in the form of *Reader's Digest* stock, which was controlled by a foundation whose board overlapped significantly with the board of the Reader's Digest Association.[20]

During the years immediately following the establishment of this fund, Scenic Hudson had to file what amounted to a grant application to the foundation for each property it was interested in acquiring. A year after

Gerald Morgan donated a conservation easement to Scenic Hudson on his property immediately north of the Franklin Delano Roosevelt National Historic Site in 1985, the organization completed the first acquisitions drawing on the Wallace Fund—the fee-simple purchase or acquisition of easements on three properties in Putnam County. In 1987 Scenic Hudson collaborated with the Open Space Institute, the DEC, the Office of Parks, Recreation and Historic Preservation, the Heritage Task Force for the Hudson River Valley, and the Hudson River Improvement Fund to acquire Sloop Hill, a 102-acre riverfront property in New Windsor, as a public park, which prevented developer Alfred J. Liverzani from building 530 condominium units on the scenic promontory. (Two and a half years after the sale, Liverzani claimed that he had been coerced and in November 1990 sued in Federal District Court seeking $15 million in damages. The suit was dismissed.) In 1987, Scenic Hudson also acquired a conservation easement on a portion of the grounds of Montgomery Place, a historic Livingston family estate in Annandale-on-Hudson. In 1990, Scenic Hudson completed the acquisition of the northern forty-three acres of Esopus Meadows Point. In two joint ventures with the Open Space Institute, Scenic Hudson acquired Manitou Point in Garrison and a sixty-nine-acre property, Eve's Point, in Ulster County. During that fiscal year Scenic Hudson also used the Wallace Fund and a grant from the Amy Scheuer Cohen Family Foundation to acquire ninety-four acres at Turkey Point, north of Kingston, which it conveyed to the state DEC.[21]

This was impressive progress for the first seven years of the land trust, and especially important was Scenic Hudson's collaboration with state agencies and other organizations, which would be a hallmark of its efforts in succeeding years. During the 1990s, Scenic Hudson acquired much of Mount Beacon, the landmark promontory on the river's east bank, as well as Fishkill Ridge, both of which were subsequently conveyed to the state, as well as land along Fishkill Creek and the waterfront in Beacon. Scenic Hudson's land acquisitions and park development were an investment in Beacon's green infrastructure that occurred as the city was recovering strongly from its unfortunate era of urban renewal and as crime and blight decreased significantly. The organization played a key role in persuading Dia to renovate the former Nabisco factory on the waterfront as Dia:Beacon, a world-class collection of contemporary art that has helped develop a thriving arts scene in the community, and Scenic Hudson's

Figure 13. Poets' Walk Park, Red Hook, New York. Photograph by Robert Rodriguez Jr. Courtesy of Scenic Hudson.

efforts have been critically important to Beacon's revitalization as a thriving Hudson River city.[22]

Scenic Hudson also completed the purchase of land at RamsHorn Marsh, as well as a 121.5-acre riverfront property in Red Hook, which it opened as a public park, called Poets' Walk, honoring Knickerbocker writers Washington Irving and Fitz-Greene Halleck and evoking the principles of nineteenth-century landscape design. It also protected Shaupeneak Ridge on the west bank, an important part of the viewshed from the Roosevelt and Vanderbilt Mansion National Historic Sites in Hyde Park. Perhaps most important, Scenic Hudson, in collaboration with Rose Harvey of the Trust for Public Land, Kim Elliman of the Open Space Institute, and the states of New York and New Jersey, along with funding from the federal government, acquired 15,250 acres at Sterling Forest to prevent that landscape from being subdivided into suburban lots. Today Sterling Forest is a state park in both New York and New Jersey. Using money from the Wallace Fund as well as other donations, in 2000 Scenic Hudson acquired a forty-six-acre property in Hyde Park directly across Route 9 from the Roosevelt home and Presidential Library, which twice had been threatened by the development of a Walmart. After the purchase of additional property, which brought the total to 336 acres, Scenic Hudson had effectively preserved the president's tree plantation. A woodland road links the president's house with Eleanor Roosevelt's Val-Kill. Scenic Hudson then transferred the land to the National Park Service, U.S. Department of the Interior, which manages the two historic sites. In the aftermath of this achievement, Scenic Hudson received the Val-Kill Medal of Honor for its conservation and advocacy efforts.[23]

The terms of the Wallace bequest remained a challenge: working through the foundation board slowed progress in land acquisition throughout the 1990s; in addition, recipients also faced restrictions on selling the stock, which declined in value in the 1990s, a time when the overall stock market soared. New York State's attorney general, Eliot L. Spitzer, was concerned that the overlapping membership of the boards of the Wallace Fund foundation and the Reader's Digest Association created at least a potential conflict of interest, and in any case he considered the arrangement perhaps in violation of the state's charities law. In May 2001 Spitzer brokered an agreement that dissolved the Reader's Digest management of the funds and gave the thirteen organizations control over how to invest and spend their respective shares of the Wallace endowment (the agreement has been sealed and apparently did not address the issues Spitzer had raised). At that time Scenic Hudson's gift was valued at approximately $115 million, as was another gift for land preservation to the Open Space Institute.[24]

With the Wallace Fund finally in hand, Scenic Hudson had the resources to begin an aggressive program of land conservation. Fee-simple acquisitions and purchases of easements accelerated in the early years of the twenty-first century. But as the quadricentennial of Henry Hudson's voyage up the river that bears his name neared, in 2007 Scenic Hudson announced an ambitious, long-term program, "Saving the Land That Matters Most," to protect the Hudson Valley's incomparable landscape. The goal was to preserve sixty-five thousand acres, at an estimated cost of approximately $500 million, that met "the state's highest standards for scenic, agricultural and ecological significance." To determine what lands to acquire, Scenic Hudson established four priorities: the land must be visible from important public viewing points; it must be biologically or ecologically significant; it must have high scenic quality; or it must contribute to the preservation of farmland corridors. To establish these priorities it assigned rankings based on a complex methodology that included whether land had been designated within the boundaries of the Scenic Areas of Statewide Significance; whether the land was visible from public viewpoints; whether it had been designated by DEC as a biologically important area; and whether the area was included in the state's listing of Natural Heritage High Priority Areas.[25]

Under the leadership of Scenic Hudson Land Trust executive director Steve Rosenberg and his staff, between the mid-1990s and 2015 Scenic Hudson preserved a range of notable sites, including the West Point Foundry Preserve and adjacent wetlands in Cold Spring. It acquired hundreds of acres to provide buffers for significant estuarine areas, protected the ecologically and culturally significant Black Creek corridor, acquired (and continues to manage) the 249-acre Franny Reese State Park in Lloyd, Ulster County, expanded its holdings at the Shaupeneak Ridge preserve in Esopus, purchased (with the Hudson Highlands Land Trust) 140 acres at Popolopen Ridge in the Hudson Highlands, acquired a trail easement at the Cat Rock estate in Putnam County that links two pieces of Hudson Highlands State Park Preserve, increased the size of the Esopus Meadows Preserve, bought a 216-acre property that links the Shaupeneak Ridge Preserve with the Black Creek Corridor, and acquired 280 acres near the top of Illinois Mountain, an ecologically important and scenic area. The list could go on for pages, but by the end of 2015 Scenic Hudson, often in collaboration with the state or private-sector groups, had conserved approximately thirteen thousand acres identified under its Saving the Land That Matters Most initiative, and its partner organizations had conserved an additional twenty-six hundred acres.[26]

One of the most creative elements of Scenic Hudson's land preservation program is its ongoing work to protect the Olana viewshed. The significance of the viewshed had been key to defeating the proposed nuclear power plant at Cementon in the 1970s and the St. Lawrence Cement plant in 2005, but other threats emerged beginning in the 1980s—the possible subdivision of farmland for development, and the construction of cell phone towers and a new generation of high-voltage electricity transmission lines. In May 1986 the National Park Service had identified Olana as a Priority 2 site, indicating that "the surrounding development pressure exhibits a greater potential threat to the resource than ever before." That fall the Scenic Hudson Land Trust began acquiring, either in fee simple or through the purchase of easements, significant properties in the viewshed. By the early 1990s Scenic Hudson was engaged in "a number of initiatives as part of a comprehensive effort to preserve the entire Olana viewshed," and at the end of 2014 it had protected fifteen hundred acres. While there is much more to accomplish in this as in other land conservation priorities, this has been a major achievement.[27]

Scenic Hudson also began a farmland preservation initiative in 1996. This became just as urgent a priority as land conservation. The American Farmland Trust estimated that New York State had lost three and a half farms a day over the previous twenty-five years, or almost half a million acres of highly productive farmland. As land prices and development pressures escalated, the historic and productive agricultural economy of the Hudson Valley was at risk. Often working collaboratively with local land trusts in Columbia, Dutchess, Ulster, and Orange Counties, but extending its efforts as far north as Albany and Rensselaer Counties, Scenic Hudson has moved energetically to purchase easements on farmland to keep it in productive use. Land trusts or governmental agencies acquire easements (or purchase of development rights) by paying farmers the difference between the land's value if protected and its value if developed. Scenic Hudson estimates that land kept in farming ranges from 50 to 60 percent of the potential value of the land if developed. This would be approximately $4,400 per acre for highest-priority farms in the Hudson Valley. These easements are permanent and could keep the land in agriculture for succeeding generations.[28]

While quality of soil is always a key determinant in farmland preservation, in 1997 Scenic Hudson adopted what it terms a "critical mass" approach to preservation, concentrating efforts in areas where it could protect enough contiguous farms to support an agricultural services industry. This strategy evolved as Scenic Hudson and local land conservancies began acquiring easements in the village of Red Hook, in northern Dutchess County, and in Columbia County to its north. Scenic Hudson uses Geographical Information Systems analysis to identify areas with important wildlife habitats to enable it to prioritize those farms for preservation. Through the easements, Scenic Hudson provides farmers capital that enables them to increase the productive capacity of their land or to transition to more ecologically sustainable practices. Combining their own resources with state funds and grants from the U.S. Department of Agriculture, by the end of 2015 Scenic Hudson and its land conservancy partners had protected more than eighty-one thousand acres of high-quality farmland. A major boost to farmland preservation and to Scenic Hudson's Foodshed Conservation Plan occurred when Governor Andrew Cuomo included $20 million in the 2016 state budget to preserve farmland in the Hudson Valley.[29]

Scenic Hudson has identified nine priority conservation areas with clusters (the "critical mass" approach) containing 614 farms designated "highest priority" for conservation, totaling 163,673 acres. It estimates that acquiring easements on these farms will cost approximately $720 million. While this is a daunting number, Scenic Hudson is committed to working with its partner organizations and governments to preserve these farms in perpetuity, both to support a sustainable agricultural economy and because it recognizes that these farms "maintain our scenic working landscapes, rural heritage and quality of life" while also safeguarding "wildlife habitat and environmentally sensitive areas." In effect, farmland preservation is an important tool in preventing unplanned sprawl.[30]

Perhaps the most important aspect of Scenic Hudson's farmland preservation program is the development of a coordinated regional Foodshed Conservation Plan, a program developed by Steve Rosenberg. This plan obviously builds on the "locavore" movement that has gained substantial traction nationally since its beginning in San Francisco in 2005, but it is remarkably ambitious, embracing eleven counties extending from Westchester north to Rensselaer County. The plan anticipates that Hudson Valley farms will be able to provide a significant portion of the fresh vegetables and fruits consumed in homes and restaurants in New York City and throughout the valley. The preservation of farmland is an essential first step in providing access to healthy food, but it also requires the creation or enhancement of existing processing facilities and an efficient distribution network, which Scenic Hudson calls "food hubs," as well as supportive public policy and effective marketing. The Foodshed Conservation Plan would strengthen agriculture throughout the Hudson Valley even as it provides healthy meals to residents. Thus Scenic Hudson as an organization advocates that the federal Department of Agriculture and the state's Department of Agriculture & Markets, as well as counties and municipal governments, significantly increase appropriations for farmland preservation. It also calls on private philanthropies to recognize the importance of farmland preservation to help match these public investments and thereby contribute to a more healthful life for millions of people. It is too early to determine how successful this program will become, but the "foodshed" program is a visionary plan that, if completely implemented, would both protect the environment and enhance the quality of life, upstate and in crowded cities and leafy suburbs alike.[31]

Still another important initiative Scenic Hudson has embraced is reconnecting people to the riverfront. This is being accomplished through a number of strategies, the most significant of which are opposition to high-rise and high-density development along the riverfront and instead urging communities to follow the guidelines presented in its *Sound Waterfront Development Principles*; and the conversion of former industrial sites into attractive public parks. When one developer proposed construction of 2,200 dwelling units and 328,000 square feet of retail space on Kingston's waterfront, and another expressed the intent to build 360 residences and 60,000 square feet of retail, Scenic Hudson joined with local opponents of the projects—which would privatize the city's last remaining open space along the river—and succeeded in scaling back plans for those projects and maintaining public access to the water. Ultimately, neither project was built. In Poughkeepsie, Scenic Hudson fought three development proposals: one where it successfully persuaded the developers of a contaminated riverfront site to reduce the project in scale and move it back from the river to create publicly accessible open space; another where it prevented development on Kaal Rock, a cliff overlooking the river; and a third, a former lumberyard along the river, where it persuaded the owners to alter their plan and follow the guidelines in *Sound Waterfront Development Principles*.[32]

In Lloyd in Ulster County, and Ossining, Tarrytown, and Sleepy Hollow in Westchester County, Scenic Hudson responded to pleas from residents to head off poorly prepared development proposals. Rather than taking a position of outright opposition, in many of these cases Scenic Hudson prepared design alternatives that would protect water quality, wildlife, and public access to the riverfront. The Sleepy Hollow project, Lighthouse Landing, was designed for the site of the former General Motors plant adjacent to the river. Scenic Hudson presented a series of recommendations to the developers and village officials, most of which were accepted, including a riverfront park and a buffer between the housing and commercial development and adjacent parkland, which could lead to the restoration of wildlife habitat along the Pocantico River, now in the early stages of implementation. In Yonkers, Scenic Hudson battled for years to modify a massive development project on a four-and-a-half-mile stretch of the river—"a virtual wall of high rises" that would cut residents off from the waterfront—and successfully argued for a vastly reduced scale for the proposed high-rise buildings and the creation of parks along the river. In Pine Plains, Dutchess County, Scenic Hudson joined with citizens in persuading a developer to revise plans for a twenty-two-hundred-unit subdivision in order to protect important wildlife habitats and create more open space. Again, the list of these initiatives could go on for paragraphs. Suffice it to state that Scenic Hudson has worked successfully with residents throughout the valley to ensure that, as much as possible, new residential and commercial development maintains the scale of historic communities and preserves public access to the riverfront. As board chair Frederic C. Rich and Ned Sullivan pledged in 2006, Scenic Hudson will work to "stop or modify every single poorly planned residential mega-project along the Hudson."[33]

Scenic Hudson codified its strategies for waterfront development in a booklet published in 2010, *Revitalizing Hudson Riverfronts*. This booklet takes a proactive and positive approach to the rapid (and in a number of cases unfortunate) development along the river and attempts to direct future development in more sustainable ways. Addressed to public officials, developers, and citizen activists, *Revitalizing Hudson Riverfronts* has as its goals "to promote the development of lively, pedestrian-friendly, mixed-use riverfronts in and adjacent to municipal centers while conserving forests, farms, wetlands, and fields" and also to promote the completion of a continuous greenway along the river. It advises that riverfront development take place where infrastructure already exists, which would help revitalize older cities, and presents strategies for connecting people to the river, protecting natural and scenic resources, and promoting good planning and sustainable design. *Revitalizing Hudson Riverfronts* effectively grafts many of the planning strategies associated with the New Urbanism—gridded streets, mixed-use development, pedestrian-friendly streets and spaces, appropriately scaled new buildings in keeping with historic architecture and community character, and a diversity of housing options—to Scenic Hudson's long-standing efforts in protecting the landscape and scenery of the valley.[34]

The development of riverfront parks is the other half of Scenic Hudson's commitment to reconnecting residents to the river. One interesting example is the fifteen-acre Long Dock Park in Beacon. Scenic Hudson had been active for years in protecting Mount Beacon and Fishkill Ridge, and has strongly supported Beacon's revitalization, but Long Dock Park represents a new twist on the strategy used by park builders such as Frederick Law Olmsted in the second half of the nineteenth century—parks as a strategy for directing and stimulating residential development—by presenting recreational development as a tool in urban revitalization. The site once was a gritty, abandoned wasteland, home to a rail ferry terminal and warehouses, and later to an oil terminal and junkyard. After suffering more than a century of pollution and neglect, the site was remediated by Scenic Hudson, which transformed it into a riverfront park that has become a center for community and individual activities. A strikingly modernist pavilion on the dock provides storage space for kayaks, while a red barn on the site has become a center for art and environmental education. The park provides expansive views south toward the Hudson Highlands, west across Newburgh Bay, and north toward the river and mountains to the west. The site's remaining eight acres were originally slated to be developed into a LEED-certified hotel, but this is no longer a part of the plan. Instead, Scenic Hudson hopes to develop the site as an attractive, lively commercial project that will bring residents and tourists to the riverfront. The project is currently in the design phase, and Scenic Hudson anticipates that construction will commence in 2017.[35]

Another extraordinary effort was Scenic Hudson's role in "daylighting" the Saw Mill River, a tributary of the Hudson that for decades had flowed underground, in culverts, through downtown Yonkers. It was, alas, a scenic and ecological resource sacrificed to conventional planning precepts generations ago. The Saw Mill once provided the water power that ran one of the mills so important to the Philipse family's manor hall, the centerpiece of a patroonship that once covered a vast expanse of 250 square miles (the manor hall, a state historic site, is adjacent to the river and near the site of the mills, which have long since been demolished). In 2005 Scenic Hudson received a grant from the state to investigate how daylighting the river could be part of an urban revitalization and habitat

Figure 14. Kayak Pavilion at Long Dock Park, Beacon, New York. Photograph by Robert Rodriguez Jr. Courtesy of Scenic Hudson.

restoration program. It saw this as an opportunity to work with the city and local stakeholders not only to restore a natural feature in the city but also to create a downtown destination anchored by a riverwalk akin to those in San Antonio and Providence. Scenic Hudson then successfully advocated for funding to transform a nearby abandoned building into loft apartments and a restaurant and helped attract investment to strengthen a pharmaceutical firm located near the river. Downtown Yonkers was an unappealing, moribund area for decades, but the daylighting of the Saw Mill and the riverwalk are making it an attractive destination.[36]

In dozens of cities and villages along the river and its tributaries, Scenic Hudson has worked with governments and citizens to transform derelict industrial areas into attractive riverfront parks. These have ranged in extent from a postage-stamp two-acre site to a park of more than one hundred acres, up and down the valley—in Cortlandt, Tarrytown, Hastings-on-Hudson, Nyack, Peekskill, Marlborough, Poughkeepsie, and Bethlehem, among many others. In Sleepy Hollow, through the contribution of Kathryn W. Davis, Scenic Hudson transformed a bathhouse in Kingsland Point Park into a center for environmental education and recreation (the center is named for Ms. Davis, who also created an endowment

Figure 15. The "daylighted" Saw Mill River, Yonkers, New York. Courtesy of Scenic Hudson.

at Scenic Hudson for park planning and community land use). By 2016 Scenic Hudson had, in collaboration with local communities, created or revitalized more than sixty parks in the Hudson River Valley.[37]

Of these, surely the most unusual is the transformation of an abandoned railroad bridge into Walkway Over the Hudson State Historic Park, an idea first proposed by William Sepe. Constructed beginning in 1873, and operational in 1888, this bridge was at the time the longest in the world and was considered an engineering marvel. As the only railroad crossing of the river south of Albany, it carried an immense amount of freight, sometimes as many as thirty-five hundred train cars a day. The bridge remained in operation until 1974, when a fire damaged the tracks. Thereafter it stood, rusting, unused, perhaps awaiting the time when its steel frame was valuable enough to be taken back to the furnace and given new life. But in 1998 a local organization, Walkway Over the Hudson, began an effort to transform the relic into an elevated pedestrian park that would link greenways proposed for the east and west banks of the river. Scenic Hudson made the first significant donation to the walkway, of $1 million. The project's major benefactor was the Dyson Foundation, also a significant supporter of Scenic Hudson. Fred W. Schaeffer, a Poughkeepsie attorney and longtime president of the Walkway Over the Hudson organization, was indefatigable in gaining public support for the project and in reaching out to state and federal officials as well as municipalities and corporations for the financial support to transform the rusting bridge into a park. Construction began in May 2008, and in October 2009 the walkway opened to the public as a park—a legacy project of the Hudson-Fulton-Champlain Quadricentennial, whose executive director, Tara Sullivan, is Ned Sullivan's spouse. The walkway has proved to be immensely popular, attracting 720,000 people in its first year. Pedestrians can stroll across the bridge, which spans a distance of 6,728 feet (1.28 miles), at a height of 212 feet above the river, and enjoy scenic views, much of the landscape preserved through the efforts of Scenic Hudson and its partners. These organizations have also linked the walkway to greenways on both side of the river and recommended modifications to existing zoning ordinances to promote tourist-oriented economic development.[38]

Still another longtime effort of Scenic Hudson has been its ongoing battle to clean up the Hudson River. Its vision is to make the river a vital recreational resource, a safe place to swim and fish, kayak or sail, its banks an inviting place to hike or stroll. To this end Scenic Hudson has been fighting pollution—insisting, for example, on the need for better sewage waste treatment facilities and on the need to remediate the thousands of tons of polychlorinated biphenyls (PCBs) released into the upper river by the General Electric Corporation. It pushed hard for the federal Environmental Protection Agency to reverse an early decision—that it was better to leave the PCBs in the riverbed and wait until subsequent siltation covered the carcinogenic threat—and instead rule that GE needed to undertake a massive, and expensive, dredging operation to remove most of the ecological damage that it caused. Phase 2 of the cleanup concluded in 2016, and Scenic Hudson is among the organizations most vocal in pushing for regulatory agencies to force GE to fund a Phase 3 to clean up the remaining PCB hot spots in the river north of the Federal Dam at Troy. Scenic Hudson joined Riverkeeper in this effort, and has also advocated strategies for abating other industrial toxics released into the river, which naturalist and writer Robert H. Boyle pointed out forty-five years ago and a subsequent study by the Environmental Defense Fund and the New York Public Interest Research Group confirmed and amplified in 1977. Those other toxic substances, including mercury and various chlorinated hydrocarbons, cadmium and other metals, as well as hundreds of other chemicals, many of which are carcinogenic, are as dangerous as PCBs to the future of the river.[39]

Environmental education became an important focus for Scenic Hudson in the first decade of the new millennium. The organization established partnerships with core schools in Kingston, Beacon, and Cold Spring in which Scenic Hudson educators visited classrooms and then took the children to one of the organization's parks for "hands-on exploration." In 2006 the core schools program involved twelve hundred students, while other programs reached more than five hundred students at levels extending from elementary school to college. Susan Hereth, then the community education coordinator at Scenic Hudson, promoted efforts to teach children the history and ecology of the Hudson Valley. In an organizational restructuring, Scenic Hudson has emphasized the creation of parks that can serve as outdoor classrooms for schools, scouts, and other groups, including those organized by Clearwater. (Consistent with its educational mission, the Clearwater organization has been more ambitious in engaging with school districts and has reached far more students, both in the classroom and on the waters.) Scenic Hudson also regularly employs Student Conservation Association interns to both learn on the job and assist in educating students. Although its educational efforts do not receive as much attention as its land conservation efforts do, Scenic Hudson remains committed to these programs and will be adding a civic engagement component to encourage young people to advocate for environmental improvements in their communities.[40]

Scenic Hudson has expanded its mission in other ways: it has developed a strong outreach program that has embraced communities and individuals who care deeply about the Hudson Valley. Its staff has organized guided hikes for adults and children through the parks and preserves it has created and festivals that bring people to the riverfront. The organization has also promoted partnerships with citizen activists, an important force in supporting Scenic Hudson's advocacy for environmental funding and legislation in Albany.[41]

In recent years Scenic Hudson has become a vocal opponent of other threats to the quality of life in the Hudson Valley. One of these is a state plan to construct a new generation of towering electricity transmission lines that would run through seven counties and twenty-five communities in the valley. This is an issue that extends back to Scenic Hudson's beginnings, in its opposition to new transmission lines through Putnam and Westchester Counties that would have been required to move electricity produced at the proposed pumped-storage plant at Storm King Mountain downstate to New York City. Together with the Hudson Valley Smart Energy Coalition, Scenic Hudson has insisted that any new lines be placed within existing rights-of-way rather than cut through new areas that would endanger the landscape, family farms, and wildlife habitats. Data presented by these two groups, and reports by experts employed by Scenic Hudson, have demonstrated that current infrastructure is adequate and that the proposed lines, which would be a blight on the landscape, are neither economical nor necessary. Scenic Hudson has been arguing before the state Public Service Commission and urging Governor Andrew Cuomo to abandon the plan.[42]

Scenic Hudson is also addressing climate change. Because the Hudson River is an arm of the sea, communities along its banks are vulnerable to rising sea levels and the increasingly frequent and intense storm surges.

Scenic Hudson property is also at risk: as a result of its efforts to protect estuarine habitats and ensure public access to the river, the organization owns more than one thousand acres along the Hudson. The riverfront parks it has worked so hard to create are threatened by rising water, and so is the quality of life in Hudson River communities.

Thus Scenic Hudson has begun to tackle the threat of climate change to ensure "a future that balances and reduces risks to people, property and nature and holds the promise of secure, thriving riverfront communities within a vibrant, healthy ecosystem." Its overall strategy focuses on two goals: mitigation and adaptation. Mitigation is an overall effort to minimize pollution and, through the ownership of thousands of acres of forests that sequester carbon, to slow the effect of global warming. Scenic Hudson is also lobbying in Albany for policies that promote smart growth and renewable energy. Adaptation is, if possible, more difficult. Scenic Hudson's goals include focusing its conservation priorities to prepare Hudson Valley communities for climate change by protecting the most threatened habitats and places. In riverfront communities it has collaborated with DEC to bring together public officials and key stakeholders to identify areas where development would be appropriate and others where flooding and storm impacts render them inappropriate. As a result, Catskill, Kingston, and Piermont have modified their master plans and zoning to reflect these new planning principles, while Kingston has received state funding to protect its sewage treatment plant from flooding. Funding from the Doris Duke Charitable Foundation is enabling Scenic Hudson to prepare a "climate resilience conservation plan" for the Hudson Valley. The organization is also working with DEC and the Department of State on climate initiatives and legislation. At Long Dock Park in Beacon and the Esopus Meadows Preserve, Scenic Hudson has erected buildings and designed landscapes to withstand periodic flooding and, it hopes, a waterfront that can sustainably survive higher water levels. Whether this is enough—indeed, whether a regional organization can control its own destiny in the face of global climate change—remains to be seen.[43]

Scenic Hudson has evolved from a single-purpose organization created to defend Storm King Mountain against Con Ed's proposed hydroelectric power facility to one that takes a much more holistic vision of the river, its landscape, economy, and communities. To do so it has forged partnerships with other environmental organizations, most notably River-keeper, Clearwater, and sixteen land trusts, and has worked effectively with state agencies in conserving land and preserving farms. It has also secured the financial resources and annual support to enable it to work quickly and effectively to protect threatened resources. The Wallace Fund for the Hudson Highlands, valued at $115 million in 2001, is now the Lila Acheson and DeWitt Wallace Hudson Valley Land Preservation Endowment. At the close of 2015 it was valued at $157.9 million, despite the monies expended for the purchase of land or easements over the intervening fourteen years. Scenic Hudson has been an effective steward of this resource, taking a 5 percent draw of the fund's value based on a three-year rolling average (this slows the increase in the draw when the market is rising, but also protects income during times of market decline and is a strategy most educational institutions and other endowed nonprofits follow). Scenic Hudson also has an endowment fund for operating purposes ($14.9 million at the end of 2015), the Kathryn W. Davis Fund for park planning ($4.7 million), and an easement enforcement fund of $1.1 million. These numbers are impressive, and testify to wise management and effective development efforts. Indeed, return from these endowments accounts for about 47 percent of Scenic Hudson's annual budget, just about two-thirds of which (65 percent) is spent in land acquisition and managing its parks and preserves. But members of Scenic Hudson's management and board of directors would undoubtedly tell us that there is so much more they could accomplish with greater resources.[44]

Scenic Hudson has grown from small beginnings into the conservation-environmental organization in New York State that speaks authoritatively to governors, state legislators, and bureaucrats in key Albany agencies. It has articulated a holistic vision for the Hudson Valley that embraces the preservation of a world-renowned and threatened landscape. It can point with pride to its role in creating parks that inspire visitors through the breathtaking views of the river or the mysteries of woodland trails or lovely creek corridors, in taking steps to support the emergence of economically vibrant communities along the river, in educating the next generation of environmental activists and citizens, and in strongly supporting creation of the Hudson River Greenway, an ambitious program of trails that link open spaces throughout the valley, as well as the Hudson's designation as one of the first American Heritage Rivers. Scenic Hudson has also begun planning for a future in which climate change will, quite literally, change everything. These are significant accomplishments. Whether Scenic Hudson can persuade a state legislature notorious for its corruption and political intransigence to adopt a vision that prepares New York for this uncertain future, whether it will have the resources and support from citizens, philanthropies, and corporations to complete its ambitious agenda and ensure a clean river with a sustainable future, is the challenge going forward.

7

Linking Landscapes and Promoting History

Two organizations that emerged in the 1990s that are essential to the economy and quality of life in the valley are the Hudson River Valley Greenway and the Hudson River Valley National Heritage Area. The Greenway is a program adopted, at the urging of Governor Mario M. Cuomo, by the state legislature in 1991. It is a local manifestation of a nationwide movement, as Charles E. Little defines it, that is predicated on the belief that a coordinated program of greenway development, together with effective planning and the promotion of historic preservation and heritage tourism, is essential to ensuring the quality of life in the valley. The National Heritage Area is a federal designation awarded by Congress in 1996. The Greenway was a strong supporter of the National Heritage Area, and in the federal legislation the Greenway's two constituent parts, the Conservancy and the Communities Council, were named the "management entities" for the National Heritage Area. In effect, from the beginning the Greenway has been the umbrella organization that provides direction for the National Heritage Area. The Greenway and the National

Heritage Area remain separate legal entities and have their own boards of directors and budgets, but share enough in common that they have a single administrative staff and offices in Albany and together are working to shape the valley.[1]

A greenway is, at its simplest, a landscaped trail that usually links public parks or other open spaces. Perhaps the first greenway proposed in the United States was included in Frederick Law Olmsted's plan for the College of California at Berkeley. Olmsted suggested in 1866 that a handsomely landscaped suburban road link the Berkeley neighborhood to Oakland and, by ferry, to San Francisco. In the same year he and Calvert Vaux recommended the creation of a series of parkways linking Prospect Park with other neighborhoods in Brooklyn and extending, by a bridge or ferry across the East River, to Central Park in Manhattan and thence northward on broad boulevards then being proposed by a commission headed by Andrew H. Green. Two years later, in urging the Brooklyn Park Commission once again to establish a parkway system, Olmsted and Vaux argued that a system of broad, tree-lined roads would extend the benefits of parks throughout the city. Equally important, the parkways would become a spine around which a new urban form would take shape: they would "constitute the centre of a continuous neighborhood of residences of a more than usually open, elegant and healthy character." Eastern and Ocean Parkways in Brooklyn; parkways linking the three parks in Buffalo, New York (Olmsted and Vaux's first comprehensive park system); and a nine-mile parkway intended to link the suburban community of Riverside, Illinois, with downtown Chicago were all proposed in 1868. Construction began on the Riverside parkway, though it was never completed, while the Brooklyn and Buffalo parkways were built as designed.[2]

Little argues that a second foundational point for modern greenways was the Englishman Ebenezer Howard's concept of new towns of limited size surrounded by a permanent agricultural greenbelt. In *To-morrow: A Peaceful Path to Real Reform* (1898; retitled and reprinted in 1902 as *Garden Cities of To-morrow*), Howard proposed to address the staggering levels of congestion and squalor in Victorian London through the creation of garden cities on six thousand acres, a thousand acres of which would be developed as a community of thirty thousand residents, the remaining five thousand acres devoted permanently to agriculture, which would prevent the new town from sprawling into the countryside. The community would consist of public buildings, markets, industries, cultural institutions, and open space as well as houses. It would be linked to other garden cities, as well as the metropolis, by railroads. Howard's book was translated into several languages, including German, French, Czech, and Russian. A Garden City Association was formed to promote Howard's ideas, and two garden cities, Letchworth and Welwyn Garden City, were constructed in the early twentieth century along the general lines he proposed in *Garden Cities of To-morrow*. Little suggests that the term "greenway" is an amalgam of "greenbelt" and "parkway." He credits William H. Whyte for the first use of the term, in his 1959 book *Securing Open Space* and, more influentially, in the chapter "Linkage" in *The Last Landscape* (1968). Little mentions others as progenitors of the greenway, including Benton MacKaye, who in 1921 proposed the Appalachian Trail as a recreational resource and (though this part of his proposal is largely forgotten) an experiment in community planning and economic revitalization, as well as the work of landscape architect Ian McHarg, whose book *Design with Nature* (1969) educated the rising generation on the importance of ecological planning.[3]

Many of the first greenways were rails-to-trails projects, in which abandoned railroad lines were converted to pedestrian and bicycle corridors beginning in the 1960s. These trails tended to be narrow and relatively flat, which made for comfortable walking, and some of them traversed significant distances. These trails proved to be very popular, and may well be considered one of the foundations of the modern greenway movement. But rails-to-trails projects did not, as a rule, connect parks or other preserved land, which has become a paramount principle of the greenway.[4]

The idea of a greenway for the Hudson River Valley emerged in the mid-1980s. Franny Reese of Scenic Hudson strongly promoted legislative adoption of the Hudson River Shorelands Study Act, which identified lands that should be preserved and linkages connecting them, and also conceptualized a "Hudson Heritage Way," which later evolved into the Greenway. Her colleague Klara Sauer, the longtime executive director of Scenic Hudson, played a key role in calling together a small group of individuals, including David Sampson, Al Appleton, Hooper Brooks, and Judith LaBelle, who met frequently to brainstorm about shaping a greenway program that would appeal to citizens as well as local and state officials. They determined that this would be a grassroots effort, with the eventual shape of the program emerging from the ideas residents expressed in a series of public meetings, rather than the top-down planning strategy employed by the long-defunct and, as Sauer put it, "not well-liked" Hudson River Valley Commission. In 1987 Frances Dunwell, Kenneth R. Toole, and Richard Halverson joined the ad hoc planning group. Sauer took minutes and sent copies to potential funders and supporters, including Laurance Rockefeller, Nash Castro of the Palisades Interstate Park Commission, Joan Davidson of the J. M. Kaplan Fund, and Henry Diamond, former commissioner of the Department of Environmental Conservation. The New York State Council on the Arts funded publication of a brochure promoting a Hudson Valley greenway, which was widely distributed and contributed to the increasing public awareness and support of the idea.[5]

The following year, Sampson brought new life to the Hudson River Valley Association, which was contemporaneously described as a kind of chamber of commerce for the valley, and Scenic Hudson hired Barry Didato, who had recently completed his studies in environmental design and planning at the University of Massachusetts, as greenway coordinator. Didato gave some two hundred presentations on the greenway idea in communities up and down the valley and, as Sauer put it, "rallied the grassroots." Didato's work, together with that of Karl Beard of the National Park Service's Roosevelt National Historic Site, who worked closely with Didato, was essential in giving the greenway idea a public presence. Beard wrote many of the early publications promoting the greenway idea, and he and Didato coauthored *Building Greenways in the Hudson River Valley: A Guide to Action*, a primer that presented twelve case studies of successful greenway development in the valley, which was published by Scenic Hudson and the National Park Service in December 1989. Scenic Hudson and the National Park Service, through its River and Trail Conservation Program, were indispensable in supporting the Hudson River Valley Greenway in its early years. Collectively, these efforts resulted in the establishment of a greenway coalition, which attracted the support of corporations, historical societies, garden clubs, think tanks, local officials, and individuals long prominent in conservation circles in the Hudson Valley, Barnabas McHenry prominently among them.[6]

Two other events in 1988 raised the profile of the greenway idea. In his State of the State address on January 6, 1988, Governor Mario Cuomo strongly advocated the creation of a Hudson River greenway, which he described as "a chain of parks, open space, and trails from New York City to the foothills of the Adirondacks." He portrayed the greenway as a "cooperative public private undertaking [that] will link the extraordinary environmental, cultural, and historical heritage of the Hudson River Valley—in the process, fostering a sense of regional identity while protecting a greenway of national and international significance."[7]

The second event was the publication of a forty-six-page booklet, *Greenways in the Hudson River Valley: A New Strategy for Preserving an American Treasure*. Henry Diamond, its coauthor, anticipated the booklet's publication in an article published in the *New York Times* on January 2, 1988. Diamond advocated a Hudson River greenway "which would link existing corridors of private and public recreation lands and waters to provide people with access to open spaces close to where they live." The time was right, he asserted, and the means were available to create a network of trails that linked parks, preserves, and the everyday life of residents. *Greenways in the Hudson River Valley*, written by Diamond and Douglass Lea and underwritten by Laurance Rockefeller's Jackson Hole Preserve Inc., incorporated the thoughts of a group of private citizens, including Diamond, Sauer, Castro, Toole, Francis Beinecke of the Governor's Environmental Advisory Board, Dana S. Creel of Sleepy Hollow Restorations, Halverson and Sampson of the Hudson River Valley Association, Patrick Noonan of the Conservation Fund, and George R. Lamb of Jackson Hole Preserve. Virtually every member of the working group was or had been associated with various Rockefeller family enterprises. *Greenways in the Hudson River Valley* begins by noting the recommendation of the President's Commission on Americans Outdoors (1987), which called for the creation of a nationwide network of greenways to connect people with the natural world. The greenways that report advocated would be "corridors of private and public recreation lands and waters to provide people with access to open spaces close to where they live and link together the rural and urban spaces in the American landscape." *Greenways in the Hudson River Valley* also cited a February 1988 report of the Regional Plan Association, which defined a greenway network as consisting of natural ecosystems and habitat preserves, parks for public recreation, and corridors that link the preserves and parks.[8]

As was true of Sauer's working group, the citizens who proposed a Hudson River greenway firmly believed that "successful greenways grow out of the grassroots." They expressed the hope that the creation, maintenance, and use of greenways would result from "a strong sense of community responsibility and . . . the willingness of each community to link its destiny to those of its neighbors." These citizens realized that a greenway strategy recognized that "open spaces play a central role in shaping the character of a region and that most of the protected land will remain in private ownership, although linked, scenically and functionally, by public parklands and other holdings." Greenways, they asserted, "are landscapes that work."[9]

Greenways in the Hudson River Valley conceded that there were daunting challenges to the realization of the ideal its proponents envisioned. These included the cost, especially of acquiring land at a time when prices were escalating rapidly in the valley; the sheer scale and complexity of a greenway that extended from Westchester and Rockland Counties at the south to Albany and Troy at the north, a distance of more than 120 miles; and the difficulties of gaining the cooperation of ten counties and almost one hundred units of local government in a region that cherished home rule as a basic precept of everyday life. Success "would require little short of a full mobilization of the region's wisdom, talent, tolerance, intelligence, and perseverance," but the citizens proposing the greenway believed that residents of the Hudson Valley were ready to embrace the challenge and implement a land ethic for the twenty-first century.[10]

A greenway was especially important because of the developmental pressures the Hudson Valley was experiencing. *Greenways in the Hudson River Valley* explained that the plan it proposed was essential because the valley was "undergoing enormous stress." Its "unique values—cultural, historical, and environmental—accelerate economic development, and its proximity to New York City brings relentless threats to open space, clean water, and clean air." An "irreversible transformation" of the landscape was "already well in progress." A greenway, proponents believed, was key to retaining the integrity of the Hudson River Valley and the best possible strategy for controlling unwise development.[11]

Mapping a greenway on the scale of the Hudson Valley began with an inventory of lands in the public domain, including the Palisades Interstate Park, the Harriman, Bear Mountain, Roosevelt, Mohansic, Fahnestock, Baird, Taconic, and Lake Taghkanic State Parks, the grounds of private organizations such as corporate headquarters and college campuses, and historic sites, many of which, like Olana, Lyndhurst, and the Vander-bilt Mansion, included extensive historic landscapes. The state could use funds from the 1986 Environmental Quality Bond Act to acquire key land that connects these public and private lands. The authors of *Greenways in the Hudson River Valley* also expected that money from the federal Land and Water Conservation Fund could be used for purchases in fee simple or other conservation techniques, such as easement acquisition (New York State had only recently provided for the enforcement of conservation ease-ments, which quickly became a powerful tool in land preservation). Dia-mond and Lea envisioned a plan that would "present the Valley's lands, waters, and human enterprises as a whole, as an integrated and working landscape—and then show the greenway as an integral part of that in-terwoven landscape." If successfully implemented, the greenway would come to define the region and reinforce its unique sense of place.[12]

As Scenic Hudson had been arguing in recent years, proponents of the greenway saw a future for the Hudson Valley defined by its natural beauty and history. With the post–World War II decline in manufacturing, pro-moters of the greenway believed that tourism was becoming the driving force in the regional economy, which would contribute to an increase in jobs, income, and tax dollars collected by the state and local municipali-ties. Increasing tourism would require more than an "I Love New York" marketing campaign: it had to be predicated on policies that protected the natural beauty of the valley and ensured public access to the river. A gre-enway could knit together parks and preserved landscapes as well as the many historic sites and other cultural attractions, making the region an attractive destination for scenic, cultural, and heritage tourism.[13]

Greenways in the Hudson River Valley pointed to two legislative acts of 1987 as foundational. One formally defined the charge of the Heri-tage Task Force of the Hudson River Valley to promote "cooperative ef-forts to protect the Valley's ecological, scenic, recreational, and historical resources." The idea of a Heritage Task Force had been suggested in a Department of Environmental Conservation report, *The Hudson River Valley: A Heritage for All Time* (1979). The report urged Governor Hugh Carey to appoint an eight-member task force "to help set priorities for action, to provide overall policy guidance," and to recommend to the gov-ernor and the legislature steps that it considered essential to protecting the scenery and heritage of the valley. Carey did create the task force the following year, and during its eleven years of existence (after 1987 as a statutory body) it promoted the establishment of a Scenic Roads program, the preservation of important Hudson River lighthouses, the creation of scenic districts, and advised the state on land to be acquired and protected for its aesthetic or ecological value, among many other activities. (With legislative adoption of the Hudson River Greenway Act of 1991 the Heritage Task Force became the Greenway Heritage Conservancy.) The Heritage Task Force was also a strong supporter of a greenway. As executive director John Doyle testified, "The Greenway concept is worth pursuing because it has the potential of fostering an attitude, an awareness, on the part of all of us that we live and work in the context of an extensive, interrelated river valley." The other legislative act of 1987 mentioned by Diamond and Lea was the creation of an estuarine district management committee to protect critical habitats and support the river's fisheries. *Greenways in the Hudson River Valley* also pointed to the significance of a 1988 bill, introduced by state assemblyman Maurice Hinchey, chair of the Environmental Conservation Committee, that would create a Hudson River greenway partnership "to effectively plan and develop projects of regional benefit that are necessary to preserve the unique resources of the Hudson River Valley, and assure the maintenance of a compatible economy."[14]

Greenways in the Hudson River Valley concluded with a series of recommendations, including the creation of a Governor's Hudson River Valley Greenway Council consisting of the heads of state agencies, including Environmental Conservation; Parks, Recreation, and Historic Preservation; and Economic Development, as well as private citizens, to work energetically to transform proposals into action. *Greenways in the Hudson River Valley* advocated a funding stream of dedicated money from a range of activities along the river—everything from fishing licenses to sand and gravel sales, fines from environmental violations, and private donations—and anticipated using that money to make small grants to planning boards and supplement Environmental Quality Bond Act funds to acquire key links in the greenway system. It also recommended using the regulatory powers in the State Environmental Quality Review Act as well as federal clean water and clean air acts, along with local zoning ordinances, "to serve notice on those who would scar the landscape and skyline that their projects will receive special scrutiny in the greenway." *Greenways in the Hudson River Valley* has encouraged the partnership of state agencies, municipalities, and private-sector organizations in establishing the Greenway. This collaborative approach has been key to the Greenway's success: it brings together important stakeholders in the valley who work together, learn from each other, and effectively advance the best interests of the valley as a deeply interconnected region. All in all, *Greenways in the Hudson River Valley* advocated an ambitious yet challenging program that its authors believed was essential to the future of the valley.[15]

Greenways in the Hudson River Valley is an important and influential report. The group that produced it had strong ties to Laurance Rockefeller, who wrote the introduction and whose fingerprints, according to historian Robin W. Winks, are all over the document, especially in its emphasis on the preservation of natural lands, expansion of recreational opportunities, and the promotion of historic sites. Together, Rockefeller and Henry Diamond were the driving force behind the creation of the Greenway. With strong support from Governor Mario Cuomo, Rockefeller, and Diamond, state legislators quickly enacted a bill creating a Hudson River Greenway Council, through which, Cuomo stated, "we can insure that the open space, scenic vistas, recreational opportunities and historic and culture resources" of the valley will be accessible for future generations. The council consisted of nineteen members, the heads of five state agencies, the secretary of state, and thirteen members appointed by the governor. The legislation called on the council to present its recommendations to the governor by November 1990. Rose Harvey, who chaired the Hudson River Access Committee, called for the creation of a Hudson River Trail in the *Draft Study for a Hudson River Valley Greenway* (1990).[16]

Barnabas McHenry, a New York City attorney who has been a staunch advocate for the protection of the Hudson Valley over the last generation, became chair of the board of the Hudson River Valley Greenway Council, a position he has held for more than twenty-five years, while David S. Sampson, an Albany attorney, was its first executive director. The council held a series of public hearings throughout the valley to listen to citizens and elected officials, and shaped its recommendations accordingly. In notes appended to the 1991 Hudson River Valley Greenway Act, the legislature acknowledged that the council had "undertaken an aggressively participatory process in formulating its report including numerous public hearings and consultations with governmental and civic leaders throughout the valley." Those deliberations revealed "a strong pride and commitment to protecting the valley's special scenic, natural, cultural and historic heritage," and the legislation expressed the expectation that the greenway act would be an effective mechanism for achieving these goals. In releasing the council's draft report in October 1990, Sampson asserted that the "Hudson River Valley now stands at a crossroads" as farms and open space were disappearing under the onslaught of development. The draft report included the expectation that the Greenway would have the power of eminent domain, but so many residents and public officials expressed concern over giving it this power that the provision was dropped from the 1991 enabling legislation.[17]

Based on the council's report, the state legislature adopted the Hudson River Valley Greenway Act of 1991 to create two new agencies given responsibility for protecting the scenic values of the Hudson, for promoting recreational opportunities for all citizens, especially along the riverfront, for ensuring the preservation of historic sites, and for the development of a regional economy based on tourism. The act created a Greenway Conservancy for the Hudson Valley, a public benefit corporation, which would have the power to acquire property. Funding would come from a 0.2 percent hotel occupancy tax in the ten counties of the greenway area, which proponents anticipated would generate $750,000 for its operating budget (the hotel tax was repealed in 1994). Additional funding from the state's Environmental Quality Bond Act would be used for the purchase of especially desirable land. The Greenway Conservancy's charge was to preserve "open space characterized by natural scenic beauty, heritage, natural resource values or conditions enhancing regional qualities of the Hudson river valley," to establish the framework of a greenway trail that linked public and private open spaces in the valley, and to connect cities and countryside in a green network. That legislation also created the Greenway Communities Council, a state agency whose purpose was to work with municipalities to develop or update local and regional master plans to better protect the valley's scenic and historic resources. The Communities Council was also charged to review the work of state agencies during environmental assessments of projects proposed within the greenway area. Despite fear in the business community that the Greenway might prove harmful to the local economy, especially among builders and developers, on December 31, 1991, Cuomo signed the legislation. According to Klara Sauer, the governor, although an early supporter of the Greenway, heard the complaints of developers and businessmen and worried about the law's impact on the regional economy. At the urging of Sauer or Hinchey, Richard K. Wager, then publisher of the *Poughkeepsie Journal*, called Cuomo and persuaded him at the last minute to sign the bill. Rockefeller's Jackson Hole Preserve Inc. would long be a major source of financial support for the Greenway Communities Council.[18]

The Greenway Act was a product of its time. Despite being supported by a liberal, activist governor, it bore the constraints of Ronald Reagan's America, with its promises of lower taxes, smaller government, and the devolution of authority to the states and municipalities. The greenway idea also appealed to those who were inspired by Reagan's successor, George H. W. Bush, who had enormous faith in the private sector—his "thousand points of light" speech is a memorable example of this—to solve problems that government could not. But it was also a product of the political culture of New York State at the time, and reflected long-standing concerns about home rule. Thus the two Greenway agencies, like the Hudson River Valley Commission, had limited power and limited funding. The Greenway Conservancy could not acquire land by condemnation, however essential a specific property might be to the overall success of the greenway system, and the Greenway Communities Council could not challenge local planning and zoning ordinances that it considered inadequate, something that the U.S. Department of the Interior had recommended for the Hudson River Valley in 1966. The success of the two Greenway agencies would come from cooperation with local governments and state agencies in promoting a vision of what the Hudson River Valley could be in the future. Given the vast scale of the Greenway, and the differences in dealing with counties experiencing rapid suburbanization in the lower part of the valley versus those, like Greene and Washington at the north, which had been stagnant economically for decades, this was a formidable task.[19]

The Greenway Act also charged the Greenway Conservancy with developing a plan for the Greenway, including a management plan to guide its implementation. Responsibilities included determining what corridors or linkages were essential to completing a greenway system, providing interpretative signage that explained the natural and cultural heritage of the region, involving students and other volunteers in the development and maintenance of the trails, and coordinating with state agencies whose responsibilities included area within the Greenway. The act instructed the Communities Council and the Greenway Conservancy to organize a symposium that brought together all interested stakeholders, public and private, to prepare a plan of action, and to submit that plan to the governor and the legislature within twenty-four months, with the expectation that the Greenway trail could be completed and open to the public by June 2005.[20]

The Greenway's organizing philosophy is the creation of linkages through voluntary inter-municipal cooperation. Its mantra is a variation on René Dubos's famous dictum, "Think globally, act locally." For the Greenway this means think regionally and plan locally. It hopes that each municipality in the Greenway area will, in revising its planning and zoning ordinances, work collaboratively with adjacent communities and that the result will be a bottom-up regional plan. The Greenway has charged each of the ten counties it embraces to develop compacts that articulate a vision to be achieved through planning. Dutchess County was the first to join the compact, in 2000, and its founding document, "Greenway Connections," is often described as a model for other counties. Twenty-nine of thirty municipalities within the county have joined the compact. The county has committed $7 million to its open space and farmland preservation initiative, through which it has purchased in fee simple 556 acres of public open space and preserved 2,465 acres of farmland through easement acquisition. Orange County's plan describes the Greenway Compact as "an innovative state-sponsored program created to facilitate the development of a regional strategy for preserving scenic, natural, historic, cultural and recreational resources while encouraging appropriate economic development and maintaining the tradition of home rule for making land use decisions." Key compact principles include natural and cultural resource protection, compatible economic development, public access to the river, regional planning, and heritage and environmental education. Orange County officials foresee that approval as a compact county will provide greater access to state-funded capital programs and grants for planning and implementation. Plans prepared by three other counties—Westchester, Putnam, and Rockland—have also been recognized by the Greenway Communities Council, while Ulster County's compact plan is in the development stage.[21]

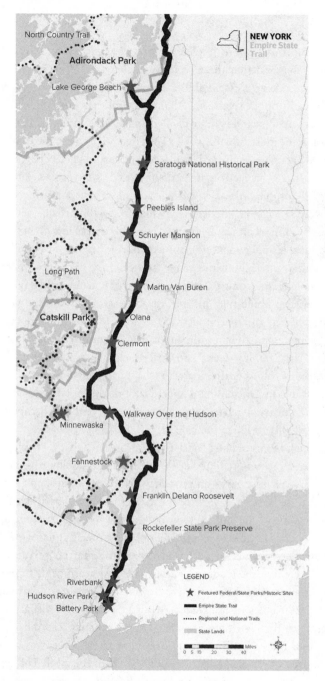

Figure 16. The Hudson River Valley Greenway, map of proposed trails. Courtesy of the Hudson River Valley Greenway.

Moving from plan to implementation is almost invariably a difficult process. The land that the Greenway backers and other proponents of open space believe is essential to their vision is also attractive to developers, especially on the riverfront. Abandoned railroad lines are low-hanging fruit; developable land is more challenging—and that on the banks of the Hudson is the most valuable of all. The Greenway's longtime (but recently departed) acting executive director, Mark Castiglione, believes that the success it has achieved to date is the result of its cooperative and collaborative philosophy. Also key was Barnabas McHenry's insistence that the Greenway agencies be nonpartisan, which has enabled them over the years to win the support of members of the assembly and senate on both sides of the political aisle. Eminent domain would have been a poison pill to most communities throughout the valley, as would the authority to challenge local planning and zoning ordinances, both of which would have affected long-cherished home rule. Instead, the Greenway has worked with local communities by offering modest grants to help them prepare or update their planning and zoning ordinances or in financially supporting conservation efforts, public access, and trail development, among other activities. It sees its role as partnering with local governments and private-sector organizations in articulating a shared vision, coordinating their various efforts, and providing catalytic support to preserve the landscape that defines the quality of life in the valley.[22]

Although in its enabling legislation the Greenway Conservancy gained the power to acquire land either through donation or by fee-simple purchase for riverfront parks and the network of trails throughout the valley, and to sell bonds to finance those purchases, its board decided that the Greenway would not take on debt. Thus, perhaps surprisingly, the Greenway does not own a single acre of land. Instead, it has worked with the state departments of parks and environmental conservation, land trusts throughout the Hudson Valley, and local governments to pursue its goals. As a result of their collective efforts, the Greenway's partners have acquired 270 miles of designated riverfront trails, with visual or physical access to the Hudson, and created approximately 770 miles of trails throughout the valley. The greatest obstacle to the Greenway's vision is the presence of railroad tracks on both banks of the river. The railroads are justifiably concerned about safety and so limit access to the Hudson across their tracks. This is the largest single gap in the riverfront greenway corridor that the organization hopes to create, and it is unlikely that in the near term the Greenway can achieve its goal of providing pedestrians a sense of ownership of the riverfront, which Clearwater and Scenic Hudson have also embraced. In September 1989, the Hudson River Access Forum, a consortium of federal and state agencies as well as nonprofit groups, published *Between the Railroad and the River*, which presented opportunities for creating and enhancing access to the Hudson's banks. But given the enormous difficulties the railroad presents, the Greenway has adopted what it considers a more achievable goal—connecting communities through trails.[23]

Some parts of the Greenway are completed, some stretches are in the design or construction phase. Others will take years to assemble and open to the public. Castiglione estimates that the trails program is approximately 30 percent complete. The most advanced piece of the extensive trail network is the Westchester RiverWalk, a 51.5-mile trail paralleling the Hudson that extends through fourteen municipalities. The River-Walk, strongly supported by the Greenway, links public and institutional land—the Old Croton Aqueduct, paths in existing parks, the Veterans Administration hospital in Montrose, and several of Scenic Hudson's riverfront parks. Approximately two-thirds of the RiverWalk is now complete and open to the public, an enormous accomplishment that required the cooperation of federal, state, county, and municipal governments as well as individuals and private-sector organizations.[24]

The Hudson Highlands Fjord Trail is another example of how complex a challenge completing the Greenway can be. The trail will extend from the train station in Cold Spring approximately seven and a half miles north to the train station in Beacon. What makes the Fjord Trail so important to complete is the safety of hikers, who park along state highway 9D or walk along the narrow roadway from the railroad station in Cold Spring to trailheads in the Hudson Highlands State Park Preserve. Coordinated by Scenic Hudson, the constituent partners in the Fjord Trail include the state departments of parks, transportation, and environmental conservation, the Metro North Railroad, the Hudson Highlands Land Trust, the towns of Philipstown and Fishkill, the village of Cold Spring, the city of Beacon, the Friends of Fahnestock & Hudson Highlands State Parks, the New York–New Jersey Trail Conference, and the Little Stony Point Citizens Association. The Greenway provided early project funding, as did the Hudson Highlands Land Trust, the Open Space Institute, and the Hudson River Improvement Fund. The Davis family is the leading private donor to the project, with additional funding from Scenic Hudson, both of which sources have been used to match capital grants from the state. With so many stakeholders, reaching consensus has been challenging, but the participants in the negotiations persevered. Planning has been under way for several years, and the first parts of the trail are nearing completion of construction and will open to the public in 2017.[25]

Still another project, the Hyde Park Greenway Trail, extends from Staatsburg to Hyde Park. Though still intermittent, the trail connects the Roosevelt and Vanderbilt Mansion national historic sites, traverses two Scenic Hudson properties, then wends through a heavily wooded ravine and ends at an overlook with spectacular views of the river, Esopus Island, and the Catskills. It is one piece of what Greenway planners envision will be a trail that connects the Mid-Hudson and Kingston-Rhinecliff bridges, one of the critical gaps in the current state of the riverfront Greenway. Also important is the Hudson River Greenway Water Trail, which Governor Pataki strongly supported; he secured a $1 million appropriation from the legislature to implement it. The water trail was developed in collaboration with several state agencies and private-sector organizations like Scenic Hudson. At the beginning of the work on the water trail, there were few places that provided public access to the riverfront. Based on the work the Greenway and its partners have completed, there are now more than one hundred points of public access, including places for launching kayaks and for marinas and riverfront parks. The water trail was designated by the U.S. Department of the Interior as a National Water Trail in 2012.[26]

One other connecting trail, the Skywalk, would link Thomas Cole's Cedar Grove, in Catskill, with Frederic Church's Olana, in Greenport, through pedestrian-friendly alterations to the Rip Van Winkle Bridge. Columbia and Greene Counties, Scenic Hudson, the two artists' houses, and the New York State Bridge Authority are collaborating on the project, made possible by substantial funding procured through the efforts of Governor Andrew Cuomo.[27]

Mark Castiglione believes that the Greenway can claim three major accomplishments. First, even if it doesn't own any land, it has effectively partnered with other organizations to promote the acquisition of key parcels that have preserved the landscape and scenery of the valley and provided recreational opportunities for the hundreds of thousands of people who hike the trails each year. Second, he believes that the Greenway has changed the conversation about land use, conservation, and development in the Hudson River Valley. Whereas in previous decades supporters of economic development and conservation/environmentalism were often at loggerheads, Castiglione is certain that the Greenway has demonstrated that development and preservation can be complementary. He points to the trails, which bring enormous numbers of tourists to the valley, as the most visible example of how conservation can promote economic development. Tourism, as Scenic Hudson has long argued, is an essential component of the postindustrial economy in the Hudson River Valley. Third, he insists that the Greenway has been key in developing the valley as a marketable brand. Whereas a generation or so ago the Hudson Valley was fragmented into sub-regions, Castiglione believes that today it is perceived as a single, special place, and most residents feel a palpable sense of regional identity. The Hudson Valley is their home, their community.[28]

These outcomes, Castiglione asserts, are direct results of the grassroots regionalism the Greenway has been promoting since its inception. He is also proud of the Hudson River Valley Ramble program, which takes place over four weekends in September each year and introduces hikers and lovers of natural beauty to the "history, culture, and natural resources" of the valley. In 2009, an estimated two hundred thousand people participated in Ramble events—hikes, craft festivals, street fairs, cultural events, harvest festivals, and historic tours that celebrate the valley's critical role in the American Revolution and its significant architecture and cultural landscapes. These and many other festivals that bring together residents and visitors are all strongly supported by the Greenway, Scenic Hudson, by the state parks and the Department of Environmental Conservation, and the Hudson River Estuary Program. Visitor spending for the 2009 Ramble had an economic impact of approximately $21 million.[29]

The Hudson River Valley Greenway is also the corporate umbrella of the Hudson River Valley National Heritage Area. The National Heritage Area's mission is "to recognize, preserve, protect, and interpret the nationally significant cultural and natural resources of the Hudson River Valley for the benefit of the nation." The area embraces ten counties and extends

from the Westchester-Bronx boundary in the south to Rensselaer County
at the north. The National Park Service proclaimed, in 1996, that the
Hudson Valley was "the landscape that defined America" and attributed
to it a series of key events and developments, from early settlement and
the American Revolution to the transformation in American taste promoted by landscape gardener and tastemaker Andrew Jackson Downing
in the mid-nineteenth century to our own time, that have defined a con-
servationist/environmentalist mission. The National Heritage Area was
introduced as part of the Omnibus Parks and Public Lands Management
Act of 1996 (Public Law 104-333) by Maurice Hinchey, then a member
of Congress. Probably more than any other individual, Hinchey was responsible for promoting legislation, in Albany and Washington, that has
protected the interests of the Hudson River Valley. He deserves a Hinchey
Park or Trail, with appropriate signage attesting to his invaluable public
service, as recognition of how hard he worked, over many years, in behalf of the people and the environment of the valley. Hinchey's purpose in
framing this legislation was to have the federal government "recognize the
importance of the history and resources of the Hudson River Valley to the
Nation," to aid the state and its communities in preserving and interpret-
ing its historic and scenic resources, and to provide general financial and
technical assistance in creating the heritage area.[30]

The National Park Service's *Hudson River Valley Special Resource
Study Report* (1996) determined that the valley qualified for federal
involvement because its resources—scenic, ecological, historical, and
cultural—were nationally significant. Although the report found that it
was not feasible to incorporate the valley as "a traditional unit" of the
National Park System, it recommended designation as an "Affiliated Area
in the National Park System as a National Heritage Corridor."[31]

The *Special Resource Study Report* recommended key interpretative
themes for presenting the Hudson River Valley to the visiting public. Central to the four broad interpretative themes in the document is the National Park Service's earlier assertion that the valley is the landscape that
shaped America's identity. The first theme is the primacy of the Hudson
Valley in defining the American landscape: the valley's scenery inspired
artists, writers, and designers who celebrated the natural environment
and fostered conservation and environmentalism, while the state, private
organizations, and individuals have preserved a remarkable number of

historic properties. Second, the Park Service has identified the river as an incomparable natural resource, a rich estuary that provides food, water, and recreational opportunities for residents, and is an "open textbook" for geologists. Third is the Hudson's role in transportation, especially the impact of Robert Fulton's first successful steamboat, *North River* (1807), and completion of the Erie Canal in 1825, which linked New York City to the interior of the nation and fostered economic development along the Hudson's banks. The fourth interpretative theme is the critical role that the Hudson River Valley played in the American Revolution.[32]

The *Special Resource Study Report* proposed the Greenway organizations as the managing entities for the National Heritage Corridor or Area, strongly endorsed the Greenway's Model Communities Program, its regional planning compacts, and the trails it was creating, as well as its record of collaborating with state agencies, other levels of government, and such private-sector organizations as Historic Hudson Valley, Scenic Hudson, Hudson River Heritage, and the National Trust for Historic Preservation. The report concluded, however, that while the National Park Service did indeed have a role to play in promoting the Hudson Valley, it should not acquire additional property or interfere with local and regional zoning matters or exercise control over local land-use decisions. In effect, the Park Service embraced the Greenway's collaborative and partnership approach.[33]

As a result, the National Heritage Area's mission parallels that of the Greenway, to create heritage trails that connect historic sites, and is organized around three themes—Freedom and Dignity (a sprawling category that includes the Hudson's role in the American Revolution, the abolitionist movement, and other social reforms in the nineteenth century, as well as Franklin Delano Roosevelt's leadership in the twentieth), Nature and Culture (especially the role of artists of the Hudson River School of landscape painters and Knickerbocker writers who celebrated the river and its environs), and Corridor of Commerce (the role the Hudson and its shipping and industries played in the nation's economic development). The hope is that the National Heritage Area's efforts will engage local communities as well as public and private agencies to create partnerships that will help conserve historic sites in the Hudson River Valley and promote heritage tourism. What isn't expressed in the management plan is how antithetical the goals of artists and writers, especially Thomas Cole, were to those of the industrialists.[34]

The key goal is to manage the diverse historic sites in the valley, which range in age from the seventeenth through the twentieth century, into a cohesive whole, to preserve and promote those sites, to foster partnerships with the private sector and increase public visitation, and to make heritage tourism a key component of regional economic development. A study commissioned by the Greenway and completed in 1995 identified historic sites as the "predominant visitor attractions" in the Hudson Valley. To accomplish the goal of increasing tourism, the National Heritage Area is partnering with the National Park Service and the state Office of Parks, Recreation and Historic Preservation to emphasize the significance of the Hudson River Valley as both a regional and nationally significant entity in the development of American culture. Scenic Hudson and other partnering organizations, including Clearwater, Riverkeeper, the Open Space Institute, the Trust for Public Land, Historic Hudson Valley, and New York Parks and Trails, are also deeply involved.[35]

The National Heritage Area embraces five national historic sites, fifty-seven national historic landmarks, eighty-nine historic districts, including the largest in New York State, in Newburgh, and more than one thousand individual entries in the National Register of Historic Places. As is true of the Greenway, addressing the divergent needs of fast-developing suburban areas in metropolitan New York along with those of economic backwaters upstate remains a challenge. And like the Greenway, the National Heritage Area is predicated on generating grassroots support for its programs and gaining the cooperation of various state agencies, as well as counties and municipalities and private-sector voluntarism and financing, to realize its goals. Supporters of the National Heritage Area, like those of the Greenway and Scenic Hudson, believe that expanding heritage tourism is a key economic development goal.[36]

The 1995 *Regional Tourism Strategy* outlined several critical challenges: sprawling acres of strip malls and fast-food franchises, exemplified along Route 9 between Fishkill and Poughkeepsie; deteriorating older riverfront cities; and above all the lack of an "articulated identity that captures the region as a unified destination." To these it adds concerns over the highly variable quality of interpretation, especially at historic sites; the lack of effective coordination among the valley's attractions (the report emphasizes the need for "cross-selling and cross-packaging between and among them"); facilities that capture and direct tourists to parks, scenic

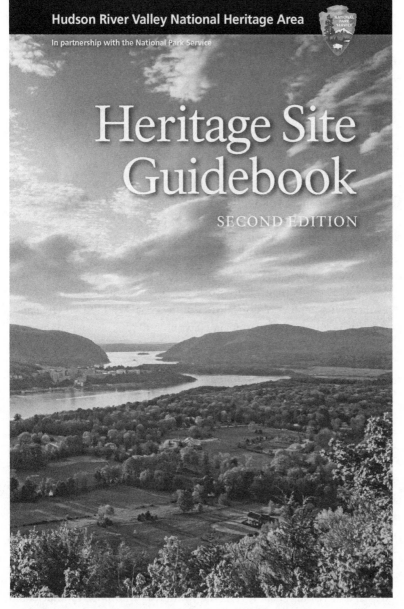

Figure 17. The Hudson River Valley National Heritage Area's *Heritage Site Guidebook* (2016). Courtesy of the Hudson River Valley National Heritage Area.

areas, and historic sites; and better training of the workforce that inter-
acts with visitors. All this, the *Regional Tourism Strategy* argued, needed
to be addressed on a regional scale. And, as was true with the Greenway, it promoted an approach that was predicated on collaboration and
partnerships.[37]

The National Heritage Area management plan builds on this earlier
tourism survey, and it has been instrumental in the development of strategies for better, coordinated signage and marketing of the valley. Perhaps
more important, the National Heritage Area has strongly supported the
development of several thematic trails to give visitors a more systematic
and in-depth experience. The first of these, the Revolutionary War Heritage Trail, resulted from the work of James M. Johnson, the Dr. Frank
T. Bumpus Chair in Hudson River Valley History and executive director
of the Hudson River Valley Institute at Marist College, which is the academic arm of the National Heritage Area. Johnson, a graduate of West
Point and a historian of the American Revolution, sees the trail as the
opportunity to link important sites in the valley. The trail extends from
the White Plains battlefield and Rochambeau's headquarters in Westchester through a number of critical sites in the contested Hudson Highlands
and Washington's headquarters in Newburgh to the Schuyler Mansion in
Albany and (just beyond the northern boundary of the heritage area) Saratoga National Historical Park, the site of arguably the most important
battle of the American Revolution. The goal of the trail is to "conserve,
interpret, manage, and develop these valuable resources."[38]

A second trail, largely the work of Elizabeth Jacks and her colleagues
at Cedar Grove, the Thomas Cole National Historic Site in Catskill, and
professional staff at Olana, is the Hudson River School Art Trail. Here
again the National Park Service's River and Trail Conservation Program
played a key role in expanding the Cole site's vision to take in the nearby
mountains. This trail introduces visitors to the two historic sites and also
leads them to places that inspired the first generation of Hudson River
School painters, including Catskill Creek, Kaaterskill Clove, Kaaterskill
Falls, North and South Lakes, the site of the Catskill Mountain House,
and Sunset Rock. These were iconic places for many nineteenth-century
artists, and visiting them is essential to tourists who hope to understand
the genesis of the American landscape tradition. The Hudson River School
Art Trail now has twenty-two trail sites and is completing a website

compatible for mobile devices. Trail markers and interpretative exhibits, including reproductions of paintings, portraits of the artists, and the history of each site, are intended to serve as "captions on the landscape" that help visitors appreciate the significance of the river and mountain scenery that captivated the artists. The Greenway and the National Heritage Area were early and effective supporters of this trail, as were state and federal agencies.[39]

There are challenges to this vision of heritage tourism as an economic driver for the valley. Two studies conducted in 2004 revealed a pattern of declining visitation for most sites. The first, by Ann Davis of the Bureau of Economic Research at Marist College, determined that 2003 was the worst year ever in terms of numbers of visits to historic sites in the National Heritage Area. Excluding the newly opened Dia:Beacon, attendance had dropped by approximately 12 percent at the other eighty-one heritage sites. The second study, by J. Winthrop Aldrich, resulted from visits to the original eighty sites included in the National Heritage Area. Aldrich, then the state's deputy commissioner for historic preservation and an adviser to the National Historic Area, expressed admiration for the high level of volunteer efforts in the operations of the many different types of sites and the professionalism he encountered among the site administrators, but he too expressed concern over the decline in visitation. All but seven of the sites had experienced fewer visitors over the preceding year, and for a number of them this was a pattern that had begun years earlier. He expressed hope that the National Heritage Area's efforts would result in greater coordination among the various sites and reverse the trend of declining visitation that he, like Davis, had observed.[40]

The most recent statewide analysis of tourism indicates a pattern of sustained growth over the last decade, save for a downturn during the Great Recession of 2008–2009. Spending by travelers in 2012 reached $62.5 million, an increase of 50 percent since 2006, and the tourism industry accounted for one in twelve jobs statewide. In the six Hudson River Valley counties included in the study (Westchester, Rockland, Putnam, Orange, Dutchess, and Columbia), visitors spent $3.3 billion, which generated an additional $1.7 billion in direct, indirect, and induced impacts. The tourism industry also contributed $219 million in local taxes and $181 million in state taxes. The results, however, were unevenly distributed throughout the six-county area, with Westchester alone generating

52 percent of tourism sales and a comparable percentage of local taxes collected. Much more needs to be done to achieve a higher and more sustainable economic impact from tourism in the other five counties, and also other counties extending to the northern reaches of the Capital District.[41]

The Greenway receives an annual appropriation from the state of approximately $500,000, which funds its administration, publications, consultants, and small grants program, while the National Heritage Area received $500,000 from the National Park Service's Heritage Partnerships Program. The Greenway also receives funding from the National Park Service ($7.8 million between 1998 and 2010), as well as additional money from the state ($16.4 million between 1996 and 2010), and approximately $2 million from individuals, foundations, corporations, and in-kind contributions. The Greenway itself has made 941 grants, in categories including capital improvements, master planning, cultural inventory, natural resource planning, waterfront revitalization, and zoning, totaling $10.5 million over the first twenty-five years of its existence. The National Heritage Area has received $7.8 million in National Park Service funding and has raised $22.5 million in matching contributions between 1996 and 2010. It is remarkable how effective the Greenway and the National Heritage Area have been in generating, from a variety of sources, the money essential to carrying out their operations. In a 2012 evaluation of the operations of the National Heritage Area, consultants hired by the National Park Service praised the overall success of its programs, which range from grants for trail making, purchase of land, support of recreational activities, and history education, to preparing maps, guidebooks, and trail guides, and the robust presence it has established on the Internet. Clearly, both the Greenway and the National Heritage Area have worked hard and effectively to enhance the quality of life in the Hudson River Valley.[42]

Still, questions remain about the effectiveness of these programs. Estimates exist for the numbers of hikers on the Greenway trails, but no one is standing at the multiple access points to the trails every day counting the numbers. Visitation at the historic sites is easier to count. The 2012 analysis of the effectiveness of the National Heritage Area conducted on behalf of the National Park Service expressed concern that "there are limited data available to measure a number of key outcomes, like visitation to the NHA and awareness of the NHA." There are no hard and fast economic data on how much its programs have contributed to tourism in the valley, no precise measurement of the economic benefits of tourism. The consultants who prepared the 2012 analysis recommended that the Greenway and the National Heritage Area, along with their partnering historic sites, develop a better methodology for tracking visitation and revenue generated through their activities, and more carefully measure the impact of their efforts on the Hudson River Valley.[43]

The difficulty of measuring the economic impact of heritage tourism on regional economic development is manifest in a number of ways. The heritage sites in the valley are far flung, and save for Historic Hudson Valley's properties in Westchester County and the Roosevelt and Vanderbilt estates in Hyde Park, they are either separated by great distances or are so small and unmarketed (Washington's headquarters in Newburgh and Knox's headquarters in New Windsor, for example) that they attract few tourists. Moreover, there are no metrics available for measuring how effectively the National Heritage Area has succeeded in marketing the valley's historic sites as a totality. Also problematic is that the hospitality industry—the hotels and restaurants and other service providers that support visitors—relies on workers who are among the lowest-paid employees in the U.S. economy. To be sure, the owners of the Mohonk Mountain House, in the Shawangunk Mountains, and the Beekman Arms, in Rhinebeck, are thriving as tourists drive into the valley in increasing numbers, but the women who clean the hotel rooms and change the sheets, or the busboys (and girls) who clear the tables are not benefiting in significant ways from the tourism economy. The recent adoption of a state minimum wage that will increase gradually to fifteen dollars an hour by 2022 will help workers, and expansion of the tourism industry, which is labor intensive, may well create a significant number of new jobs. The appeal of heritage tourism in helping to preserve the landscape, scenery, and historic sites of the Hudson River Valley is important to acknowledge. And it appears that after the deindustrialization of the post–World War II years and the more recent downsizing and the demise of IBM as a manufacturing entity in the valley, there are few alternatives. With attractive incentives, some companies may choose to move to or expand in the Hudson Valley, but the era when it was an industrial powerhouse is over. Tourism may well be the best, or the only, way forward in achieving a preserved river valley and a thriving economy. And heritage or scenic tourism has other economic benefits. Tourists patronize small businesses, from bed and breakfasts to restaurants to antiques shops and bookstores to art galleries. They purchase supplies and camp in the state parks and the many privately owned campgrounds in the Greenway area. How successful the Greenway and the National Heritage Area, together with their partners, will be in developing a thriving tourism economy—without putting strain on the scenic, cultural, and historic places that attract those visitors—will undoubtedly do much to determine the future of the Hudson River Valley.

Perhaps the greatest challenge the Greenway faces is that, despite its efforts, zoning in the mid- and upper Hudson Valley remains remarkably weak. Unless municipalities significantly strengthen their zoning ordinances and appropriate funds to defend their communities against determined developers, it is possible that the Greenway might succeed in creating the hundreds of miles of trails it envisions but that its success will be severely compromised. Instead of looking out over pastoral farmland or handsome stands of trees or the majestic river itself, hikers will confront the scarred landscape of condominiums, residential subdivisions, office parks, and shopping malls—hallmarks of the suburban sprawl that has already begun to transform the valley and will only intensify in the years to come. Anyone who has witnessed much of the residential and commercial development that has taken place on the banks of the Hudson over the last twenty years should realize how much is at stake and work to strengthen planning and zoning. Only aggressive steps to strengthen zoning will ensure a high quality of life for residents of the Hudson River Valley for generations to come.

8

A Poisoned River

In December 1971 the Niagara Mohawk Power Corporation applied to the state Department of Environmental Conservation (DEC) for a permit to remove a small old dam at Fort Edward that was producing very little electricity and needed expensive repairs. The application was also reviewed by John Seddon, a member of the staff of the Hudson River Valley Commission. Seddon reported that "there is not yet sufficient data available to assess its impact on the area after removal." He cautioned the commissioners that DEC "issues a permit on adequacy of need, not taking into consideration other consequences that may result." This was the final meeting of the commission, as its funding had been cut drastically and its staff reduced to a small handful, and there is no record that the commission ever deliberated on Niagara Mohawk's request or that its members were alarmed by Seddon's report. The lack of action on Seddon's presentation was one of a series of enormously consequential blunders that collectively unleashed what is usually estimated as 1.3 million pounds of polychlorinated biphenyls (PCBs) into the Hudson River, though in all likelihood the total amount was much, much larger, perhaps four times as much. An internal General Electric document from 1970, obtained by an *Albany Times Union* reporter through a Freedom of Information Act petition, estimated that approximately half a million pounds of PCBs were discharged directly into adjacent waterways each year, with the Hudson "the major receiving stream."[1]

PCBs were first produced by the Swann Chemical Company in 1929. Six years later Swann was acquired by Monsanto, the multinational agricultural and biotechnology corporation at the forefront of genetically engineered seeds. PCBs are humanly created chlorinated hydrocarbons that, because of their nonflammability and heat resistance, were used in hundreds of industrial and commercial applications, including transformers, capacitors, voltage regulators, electromagnets, wiring, and fluorescent lighting fixtures. Because of their chemical structure, PCBs do not decompose readily, so if released they remain in the environment for a very long time. Given variations in their chemical structure—the amount of chlorine and its placement on the carbon molecules—scientists estimate that there are potentially more than two hundred different types of PCBs. They have entered the food chain, and bioaccumulate in the fatty tissue of the meat and fish we consume, thus increasing the risk to humans. Exposure to PCBs probably affects every American and countless others across the world. In 1979 the federal government banned the manufacture of PCBs, and in 1987 the Environmental Protection Agency determined that they were probably carcinogenic and the likely cause of numerous other health problems, adversely affecting thyroid and reproductive functions as well as posing increased risk for cardiovascular and liver disease and diabetes. Two years before the federal government's ban, Monsanto had ceased production of PCBs because it recognized the numerous health and environmental problems they had caused. PCBs are not limited to the Hudson River Valley but have become a global environmental and public health concern. Perhaps five million pounds of PCBs were discharged into the Hudson River between 1947 and the banning of their use in the late 1970s.[2]

The demolition of that small dam at Fort Edward sent a torrent of PCBs that had settled in the sediment behind it south down the river. In addition to Seddon's unheeded recommendation that the Hudson River Valley Commission study the potential consequences of dam removal, there were warning signs before Niagara Mohawk's application to DEC that PCBs had already become a problem in the Hudson River and across the globe. In 1968 more than one thousand Japanese were poisoned as a result of eating rice cooked with oil contaminated by PCBs. In 1969 GE's Corporate Engineering Department completed an in-house review, "PCB: An Industry Problem?" The report estimated that the Industrial and Power Capacitor Department facility at Hudson Falls used ten million pounds of PCBs annually. Waste totaled a little more than one million pounds a year. Of this waste, the report noted, two hundred thousand pounds were returned to Monsanto, eight hundred thousand pounds of "badly contaminated material" was collected and removed by a scavenger, and sixty thousand pounds were disposed of in town dumps. The report did not mention the amount of waste dumped into the Hudson River, though it did concede that "our knowledge of chlorinated biphenyl formulations and possible deleterious effects is not as complete as is desirable in today's climate of concern for maintaining and improving the quality of life in its environmental aspects." GE then organized a Pyranol Task Force to examine the consequences of its use of PCBs (Pyranol was the name GE used for its version of the chlorinated hydrocarbon).[3]

Other evidence of the dangers of PCBs came from the fisherman and naturalist Robert Boyle. In 1970 Boyle caught five striped bass at his favorite fishing ground, near Verplanck's Point. He packed them in dry ice and shipped them to the Warf Institute, an independent testing laboratory in Madison, Wisconsin, which determined that the fish had unusually high levels of PCBs, an estimated 4.01 parts per million (ppm) in the flesh and 11.4 ppm in the eggs. At the time the federal Food and Drug Administration had determined that fish with 5 ppm or more of PCBs were unsafe to eat (the FDA subsequently lowered the limit to 2 ppm). Boyle published these and other results from fish sent to the Warf laboratory by fellow anglers across the nation in an article in the October 26, 1970, issue of *Sports Illustrated*. Boyle sent the article, "Poison Roams Our Coastal Seas," along with the results of the tests on the striped bass he had caught, to the director of fisheries at the DEC, who secretly had his lab replicate the testing, which found even higher levels of PCBs than those in the striped bass Boyle had tested. But instead of publishing the findings, that director, Carl Parker, did not make the results public, which allowed GE to continue its discharge of PCBs into the river. A man entrusted with protecting the health of the river and its people instead protected GE.[4]

General Electric had begun using PCBs in the process of manufacturing electrical capacitors at a factory next to the Hudson River in Fort Edward in 1947. Five years later, GE started using PCBs in manufacturing operations at its plant at Hudson Falls, a few miles to the north. The corporation also built a manufacturing facility to produce capacitors in Pittsfield, Massachusetts, which resulted in the release of hundreds of thousands of pounds of PCBs into the Housatonic River there. A capacitor (once called a condenser) is a unit for storing energy in an electric field, and the capacitors GE manufactured at Fort Edward were widely used by a number of industries. GE coated the capacitors with PCBs to prevent combustion when operational. Of the approximately ten million pounds of PCBs the Hudson Falls plant used each year, 10 percent was waste that ended up in the Hudson River or was buried in landfills not adequately designed and prepared for handling toxic waste. Indeed, an internal GE memorandum written by Dr. Kenneth R. Murphy, an engineer with the company's Environmental Pollution Control division, to the Pyranol Task Force demonstrated that "PCB: An Industry Problem?" seriously underestimated the amount of PCBs released into the environment. He reported that approximately nine hundred thousand pounds of PCBs each year were removed by scavengers who disposed of the waste in what one GE official described as an "out of sight, out of mind" manner. The GE official added that "few, if any, scavengers give consideration to proper disposal of hazardous wastes." It is unlikely that anyone today knows where all this toxic waste is buried, and what effect those landfills are having on the health of nearby residents or the environment. Half a million pounds "were discharged directly to bodies of water," with the Hudson River as "the major receiving stream." Only a "relatively minor amount" had been returned to Monsanto for reprocessing.[5]

Fort Edward and Hudson Falls are villages approximately forty miles north of Albany, in what has for decades been an economically depressed area. GE's two plants were important to the local economy, and at least for several years the corporation used PCBs in production and released a small amount into the river under a state license. GE's shuttering of the two plants left approximately twelve hundred workers unemployed, and a two-hundred-mile stretch of the Hudson River was designated a Superfund site by the EPA because of PCBs released in the upper river.[6]

Figure 18. General Electric's Hudson Falls facility, which was one of the two main sources of PCB contamination in the Hudson River. Photograph by Joseph Squillante. © Joseph Squillante.

The key event in this disheartening development, the demolition of the Fort Edward Dam in 1973, was a tragic and avoidable mistake. At the time, no one other than John Seddon apparently thought this might be important or decided to investigate what was in the sediment stored behind the dam. When the dam came down, so did the PCBs trapped in the sediment behind it, much of the perhaps five million pounds of PCBs released into the river by the two GE plants over a thirty-year period. The PCBs traveled almost forty miles south to the Federal Dam at Troy, where some of these waterborne carcinogens were impounded for a second time, but along the way much of the release settled in the riverbed over the course of almost the entire forty miles. Worse, during spring freshets and rainy summers, water flowed over the Federal Dam, carrying with it tons of PCBs—Boyle estimates ten thousand pounds each year—which have affected the river all the way down to the Battery, the southernmost point on Manhattan Island, and New York Harbor. This was an unprecedented environmental disaster. The Hudson River is now the largest Superfund site in the United States.[7]

It would have been so much easier, and cheaper, and less destructive of the river and its fisheries, not to mention other wildlife and the health of residents, to clean up the impounded sediment behind the Fort Edward Dam before demolishing it, but no one had that foresight.

The effect of the release of the PCBs was immediate: in 1974 an EPA study reported high levels of PCBs in Hudson River fish, and on August 8 of the following year the *New York Times* reported that DEC commissioner Ogden Reid warned consumers not to eat striped bass caught in the Hudson River or salmon from Lake Ontario because the flesh contained dangerously high levels of PCBs. In making the announcement, Reid stressed that the warning was necessary in order to protect the public's health. Federal researchers who tested shiner minnows and rock bass from the vicinity of the plants at Fort Edward and Hudson Falls found astonishingly high levels of PCBs. They also reported that the flesh of six striped bass caught near the Tappan Zee Bridge, approximately 150 miles south of the Fort Edward Dam, had an average level of 5.7 ppm. According to federal officials, Hudson River fish caught near Poughkeepsie in 1975 had "the highest PCB levels of any point monitored in the United States by the Department of the Interior."[8]

Commissioner Reid's announcement of PCB contamination in the Hudson was devastating for the many individuals who had worked so hard to clean up the Hudson and its banks. A coalition of environmental groups, including the Natural Resources Defense Council, the Hudson River Fishermen's Association, Scenic Hudson, Hudson River Sloop Restoration, the citizen-owners of *Clearwater*, and the Atlantic chapter of the Sierra Club, largely carried on the fight against PCBs. The Natural Resources Defense Council, the Fishermen's Association, and Clearwater formally intervened in the state Department of Environmental Conservation's enforcement action against GE. In August 1975 Walter Schwanne, a director of Clearwater, wrote to EPA administrator Russell Train to demand an immediate halt to the discharge of PCBs into the Hudson and its tributaries. A month later Pete Seeger took up the issue, urging the Hudson River Sloop Restoration board to mount a "full scale campaign against PCBs." In 1976 the executive committee of the sloop's board passed a motion demanding an immediate end to the discharge of PCBs into the Hudson and authorized the organization to join "any responsible lawsuit against General Electric to recover damages resulting from their discharges," but John Cronin, then the organization's environmental director, felt that it wasn't doing enough. The sloop organization joined with other environmental groups that had emerged from the Storm King battle against Consolidated Edison to sue GE.[9]

There are three parts to this environmental disaster. One is how long GE knew that PCBs posed a threat and did everything within its power—including spending hundreds of millions of dollars—to avoid and minimize its responsibility for remediation. A second is how reluctant state and federal officials have been in demanding effective remediation of the perils PCBs pose to our well-being and our environment. The third is the effort of regional and national environmental groups to push state officials to force GE to clean up its mess.

GE was aware of the dangers associated with PCBs as early as 1968, when state Health Department inspectors visited its manufacturing operations on the upper Hudson, but probably much earlier. In 1968 a staff engineer, Kenneth H. Harvey, wrote to his supervisors stating that "we intensionally [sic] omitted some information from this report which would have greatly compounded the problem in the eyes of the regulatory people." It is hard to imagine a more damaging statement, really a concession that GE knew that what it was doing was terribly wrong yet concealed the true impact of its actions from officials responsible for protecting the public's health.[10]

In September 1975 Reid ordered General Electric to completely eliminate the dumping of PCBs into the Hudson by September 30, 1976, but GE resisted, claiming that it would be impossible to "achieve 'zero discharge'" because, according to a company spokesman, "we know of no method of achieving such a goal." Reid, who believed that the state was "faced with what may be irreversible damage" to the Hudson River commercial fisheries, insisted on the deadline, though critics demanded an immediate halt to the discharges.[11]

By November 1975 Assistant Secretary of the Interior Nathaniel P. Reed called for immediate restrictions on industrial and other uses of PCBs, which had severely damaged the nation's rivers and the Great Lakes. Reed was particularly distressed by the "exceedingly high levels [of PCBs] found in fish from all our drainage systems." As a nation the United States was literally poisoning itself and needed to take immediate steps to halt the dumping of PCBs into its waterways. Russell Train of the EPA was more circumspect: he was reluctant to act against PCBs using the Federal Water Pollution Control Amendments Act of 1972 (the Clean Water Act) because he was unsure whether the act would stand up to a legal challenge. Instead, he called on Congress to quickly enact a toxic substance control bill that had been bottled up on Capitol Hill for several years.[12]

As the dimensions of the PCB crisis became clearer, in February 1976 the state DEC banned all fishing in the upper Hudson from Fort Edward south to the Federal Dam at Troy. The DEC also closed the commercial fisheries throughout the river and reiterated its warning to residents about the dangers of eating fish from the Hudson. Even below the Troy dam, fish were showing high levels of PCBs in their tissue. Two months later, the worst flood in a century carried a large amount of PCB-laced sediment over the Troy dam and south throughout the river, worsening the problem.[13]

Ironically, the federal government released its study of the effects of PCBs on the river at a time when, thanks in large part to construction of sewage treatment plants built with funding from the state's Pure Waters Bond Act of 1965, which Governor Rockefeller strongly supported, as well as the impact of the federal Clean Water Act and the closing of many of the worst industrial polluters along the river, the Hudson was actually becoming much cleaner—clearer and less polluted by human and industrial waste than at any time since the first half of the nineteenth century. When Ogden Reid met with commercial fishermen in October 1975 to explain the dangers PCBs presented, the fishermen told him that the river was cleaner, and the fish more abundant, than at any time in their collective memories. The fishermen and recreational users and other residents were eagerly anticipating fulfillment of Carl Carmer's vision of a river defined by clean water, parks, parkways, and other recreational amenities, a people reconnected with their river. "After three centuries of struggle and waiting," Carmer concluded *The Hudson* in 1939, residents "will rejoice at last in a valley of happy reality served by a free and mighty river." Instead, PCBs became the newest, and perhaps most enduring, human violation of the river.[14]

Even after the emergence of widespread concern over PCBs for their impact on human (and animal) health, the State of New York continued to license GE's release of thirty pounds of the chemical into the Hudson each day. The downward spiral continued. Although in 1977 the EPA banned the discharge of PCBs into any navigable waters in the United States under provisions of the Clean Water Act, the discharge of PCBs, especially from GE's Hudson Falls plant, would continue, and it continues to this day, though at a much reduced rate, largely because PCBs have seeped into rocks and groundwater and soil, and eventually find their way to the river. DEC has estimated that 1.5 million pounds of PCBs remain in the ground beneath the Hudson Falls site, and that 600,000 pounds remain beneath the Fort Edward site.[15]

The EPA issued regulations for the manufacture, processing, and distribution of PCBs, and for their disposal, in 1978. That year it asked the National Research Council, a division of the National Academies, to study the "hazards posed to human health and the environment by polychlorinated biphenyls." The resulting report, *Polychlorinated Biphenyls* (1979), was notably cautious in its conclusions and recommendations because of the wide variation in sampling techniques used in the many studies it reviewed, which resulted in data that were often inconsistent or at least not comparable. Nevertheless, the council's report noted the "extensive global environmental contamination" caused by PCBs and described the Hudson River as "the most contaminated water system in the Atlantic Coast area." Four years later, in 1983, the EPA included the upper Hudson River in its Superfund National Priority List. But on September 25, 1984, the EPA issued a Record of Decision that, while recognizing the high concentrations of PCBs in the Hudson, recommended no remediation: the EPA was persuaded that dredging technology was not sufficiently effective and that dredging, if undertaken, would release more sediment, and PCBs, in the river and thereby worsen the problem. Despite Governor George Pataki's insistence that GE be required to remove the PCBs, the EPA effectively adopted the corporation's argument, presented in a major national public relations campaign, that dredging would be a "horrible assault" on the Hudson. Better to allow, over time, newly deposited sediment to cover up the PCB-contaminated river bottom, the argument went. Let nature take its course, and the problem would go away.[16]

Unfortunately, PCB contamination didn't go away. As the EPA eventually conceded, "the river was not cleaning itself and PCBs in the sediment posed a serious risk to human health and the environment." Indeed, the dimensions of the problem kept getting larger and larger: scientists began discovering that riverine mammals, such as otters, and birds (among them the bald eagle), that include Hudson River fish in their diet had elevated PCBs in their tissue. In 1997 a sixteen-week-old bald eagle, found dead, was tested and had a level of 71 ppm in its body fat, more than fourteen times the level then considered acceptable for human consumption. That year, a U.S. Fish and Wildlife Service study demonstrated that tree swallows nesting near Hudson Falls had PCB levels of 55 ppm in their bodies. That eagle and those tree swallows were legally hazardous waste. There is also evidence that as sediment dries, PCBs can enter the atmosphere and enter people's lungs miles from the Hudson River. The use of oils contaminated by PCBs to coat dirt roads in rural America, to prevent dust, has surely contributed to atmospheric pollution, as have other applications of PCBs. The Hudson River Natural Resource Trustees concluded in 2013 that "numerous studies have documented PCB contamination in the surface water, groundwater, sediments and floodplains of the Hudson River, as well as in living resources at every level of the Hudson's aquatic, terrestrial, and wetland-based food chains." The dimensions of the disaster continued to become clearer, even as congressional Republicans attempted to eviscerate the Superfund law as well as other 1970s environmental protection legislation to let corporate polluters like GE avoid financial responsibility for their actions.[17]

All the while GE was continuing a massive public relations campaign, claiming that it had done nothing wrong, that it was only following the law. In 1991 GE circulated an in-house "Status Report and 1991 Strategy," which asserted, among other claims, that "natural processes in the upper [Hudson] River are dechlorinating PCBs to less toxic forms and breaking down PCB materials completely"; that PCB levels in Hudson River fish were decreasing; and that the upper Hudson, where PCB concentrations were highest, was not affecting the river below the Federal Dam at Troy. Environmental groups investigated, and the research they produced continually disproved the corporation's claims. Scenic Hudson produced a report on the proven remediation technologies then available that could be used to clean up the Hudson, *Advances in*

Dredging Contaminated Sediment (1997), and collaborated with River-keeper, Clearwater, the Sierra Club, and the Natural Resources Defense Council to mobilize pressure on the EPA to require GE to undertake a cleanup. These groups secured resolutions from dozens of communities along the river, held demonstrations, and lobbied Pataki to insist on a thorough cleanup of the river. Ned Sullivan met with EPA administrator Christine Todd Whitman in her Washington office shortly before her decision to order a cleanup. Finally, in 2002, the EPA issued a Record of Decision that squarely placed the blame on GE and ordered a massive dredging operation to clean up the river and the affected marshes and shorelines.[18]

The Record of Decision involved analysis not just of the extent of PCB pollution but also the effectiveness (and cost effectiveness) of five different remediation strategies. These ranged from No Action to Monitored Natural Attenuation, which would rely on naturally occurring processes, especially sediment flow, which ostensibly would cover PCB-contaminated sediment and thereby reduce the concentration of PCBs in the river, to dredging and capping. The EPA recommended the fourth alternative, "REM-3/10/Select"—the dredging of large stretches of the upper Hudson to remove approximately 2.65 million cubic yards of PCB-contaminated sediment. In addition, REM-3/10/Select would require upstream source control—that is, eliminating the flow into the river of PCBs from the porous rocks and soil beneath and adjacent to the two shuttered GE plants—as well as monitored natural recovery. The EPA subdivided the forty miles of the upper Hudson into three project areas, and adopted different standards of remediation for section 1 (a six-mile stretch of the river that was the farthest north, closest to Fort Edward), and sections 2 and 3 (approximately thirty-five miles south to the Federal Dam at Troy. The EPA's plan accepted a higher level of PCBs in surface sediment for river sections 2 and 3, which would have resulted in a much longer time for the ultimate remediation of the problem. Indeed, even the EPA conceded that the major dredging operation it authorized would remove only about 65 percent of the PCBs present in the upper Hudson. The EPA added that it chose REM-3/10/Select because the duration of time before river fish were safe for human consumption was much more reasonable than in the non-remediation alternatives, and because it was more cost effective than the most expensive alternative.[19]

GE didn't give up easily, and continued its delaying tactics. In 2006 the Federal District Court for Northern New York issued a consent decree in which GE would dredge the worst affected areas of the forty-mile stretch of the river between Hudson Falls and the Federal Dam at Troy. However, shortly after GE accepted the responsibility for dredging the areas designated in the consent decree, a study of more than eight thousand core samples collected in the upper Hudson between 2002 and 2005 revealed that the amount of PCBs in the river sediment far exceeded previous estimates. Moreover, the samples demonstrated that the rate of sediment recovery was much slower than anticipated, and that the flow of PCBs into the lower Hudson River was greater than the EPA had predicted. The National Oceanic and Atmospheric Administration (NOAA) reported in 2011 that the data on which the EPA had relied had seriously "underestimated" the volume of PCBs in the river and that the dredging plan approved by the EPA was woefully inadequate. Despite this evidence, the EPA did not revise the scope of work to be done. Instead, it attacked the NOAA for using old data—the very data the EPA had used in its initial report. EPA Regional Administrator Judith Enck told a reporter that her agency could compel more dredging only "if conditions in the river have changed, if there are things in the upper river that we didn't know about when we issued our cleanup plan," or "if we determine that previously unknown conditions are not protective of human health and the environment." Then, she added, "Neither of these things apply here." In assessing the success of the dredging program in January 2016, Enck noted that "GE conducted the dredging that it was required to do under the agreement, and the conditions under which EPA could require more dredging have not been met."[20]

Enck's statements represented the EPA's position at the time, an inexcusable refusal to acknowledge that circumstances had indeed changed. The more recent studies of PCBs in river sediment had revealed that the problem was far greater than the EPA believed at the time it reached agreement with GE on the scope of the dredging and that the solution it had agreed to with GE was simply not adequate. This was the occasion for revisiting that earlier agreement and standing up for the Hudson River and its residents. Instead, the EPA refused to do so.

Identifying PCBs as a threat to public health and the environment was a long, tedious process. Complicating efforts to resolve the problem has been GE's decades-long determination to refuse responsibility for what it had done. In certain respects GE had the right to defend its dumping of PCBs into the Hudson. After all, it began doing so long before anyone was aware that PCBs would prove so destructive to the ecology of the river or present a significant danger to public health, and in some years it had permits allowing it to do so. But as Peter Lehrer, New York's assistant attorney general in 2001, stated, GE's very large discharges prior to 1975 were not authorized by any permit, and "the seepage of PCB's into the river from the bedrock and soil beneath its Hudson Falls plant—the same discharge GE claims are significant sources of PCBs to Hudson River fish," were continuing. Lehrer added that most of GE's discharges both before and after 1975 have been unlawful, so GE's claim that what it was doing was lawful is, at best, tenuous, if not simply untrue. Worse, the cost of the delay—almost thirty-five years from the first alarms about PCBs in the river's fish to the commencement of Phase 1 of the cleanup—allowed the problem to worsen and spread throughout the entire river. Thus even if the dredging is as successful as EPA scientists hope, there is still the matter of PCB pollution of the other 150 miles of the river south from the Troy dam to Battery Park, which the EPA did not address in its Record of Decision because it assumed that remediation of the upper Hudson would reduce the environmental consequences of PCBs in the river below Troy. Admittedly, the lower river doesn't have the alarmingly high levels of PCBs found in the area above the Troy dam, but the PCB levels are high enough to remain in the aquatic food chain.[21]

No one will be fishing commercially in the Hudson River for a generation or more to come. Commercial fishermen who relied on the river for their livelihoods, recreational fishermen who loved heading down to the river to cast their lines or try their luck with a seine, residents who had relied on Hudson River fish as a key part of their diet, now look out upon a seemingly cleaner river that nonetheless harbors a dangerous threat to human health, and to the health of our biota. "Of all the bodies of water in the world," Robert Boyle has argued, "none has been worse hit [by PCBs] than the Hudson."[22]

The battle over PCBs and the river has pitted one of the nation's largest, most powerful corporations against environmentalists, scientists, and at least some government officials. Remediating the effects of PCBs has been fraught with challenges. The Superfund law (the Comprehensive

Environmental Response, Compensation, and Liability Act of 1980) was enacted by Congress in 1980, after toxic industrial waste rendered uninhabitable more than one hundred houses and an elementary school adjacent to the Love Canal, southwest of Niagara Falls, New York. Superfund differs from the Clean Water and Clean Air acts. Whereas those two acts regulate the discharge of pollutants into the waterways and atmosphere, Superfund gives the federal government the power to force polluters to clean up the mess they have created. Unfortunately, many Superfund sites have had multiple owners, and polluters, over the years, with the result that the allocation of financial responsibility for remediation has often ended up in long, drawn-out court battles. In the case of the upper Hudson River, however, GE was the sole source of PCBs, so it might be reasonable to assume that remediation would have proceeded smoothly. Under Superfund, the EPA is responsible for cleaning up the pollution, and another federally appointed body, the Hudson River Natural Resource Trustees, has the responsibility for the restoration of the site and compensation for individuals and groups that were denied use of the resource as a result of the pollution.[23]

Unfortunately, little has gone smoothly. After considerable planning and construction of facilities—a sediment dewatering building, a water treatment plant, and a rail support building on a 110-acre site at Fort Edward—the EPA approved Phase 1 in 2008, and dredging took place between the spring and fall of 2009. Initially Phase 1 was to dredge eighteen "hot spots" of approximately five acres each, but because the amount of PCB-contaminated sediment was greater than anticipated, only ten areas were dredged. Dredge operators removed 282,000 cubic yards of sediment, which was carefully placed on hopper barges and removed to the dewatering facility. Although the EPA conceded that the concentrations of PCBs in the sediment were much greater than expected, it nevertheless concluded that Phase 1 was a success, as did GE. During the following year, experts at the EPA and GE assessed the results and concluded that the dredging had been accomplished with a generally acceptable level of release of PCBs from the sediment (there were three occasions when dredging had to be stopped because the PCB release was too great). The EPA and GE also proposed modifications to the remediation process going forward. A peer review panel, however, identified significant shortcomings in Phase 1 and urged major revisions to the dredging strategy that the EPA and GE proposed for Phase 2. The panel specifically mentioned the unacceptably high rate of resuspension—PCBs released into the water column as a result of dredging—as well as the need for a more successful dredging program based on a clearer sense of where PCBs were concentrated in river sediment. The panel also recommended a much faster and more thorough program of covering dredged areas with at least three inches of sand to control the subsequent release of PCBs.[24]

After additional studies to figure out how to reduce the sediment released during dredging, a much more ambitious Phase 2 began in May 2009. The goal was to remove roughly 2.65 million cubic yards of contaminated sediment from the forty-mile section of the upper Hudson extending from Fort Edward to the Federal Dam at Troy. The entire dredging project, from Fort Edward to Troy, took six years (after seven years of planning and negotiations between the EPA and GE) and proved to be expensive. In October 2015 GE claimed it had spent more than $1 billion in its operations to remove PCBs from the upper Hudson. Work took place from the spring to the fall until 2015, when GE announced that it was nearing completion of the work agreed to in the consent decree and intended to dismantle its operations and remove its equipment from the upper Hudson River. GE's engineers were praised for the effectiveness of the operation, and indeed they used state-of-the-art technology in plotting the areas to be dredged and the techniques to do so as efficiently as possible. GE heralded the remediation as a great success. CEO Jeffrey Immelt stated that his corporation "brought world-class GE engineering and technology to the task" and asserted that "we met every obligation on the Hudson and will continue to do so." The EPA also praised GE for its work. "This project is the most extensive dredging project undertaken in the nation," the agency stated, "and its success is a historic achievement for the recovery of the Hudson River."[25]

However, as completed, GE's dredging of the forty-mile stretch of the upper Hudson is only a partial success. The 35 percent of the PCBs left undredged are still in the river, still affecting aquatic life, still accumulating in fish tissue, and still, during periodic flooding, flowing over the Federal Dam at Troy and contaminating the lower river. The significantly high levels of PCBs in river sediment remaining after dredging resulted in a heated dispute between federal agencies: the EPA on the one hand, and, on the other, the NOAA and the Fish and Wildlife Service (FWS), two of the "natural resource trustees" charged with overseeing the restoration of the river (the state DEC is the third). In comments submitted after evaluating Phase 1 of the dredging, the trustees challenged the effectiveness of the operation the EPA had approved and the agency's claim that the program would eliminate the health and environmental effects of PCBs in the river. The trustees asserted that Phase 1 results revealed that levels of PCBs in the sediment were "higher, more widespread, and closer to the surface" than the EPA had predicted and that PCBs were not being buried under new sediment (the natural attenuation or recovery process), as the EPA had asserted. Even after the completion of dredging, the level of PCB concentration in river sections 2 and 3 would be "approximately five times higher than the [EPA] models predicted."[26]

Similarly, the scientists who provided the peer review assessment of Phase 1 concluded that the models the EPA used in reaching the Record of Decision were outdated and could not accurately predict the river's recovery or that of its aquatic life. On December 2, 2010, they strongly urged the EPA to update its plan to achieve the results promised in the Record of Decision and specifically recommended that the same standards the EPA had adopted for PCBs in sediment in river section 1 also apply to sections 2 and 3, which would necessitate the dredging of an additional 136 acres of river bottom. Failure to do so would leave what were effectively Superfund-caliber sites in the upper Hudson. Despite these powerful challenges to its conclusions, the EPA effectively ignored the evidence that the NOAA and the FWS presented and went ahead with commencement of dredging of Phase 2 beginning in the spring of 2011. Critics also complained that GE had no intention to dredge the thirty-two-mile Champlain Canal, which had been important to the economy of northern New York. The New York State Canal Commission, which oversees the operations of the canal, cannot afford the conservatively estimated $180 million it would cost to remove the PCBs.[27]

As GE began its sixth year of dredging in 2015, the *New York Times* joined environmental organizations and citizens in calling for the corporation to expand the scale of its operations. Unless an additional 136 acres of contaminated sediment were removed, the *Times* editorialized, "the river's degraded health will persist decades longer." GE was "sticking to the letter of its obligations to the Environmental Protection Agency" made in 2002 and leaving the job unfinished. While it praised the quality of work GE's engineers had accomplished, the *Times* noted that the company was "turning aside calls to slightly expand its work in the interest of a more thorough cleanup and a healthier river." When GE announced that it was completing the dredging and ending its operations, the *Times* called on Immelt and GE to fulfill the company's moral obligation—not just its legally binding agreement with the EPA—and finish the job properly by dredging the remaining hot spots in the upper river.[28]

Despite the arguments of the *Times* and environmental groups, on October 5, 2015, GE declared its cleanup of the upper Hudson complete and then applied to the EPA for authorization to dismantle its decontamination facility at Fort Edward. The buildings at Fort Edward were no longer needed, GE asserted, and should be removed rather than fall into disuse. This was an application that could have fateful consequences. If GE were allowed to dismantle the facility while 35 percent of the PCBs still remained in the sediment of the upper Hudson, it would become highly unlikely that the state or adjacent counties and municipalities could afford to finish the job. GE would effectively walk away, and if governmental agencies decided on further remediation, as the Hudson River Natural Trustees and other defenders of the river insisted was essential, they would have to reopen legal proceedings against GE or bear the huge cost of replacing the dewatering and decontamination facilities, as well as that of the additional dredging.[29]

The trustees strongly opposed GE's plan to decommission the Fort Edward facility, as did the most important Hudson River environmental and conservation organizations—Scenic Hudson, Riverkeeper, Clearwater, the Atlantic chapter of the Sierra Club, and the Natural Resources Defense Council, which together petitioned the EPA to reconsider GE's application and indeed to expand the dredging program agreed to in the Record of Decision. In a thorough and fully annotated analysis of the history of the case, the petition asserted that the EPA was failing to carry out its statutory authority and had "violated its non-discretionary duty under CERCLA [the Superfund law] to ensure that selected remedies are protective of human health and the environment." Nevertheless, on November 12, 2015, the EPA approved GE's plan to decommission the treatment facility at Fort Edward. In its statement approving the decommissioning, the EPA asserted that no additional dredging was likely, and that if other parties—that is, the state—undertook further work, or forced GE to do so, a temporary dewatering facility could be constructed. The EPA still has not responded formally to the environmental groups' petition, though it has begun a five-year review to assess the effectiveness of the dredging as completed, a process that it now under way.[30]

The EPA's Enck declared the dredging a success in an op ed piece in the *Albany Times Union* even before initiating the 2017 Five Year Review mandated by Superfund to determine if the remediation had met its goals. Ned Sullivan and Aaron Mair, president of the Sierra Club, challenged Enck's assertion in a follow-up piece in the *Times Union*, citing the prevalence of consumption of PCB-tainted fish by poor and minority residents along the Hudson, among several other ways in which the cleanup fell short of its goals. Moreover, the decision to authorize the decommissioning of the cleanup operations shocked environmentalists as well as Enck's counterparts at the NOAA and FWS, who had publicly called on her to leave the equipment in place to facilitate additional dredging.[31]

Legislators and conservation groups, led by Scenic Hudson president Ned Sullivan, called on Governor Andrew Cuomo to intervene with the EPA on the state's behalf, but Cuomo refused to act. "I know there are claims for [GE] to do more above and beyond" what it had agreed to do in 2006, he conceded, but added, "I haven't really looked into that." For a hands-on, activist governor, this was a remarkable concession—that the future of the Hudson River Valley, and the lives and livelihoods of residents of New York State, was simply not worth his attention. David Sirota, an investigative reporter for the *International Business Times*, has claimed that in his political campaigns Cuomo was the recipient of more $466,000 in contributions from GE, which he implies explains the governor's hands-off response to the question. A more likely motive for his inaction might be that Cuomo was at the time publicly encouraging GE to move its corporate headquarters back to New York State (though the corporation ultimately decided to relocate to metropolitan Boston instead). The result was that when the NOAA and the FWS, acting as natural resource trustees, challenged GE's plans to decommission the Fort Edward facility, the state Department of Environmental Conservation, the third trustee, stood on the sidelines. The EPA claims that it approached the DEC about joining in its effort to persuade GE to undertake additional dredging and that Cuomo's appointees at the head of the agency responded with what the EPA could only describe as "radio silence."[32]

Removal of the dewatering facility was under way in 2016. Much of the equipment has been removed. When the buildings are demolished and the site decontaminated and restored, the dredging program will be complete. The EPA will then oversee an Operation, Maintenance, and Monitoring phase to "track the ongoing recovery of the river and the effectiveness of the cleanup over time." The EPA is also overseeing a study, by GE, of the wetlands and adjacent surface soil of the forty-mile extent of the Hudson above the Troy dam, to determine if periodic flooding has contaminated those soils with PCBs. Superfund requires periodic (usually five-year) reviews of the monitoring program, so it is too early to make an objective assessment of how effective the dredging has been and to anticipate with confidence when the river will have recovered, when its fish are safe to eat, and when Carmer's vision of a people reconnected with the big stream, as he called it, will become a reality. But if the findings of scientists at the NOAA and FWS are correct, that day will not come during our lifetimes.[33]

As dispiriting as all this is, the fight for a cleaner, healthier Hudson isn't over. Scenic Hudson, Riverkeeper, and other environmental organizations have continued to insist publicly that GE fulfill its responsibility to remove the remaining PCBs from the river. The natural resource trustees continue to pressure the corporation to comply with Superfund requirements, which have not ended with the dredging already completed. And, in a remarkable turnaround from its earlier reluctance to hold GE accountable, the DEC has belatedly recognized that, as its name states, it is indeed responsible for protecting the environment. Basil Seggos, appointed DEC commissioner in October 2015, has placed his agency where it should have been all along—defending the Hudson River against GE's resistance to finishing the job.

Seggos, a former investigator for Riverkeeper and an adviser to Governor Andrew Cuomo on environmental issues, recently wrote to EPA regional administrator Enck and asserted that "the work is not done." He called for the dredging of the remaining 136 acres of PCB-contaminated sediment in the upper Hudson. Seggos is convinced that the EPA erred in declaring that the job was finished: "Both the amount of sediment and the fish are suggesting that the initial goals of the remedy have not been, and may not be met, for decades," he stated in an interview in the *New York Times*. In her response, EPA spokeswoman Deirdre Latour stated that as a result of the dredging already completed, "PCB levels in the

Upper Hudson have already shown significant declines." She expressed the agency's confidence that subsequent studies will demonstrate that "the dredging project achieved the agency's goals of protecting public health and the environment." Of course this statement fails to state the obvious: that, as Superfund mandated, a formal five-year review concluding that the cleanup had indeed met its goals was required before any assertion that the remediation had been completed.[34]

In the midst of this bureaucratic infighting, the Hudson continues to flow from the Adirondacks to the ocean, but it remains a poisoned river. Scenic Hudson, Riverkeeper, and other environmental organizations have continued to insist publicly that GE fulfill its responsibility to remove the remaining PCBs from the river. During the final weeks of the Obama administration, Scenic Hudson pressed the White House and EPA administrator Gina McCarthy to adopt New York's finding that the cleanup had failed to achieve Superfund's protectiveness standard.[35]

Unfortunately, the reality is that the trustees' scientists, who have produced an impressive body of evidence of the harm inflicted on the river and its biota, or the DEC, or Scenic Hudson and other groups, cannot, without cooperation from the EPA, force GE to undo the damage it has caused to the river's ecosystem. Given that 35 percent of the PCBs GE dumped into the river still remain in the sediment, it is not possible to reintroduce the otters and mink, the mallards and other waterfowl, or the tree swallows and bald eagles. It would be an act of sheer folly to place these and other species into a Hudson River Valley that will poison rather than sustain them.

The use of PCBs at GE's manufacturing operation at Fort Edward in 1947 was the first of a series of terrible steps that have devastated the Hudson River Valley. Decisions by GE to dispose of its toxic waste by dumping it in waterways or having scavengers transport it to dumps not adequately prepared to accommodate it worsened the problem. The demolition of the dam at Fort Edward and the long years in which GE resisted accepting responsibility for the damage it caused to the Hudson River Valley have allowed toxic pollution to spread throughout the valley to New York Harbor and the Atlantic Ocean. It has taken more than forty years of heroic effort by individuals and environmental organizations in defense of the river to reach an agreement and have GE dredge the worst areas of contaminated sediment.

What is most troubling about this account of PCBs and the Hudson River is that the steps taken to date have not yet solved the problem but have left it to future generations. At crucial points the two agencies most responsible for protecting the environment and human health—the federal EPA and the state DEC—simply did not act in the public's interest. In the new chapter he added to the 1979 edition of *The Hudson River*, Robert Boyle stated that the EPA really stood for "Everyone's Polluting Again." It would be easy to dismiss Boyle's remark as hyperbole, or sarcasm, and, indeed, he wrote it long before the full dimensions of the environmental disaster caused by GE were evident and before the partial remediation was undertaken. But the EPA's role in the resolution of the problem of PCBs that have fundamentally altered the ecosystem of the Hudson River Valley makes Boyle's words seem prescient.[36]

The EPA completed its second five-year review of the dredging operations on May 31, 2017 (the first, undertaken in 2012, was basically worthless, because the dredging was still ongoing). Predictably, the EPA's report called the work a success, claiming that the "models used to support decision making were well-designed, remedial action objectives (RAOs) were appropriately developed, and remedy implementation is proceeding as planned." Although the EPA's analysis conceded that "human health and ecological remedial goals have not yet been achieved," it expressed confidence that the dredging program had successfully met the goals established in the Record of Decision. What the report did not state was that the ROD was based on data that was rendered obsolete because subsequent sampling of sediment revealed that PCB contamination was far more extensive than previous studies had revealed. When the EPA released its report, Riverkeeper and Scenic Hudson hired a consultant, Remy Hennet, a Princeton PhD in geochemistry, who concluded that the report was deeply flawed. EPA had presented a high rate of recovery in soils, water quality, and fish tissue concentrations of PCBs, but the evidence it presented led Hennet to judge its conclusions as unwarranted. The recovery rate for fish tissue, he stated, was "so uncertain as to be meaningless." Riverkeeper and Scenic Hudson called on the EPA to delete its finding that the dredging "will be protective" of human and animal health within fifty years. An independent study of the dredging program, prepared by consultants hired by the Hudson River Foundation, concluded that in a number of respects the dredging had been successful, but it recognized that it was simply too soon to tell if the program will remove the threat of PCBs. The Hudson remains at risk.[37]

PCBs are only the most notorious poison to have harmed the Hudson. Indeed, long before modern environmentalism came of age, industries and municipalities along the river routinely dumped their waste into its waters, with disastrous results. Unfortunately, as the use of chemicals by industry increased dramatically in the years since World War II, the Hudson, as well as rivers and lakes across the nation, have been the dumping ground for toxic and, in many cases, carcinogenic chemicals. In his article "Poison Roams Our Coastal Seas," Robert Boyle demonstrated that "coastal waters are infested with pesticides, metal and other toxic pollutants, and these poisons can kill fish, their young and the organisms they feed on." They can also kill, or seriously harm, those of us who eat the fish. The Warf Institute analysis of the fish Boyle's readers sent revealed the presence of high levels of mercury, chlorinated hydrocarbons such as DDT, as well as PCBs, whether the fish were caught in the Hudson or along the Atlantic Coast, in the Gulf of Mexico, or in the Pacific off California and Washington State. Drawing on the research of biologists at major research institutions, as well as the findings of the Warf Institute, Boyle concluded, as have federal environmental officials in the years since, that toxic pollutants in our waterways are a threat to human health as well as to our environment. We are literally poisoning ourselves.[38]

In 1977 the Environmental Defense Fund (EDF) and the New York Public Interest Research Group (NYPIRG) released a study of toxic chemicals in the Hudson, *Troubled Waters*. The report directly challenged the success of former governor Nelson Rockefeller's Pure Waters Program. While conceding that the construction of sewage treatment plants had reduced the amount of human waste in the river, the study found that the governor's program had "ignored the pollution caused by the discharge of chemically-laden industrial wastewater." The EDF and NYPIRG hoped that publication of *Troubled Waters* would force the state to "address the ever increasing extent of chemical pollution," especially organic chemicals and heavy metals, which the study identified as a direct and increasing threat to public health. Among the toxics found in the river the study identified benzene, chloroform, methylbenzanthracene, and tetrahydrofuran, all likely carcinogenic, as well as PCBs. Much of these toxic substances were not dumped profligately by industries but entered the river indirectly, after passing through municipal sewage treatment plants, which were not designed to remove organic chemicals and heavy metals. And those deadly elements have a much longer life in the environment than what we blithely flush down the toilet. Riverkeeper is deeply concerned over the amount of toxic micropollutants and pharmaceutical waste that has flowed into the river.[39]

Most of the sewage treatment plants along the Hudson are not only inadequate to the task of removing harmful chemicals: they are aging. Many are now fifty years old or more and are on the verge of obsolescence. In addition, most cities have combined systems, in which rainwater from storm drains flows into the sewage treatment facilities and during periods of heavy rain or snowmelt overwhelms their capacity. As a result, vast amounts—surely more than thirty billion gallons—of untreated sewage and polluted stormwater flow directly into the Hudson and other waterways every year. As the Pisces Report demonstrated, pollution is the largest single contributor to the drastic decline of ten of the Hudson's signature fish species in recent years.[40]

Thus in 2015 the New York State Legislature adopted a Water Infrastructure Improvement Act that allocated $425 million for grants to municipalities to upgrade their wastewater and drinking water facilities. Most of that money has already been allocated, and some experts have pointed to the need for an additional $1 billion over the next five years to complete the job. In supporting this additional funding, Ned Sullivan of Scenic Hudson stated that "continued investment in the region's water and wastewater infrastructure is crucial to the safety and health of our waters—for fishing, swimming and drinking and to meet the basic provisions of our environmental laws." Paul Gallay, president of Riverkeeper, also urged significant additional funding to fulfill the goals of the Water Infrastructure Improvement Act: "To improve water quality the state must continue to expand this transformative grants program to help communities make these critical investments." Other conservation and environmental organizations similarly support this initiative, including Audubon New York and the Citizens Campaign for the Environment. The construction industry endorses this additional funding as well, claiming that a $1 billion investment in infrastructure will create between thirty thousand and forty-seven thousand direct and indirect jobs.[41]

Even if the additional $1 billion is appropriated and successfully spent in upgrading water and sewage treatment facilities, it will only prevent this very serious problem from worsening. Just as 35 percent of the PCBs remain in the sediment of a forty-mile stretch of the upper Hudson, chemicals and toxics, including pharmaceutical waste, micropollutants from cosmetics and other products, as well as endocrine disruptive agents already released into the river, will persist for decades, in some cases for generations to come. Pharmaceuticals are not currently regulated by the EPA and thus present an unknown long-term risk to the health of the river's ecosystem, though scientific research has demonstrated that even low levels of pharmaceuticals have "alter[ed] hormone levels" in aquatic species. These are potentially dangerous compounds, yet they pass through sewage treatment plants and enter our water supplies. No one has yet determined what effects discharges of such substances will have on public health in the decades to come, and yet their release into the waterway continues. The Hudson will long be a poisoned river.[42]

A River Still Worth Fighting For

The Hudson continues to flow from the Adirondacks to the sea, and along the way passes through some of the most beautiful scenery in the eastern United States. Much of the landscape is pastoral, with centuries-old farms lying just beyond the river's banks. The Catskill Mountains, the Highlands, and the Palisades are exclamation points to a partnership landscape, where human settlement has largely worked in harmony with the natural world. To be sure, older industrial cities and villages line the river, but the landscape still retains much of its remarkable beauty and charm. But as Robert Boyle and others have demonstrated, the Hudson is also one of the most abused natural resources in the nation. We have poured human waste into it, we have choked it with the outflow of industries and poisoned it with toxic chemicals. We have, as they say in corporate suites, outsourced our expensive waste into the river. Throughout most of the twentieth century the river was unsafe to swim in and really wasn't very appealing even to walk along. It has gotten much better. The Hudson has been healing over the last forty-five years. For this we can be thankful for the construction of sewage treatment plants, the Clean Water Act and other legislation, the closing of many once-polluting industries, and the passionate commitment of organizations such as Scenic Hudson, Riverkeeper, and Clearwater. But despite real gains, the outflow of untreated sewage into the river during storms is still a major problem: in *The State of the Hudson 2015*, the Hudson River Estuary Program reported that combined sewage overflows result in the release of 1.2 billion gallons of untreated sewage and polluted stormwater into the Albany Pool and 27 billion gallons into New York City's waters annually. The Hudson is still an imperiled resource.[1]

There is much to be pleased about, proud of, in what has occurred along the Hudson in recent decades. But the essential reality is that defeating one threat, one nuclear plant proposed at Cementon, for example, is not a final solution. It is not a complete victory for the river but a stay of execution. Other threats loom, just as a natural gas power plant was constructed at Athens, the alternative site proposed for the Cementon project, or will appear, simply because the Hudson River Valley is such an attractive place to live and work and, for developers, to invest in by buying property and building. The threat could be a subdivision that consumes

Figure 19. A train carrying Bakken shale crude oil down the Hudson. Photograph by Matt Kierstead. © Matt Kierstead.

cherished pastoral farmland, or a shopping mall, or fast-food restaurants along what had once been a lovely rural road, or another power plant. The list could go on. The threat is real and omnipresent.

One immediate threat is the increasing use of the Hudson Valley as a highway for the shipment of oil from the North Dakota Bakken shale basin down the river to refineries along the East Coast, which Riverkeeper Paul Gallay has termed "an unprecedented threat." Much of the oil is shipped by rail. Trains of tank cars stretch a mile or more long, each car filled with approximately thirty thousand gallons of crude. This fracked shale oil is a highly polluting, highly flammable crude, as has been demonstrated by recent rail disasters in Lynchburg, Virginia, where the James River actually caught fire, and Lac Mégantic, Quebec, where forty-seven people died as a result of a fireball. Moreover, should a spill occur, Bakken crude oil is extraordinarily difficult to clean up, so the increasing train traffic presents a dire potential threat to water quality and aquatic life in the Hudson. All the more distressing is that most of the train cars carrying the crude, DOT-111s, are a generation old, and the industry has largely been successful in resisting efforts to upgrade to new cars that are less susceptible to puncture or combustion. Equally important, the oil industry has resisted efforts to remove the volatile gases in the oil before loading it into railcars, even though, should an accident occur, it is those gases that erupt into flames and could potentially cause cataclysmic loss of life and property damage in a densely populated area.[2]

Scenic Hudson and Riverkeeper have worked with other environmental groups to oppose the transport by rail of Bakken crude through the valley. Scenic Hudson estimates that a worst-case disaster involving rail shipments could cause more than $1 billion in damage. Gallay has warned that "a spill could negate all the progress we've made to clean up PCBs and other toxic wastes, which has made the river safer for swimming and has opened the Hudson to the public." Thus, in partnership with other groups, Scenic Hudson and Riverkeeper have strongly opposed this increased train traffic: Scenic Hudson has sued to force the federal government to require the new generation of tank cars and challenged a state permit that allows transport of the crude by rail on the banks of the Hudson.[3]

Scenic Hudson and Riverkeeper have also opposed expansion of Global Companies LLC's oil terminal in Albany that would enable the more efficient transshipment of crude by rail, arguing that Global was operating in violation of the Clean Water Act. As a result of this challenge, the state Department of Environmental Conservation has reversed course and is now planning a full environmental review of the plan to make the Port of Albany a major transshipment point for oil, possibly including the even more volatile tar sands oil from Canada in the form of diluted bitumen. The National Academy of Sciences in 2016 issued a study, *Spills of Diluted Bitumen from Pipelines*, that reported that the United States was completely unprepared to address the environmental consequences of a major spill of tar sands oil. But there is little that New York State can do to ensure the safety of its residents, other than inspecting track and railcars, as the railroad industry is regulated by the federal government, and the Department of Transportation has been slow to require the upgrading of the fleet of tankers carrying the oil and thus is not acting to ensure the well-being of those who live near the river.[4]

Oil from the Bakken field also flows down the Hudson River in barges. These are not the quaint, slow-moving barges that carried trap rock down the river in years past but enormous, six-hundred-foot-long tankers that hold as much as four million gallons of oil. In 2016 the Maritime Association of the Port of New York and New Jersey, the Hudson River Port Pilot's Association, and the American Waterways Operators petitioned the U.S. Coast Guard for permission to construct ten new anchorage sites between Yonkers and Kingston with berths for forty-three barges. The maritime organizations argued that the berths would provide for greater safety by allowing barges to anchor during times of intense fog or inclement weather. (The prospect of a pilot trying to parallel park one of those barges in a heavy fog should cause a lot of people to have nightmares about the ecological disaster that a major spill could cause.) The Maritime Association also informed the Coast Guard that it expected that barge traffic will increase "significantly over the next few years with the lifting of the ban on American crude exports for foreign trade." Predictably, environmental groups were quick to protest the plan, as were many communities along the river. The challenge is daunting, because the Coast Guard's proposal is exempt from compliance with the Environmental Protection Agency and is not required to demonstrate need or consider alternatives.[5]

The Hudson has been a transportation thoroughfare since European settlement more than four centuries ago, yet the barge proposal has provoked intense and perhaps predictable opposition. Many riverfront communities, especially on the east bank, have invested considerable resources in reconnecting with the Hudson, clearing derelict industrial buildings and warehouses as well as dumps and creating new park spaces that bring people to the river. Dobbs Ferry, for example, spent $7 million in renovating its waterfront park in 2015, and the village's mayor, Hartley Connett, responded vehemently to the Maritime Association's proposal: "People are kayaking more and canoeing more. The idea that you'd have these giant floating structures is at odds with that. We are going to do everything we can to fight it." The city of Yonkers has benefited from considerable investment in housing and new commercial buildings that take advantage of river views as community amenities, as have other cities and towns. So for some opponents of the barge plan, quality-of-life issues are paramount. For others there are environmental concerns—that the barges would create noise and light pollution, that their anchors would harm important fish-breeding areas, especially for sturgeon, which was listed as an endangered species in 2012, and of course the threat of accidental spills. John Lipscomb, Riverkeeper's boat captain, has been perhaps most vocal about the potential consequences of a spill. "Trying to corral crude oil in a moving river is virtually impossible," he stated, pledging that Riverkeeper and its allies would work to "prohibit any transport of crude oil on the river." The New York Times editorialized that "the fragile Hudson, many fear, will inevitably become—like streams and farmlands in North Dakota—an environmental casualty of the oil boom." State Senator Terrence Murphy even expressed concern that oil-laden barges parked on the river would be an attractive target for terrorists.[6]

The safety of the transport of oil in railcars has gathered increasing scrutiny at the federal level recently, but the issue remains unresolved, really an accident waiting to happen. So too is the Maritime Association's proposal for barge anchorages. These are examples of the continuing threats to the ecology and quality of life along the Hudson River.

Another recent example of the ongoing threats to the valley involves the Palisades. In March 2011 the South Korean electronics manufacturer LG filed an application with the zoning board of Englewood Cliffs, New Jersey, seeking a variance that would enable it to construct its North American corporate headquarters. LG had a smaller facility in the northern part of the borough, but it had acquired a twenty-seven-acre property at 111 Sylvan Avenue, immediately west of the Palisades Parkway, where it intended to construct a modern building that would house all its corporate workforce, then scattered in several locations in the borough. The problem was that LG and its architects, the internationally prominent firm HOK, proposed erecting a 143-foot-tall building, which far exceeded the height limitation of thirty-five feet already in place in the borough and thus would require a variance. Moreover, the proposed location is just a mile north of the George Washington Bridge and is at the top of the Palisades—the sheer wall of diabase formed in the Triassic period when lava forced its way through sandstone and hardened—that reaches more than five hundred feet in height and extends approximately fifteen miles from Fort Lee, New Jersey, north to southern Rockland County, New York. Thus began what might be called the second battle for the Palisades.[7]

The first battle for the Palisades began in the 1890s, when quarrymen using dynamite were literally blasting away at the face of the great cliff. The American Scenic and Historic Preservation Society, along with other groups, sought to end what it considered the desecration of this visual landmark, which for centuries had awed and delighted New Yorkers as well as prominent visitors from abroad. The English traveler James Silk Buckingham likened the cliff to "rude basaltic columns, or huge trunks of old and decayed trees, placed together in a perpendicular form for a barricade or defense." The Palisades, Washington Irving wrote, "spring up like everlasting walls, reaching from the waves unto the heavens." William Cullen Bryant described them as a "brow of rock on the Hudson's western margin," while the naturalist John Burroughs wrote that the Palisades were "the precise spot where this son of Vulcan sat down so heavily and so hot upon his brother of the sedimentary deposits." As the rate and destructiveness of quarry operations increased, many prominent New Yorkers rushed to the defense of the Palisades. In 1895 a writer in the *New York Times* called the Palisades "one of the uncommon beauties of an uncommonly beautiful river." These and many other, similar statements captured the stunning beauty of the Palisades and also pointed to the fact that they were worthy of preservation, the closest thing to a national park in greater New York.[8]

The battle to preserve the Palisades was one of the first and most important early land conservation struggles in American history. It was especially difficult because that sheer wall of rock, so imposing a view to New Yorkers, was largely out of sight to residents of New Jersey, especially those who lived in the central and southern parts of the state. As a writer in the *New York Times* explained, "The Palisades turn their backs on New Jersey, their faces to New York. Their beauty and picturesqueness is all for us, but they are wholly within the control of the State across the river." As the destructiveness of the quarrying increased, patrician New Yorkers and some residents of New Jersey rose to the defense of their cherished landmark. John H. Stoddard, who lived atop the Palisades, described the quarrying as being "as much of a sacrilege as would be a similar destruction of Niagara Falls." As governor of New York, Theodore Roosevelt was a powerful voice for the preservation of the Palisades, as was Andrew Haswell Green of the American Scenic and Historic Preservation Society. Other groups were also important, including the New Jersey State Federation of Women's Clubs. Despite Roosevelt's strong support in promoting the bi-state legislation that in 1900 created the Palisades Interstate Park Commission, it was the private sector that was most responsible for defending the Palisades. George W. Perkins, the visionary first chairman of the Palisades Interstate Park Commission, persuaded J. P. Morgan to donate $125,000 to the land acquisition and preservation effort, and other wealthy New Yorkers did so as well, including John D. Rockefeller, who also gave approximately eighty acres to what became Palisades Interstate Park, which was designated a National Historic Landmark on January 12, 1965. Rockefeller's great-grandson, environmental lawyer Laurance Rockefeller Jr., would be a key player in the second battle to preserve the Palisades.[9]

LG had acquired the Sylvan Avenue property in 2010. On the site was a 410,000-square-foot, three-story building erected in 1953 that was used by Citicorp for its check-processing operations. That building was demolished in 2014 to make way for the larger, taller structure LG envisioned for its corporate offices. LG proposed to construct a 490,000-square-foot building, at a cost estimated at $300 million. It would be an LEED-certified structure, with some 85,000 square feet of solar panels that would provide the electricity used within its walls. Announcement of LG's plans to erect a tall building on the site was applauded by Englewood Cliffs officials, who welcomed the tax revenue it would generate, and of course by labor unions that anticipated the jobs that construction would produce.

Figure 20. Saratoga Associates, project visualization schematic showing the impact of the proposed LG office tower atop the Palisades, as seen from Fort Tryon Park. Courtesy of Scenic Hudson.

It also sparked an immediate outcry from important conservation groups, most notably the Palisades Interstate Park Commission, Scenic Hudson, and the Natural Resources Defense Council, as well as some residents, who feared that the tall building would forever change the smaller scale they cherished in their community.[10]

The borough's zoning board considered the application for variances, which included not just the height and bulk of the proposed structures but also the number of parking spaces, and on November 30, 2011, approved LG's plan. Four months later two individual plaintiffs filed lawsuits challenging the zoning board's approval of the application, and conservation and citizen groups collectively referred to as the Palisades litigants—Scenic Hudson, the New Jersey State Federation of Women's Clubs, the Natural Resources Defense Council, and others—similarly filed suit to block the variance. The Metropolitan Museum of Art also opposed LG's building because of its potential impact on the view from the Cloisters, its medieval outpost in Fort Tryon Park. The Palisades litigants argued that Englewood Cliffs had engaged in spot rezoning, which basically changed the zoning ordinance for a single property and which is illegal in many jurisdictions—it can benefit one property owner at the expense of all others, thereby violating the foundations of zoning law—and is really a concession to poor urban planning. Thus began a contentious battle, both within Englewood Cliffs' planning board and borough council and in the courts. In February 2013 the zoning board again approved LG's application for a variance on the height restriction and stated that the increased height "enables substantially more landscape amenity and buffer features for nearby residents." The borough subsequently adopted an amendment to its zoning ordinance creating a new overlay zone, described as B-2A, which basically applied only to the property LG owned and would have enabled construction of a building up to 150 feet in height. In their appeal, the Palisades litigants challenged the variance for its failure to consider the project's impact on "the surrounding neighborhood," both the Palisades and the region. In short, plaintiffs argued, this was not a local decision for a borough's zoning board but one that had much broader significance.[11]

The Superior Court of New Jersey, Law Division, upheld the zoning variance. But in October 2015 the appellate division of the same court overturned that ruling. In the appellate ruling, Judge Douglas Fasciale asserted that because of the significance of the Palisades, the zoning board should have considered the impact of the proposed structure on surrounding communities and weighed how the building would affect the historic and scenic Palisades. The zoning board's decision, Fasciale ruled, would "undoubtedly have a visual effect on the area, especially because of the placement of the building in close proximity to the Palisades Cliffs, a historic, renowned natural and dramatic geological feature." Fasciale remanded the decision to the zoning board for reconsideration.[12]

Fasciale's ruling effectively established a new precedent for local zoning boards in New Jersey. It required that the Englewood Cliffs zoning board "consider the impact that the structure would have on more than the municipality itself or the immediate vicinity of the structure." In directing that the zoning board reconsider the application, Fasciale ruled that "'surrounding neighborhood' means all reasonable visual vantage points"—not just adjacent communities but, in this case, the viewshed from New York City and its suburbs as well.[13]

Before the zoning board could reconsider the approval it had granted to LG, that board had been subsumed within the borough's planning board. And before the planning board could act, opponents of LG's tall building and defenders of the Palisades had commenced a lengthy negotiating process with the corporation that resulted in a remarkable settlement. Significantly, this negotiation did not involve the borough's council or its planning board, the county, or the state, each of which had approved the original variance and paved the way for construction. It was the work of dedicated conservationists, led by Laurance Rockefeller Jr. and Ned Sullivan, as well as attorney Albert K. Butzel, and people at LG who were willing to work out an alternative to the initial plans.[14]

The settlement agreement, as it is called, was reached on June 17, 2015. In it LG basically agreed to reduce the height of the proposed building to less than 70 feet, so it would be below the tree line and thus not violate the viewshed from New York City. The agreement also contained other restrictions, for example by requiring that the building be effectively camouflaged to reduce visibility and the use of native plants in the landscape to mitigate visual impact. It also mandated that neither LG nor later owners of the site could increase the height of the building.[15]

The result, almost everyone cheered, was a "win-win" settlement. LG will construct a shorter building that will not violate the Palisades, with a much wider footprint to provide the floor space to accommodate its approximately eleven hundred employees. Englewood Cliffs will have the economic benefits of a major corporation and a larger workforce in its community. And the conservation groups, led by Sullivan of Scenic Hudson and Rockefeller, have preserved an iconic place.[16]

Important as is the ongoing battle to prevent the Hudson River Valley from becoming a superhighway carrying crude oil from North Dakota to refineries along the Atlantic Ocean, as well as the successful fight to protect the Palisades from LG's proposed skyscraper, other threats will surely emerge in the years to come. Thus it is important to recognize the efforts of individuals and organizations that continue to defend what Frances Dunwell and so many others have called America's river. Although the three principal groups—Clearwater, Riverkeeper, and Scenic Hudson—usually join together in opposing threats to the Hudson, they have distinct but complementary missions. Clearwater has concentrated its energies on environmental education, while Riverkeeper has focused especially on the Hudson's water quality and its fisheries. Scenic Hudson has evolved from a small group of individuals defending Storm King Mountain against Con

Ed's proposed pumped-storage power plant to become a land conservation organization that embraces a holistic view of the valley—not just its spectacular scenery but the economic and social well being of its communities and their residents.

Other private-sector groups that lack the resources or membership of Riverkeeper or Scenic Hudson are nonetheless important. The Hudson Valley GREEN (Grass Roots Energy and Environmental Network) Coalition was organized in January 1981, when the Mid-Hudson Nuclear Opponents, the Citizens for Safe Power Transmission, and the Concerned Citizens for Safe Energy merged. It publishes a newspaper that carries "local news related to sustainable urbanism, the environment, transportation and infrastructure issues," as well as a calendar of events and meetings. The Hudson River Environmental Society, a nonprofit membership organization founded in 1970, conducts and publishes research on the river and environs, including such topics as PCBs, acid rain, the state of the river's fisheries, cultural resources, and scenic and historic preservation. The society also organizes symposia and workshops addressing environmental issues that affect the Hudson River Valley. The theme of the spring 2015 symposium was "Seeing the Hudson River in the 21st Century," while in 2016 the topic was "The Hudson River Estuary and the Mohawk River: 'The Coming Together of the Waters.'" These symposia bring together elected officials, leaders of private nonprofit organizations, and citizens in a collegial atmosphere that promotes the sharing of information and the building of alliances.[17]

Land trusts and smaller conservation organizations are other keys to the preservation of the Hudson River Valley. The Open Space Institute, like Scenic Hudson the beneficiary of a $115 million bequest from Lila Acheson and DeWitt Wallace, has preserved more than 116,000 acres in New York, principally in the Hudson Valley and the Adirondacks, either through fee-simple acquisition or purchase of conservation easements. OSI has added five thousand acres to Fahnestock State Park and fifty-four hundred acres to Minnewaska State Park Preserve, supported the Hudson River Valley Greenway, and has developed a "River to Ridge" connection from the Wallkill River to the Shawangunks. OSI is also a significant contributor to the Mohonk Preserve, which was established in 1963 with the gift of five thousand acres from the Smiley family. Over the last fifty years the preserve has purchased approximately thirty-five hundred additional acres in the Shawangunk Mountains. The Nature Conservancy's Shawangunk Ridge Program has focused on climate change and resiliency. Laurance Rockefeller's Jackson Hole Preserve acquired 670 acres on Breakneck Ridge, the site Central Hudson Gas & Electric intended for a pumped-storage power plant opposite Storm King Mountain, and conveyed it to the state for what, following additional land acquisition, became the Hudson Highlands State Park Preserve. Working with the state and local governments, the Trust for Public Land has protected more than fifty-one thousand acres of the valley, and the Nature Conservancy has established twenty-seven preserves.[18]

Smaller, more locally oriented land trusts are also important. Every county has a land conservancy, and the state has been awarding grants from the Conservation Partnership Program funded through the Environmental Protection Fund to support their efforts ($480,550 for the Mid-Hudson area in 2016). The Hudson Highlands Land Trust owns 39 acres, has conservation easements on nineteen properties, and has preserved 1,300 acres. The Catskill Center for Conservation and Development owns nine properties (367 acres) and has acquired seventeen easements (2,550 acres). The Winnakee Land Trust, established in 1989, often working with Scenic Hudson and the Dutchess Land Conservancy, has preserved more than 2,500 acres of northern Dutchess County through gift, outright purchase, or acquisition of easements. Winnakee has also taken on maintenance of a park in Rhinebeck and has established a nature preserve and arboretum in Hyde Park. The Pound Ridge Land Conservancy owns eighteen preserves and more than 360 acres, and also works collaboratively with the Westchester Land Trust in securing easements on important land. The efforts of these and other local organizations have been essential to landscape preservation in the Hudson River Valley.[19]

The role of public agencies is also critically important. After local citizens opposed the Marriott Corporation's plan to develop a resort at Lake Minnewaska, the state acquired much of the land in 1987 and established Minnewaska State Park Preserve, which opened in 1993. The original purchase was enlarged three years later when the Open Space Institute transferred fifty-four hundred adjacent acres it had acquired to the park preserve, an area known today as Sam's Point Preserve. The state Department of Environmental Conservation's Hudson River Estuary Program was created following legislative adoption of the Hudson River Estuary

Management Act of 1987, which was written by John Cronin and introduced in the state assembly by Maurice Hinchey and in the senate by Jay
Rolison. The Estuary Program embraces the entire watershed of the river,
a massive area of 13,400 square miles extending from the Verrazano Narrows Bridge at the south to the Federal Dam at Troy at the north. The
program coordinates the management of the four federally designated estuarine research reserves along the river. Based on extensive meetings with
stakeholders, it has identified six key goals: clean water; resilient communities; protection of the estuarine ecosystem; conservation of aquatic
and terrestrial animals and their habitats; scenic preservation; and greater
opportunities for river access, recreation, and education. According to
Frances Dunwell, director of the Estuary Program, it addresses not just
these issues but represents a new way of doing business, a holistic interdisciplinary approach to managing the Hudson's ecosystem and a willingness
to collaborate with other public and private efforts.[20]

In its emphasis on environmental education, water quality and fisheries, land preservation, recreation, and public access to the river, the Hudson River Estuary Program overlaps with and supports the efforts of the
three major conservation organizations in the Hudson Valley, as well as
those of the smaller land trusts. Its structure is strikingly similar to that
of the Hudson River Valley Greenway and the National Heritage Area. It
has a modest budget—$4.2 million in 2016—but the annual appropria-
tion from the state for its support has fluctuated from a high of $6 mil-
lion at the beginning of this century to a low of $3 million between fiscal
years 2010–11 and 2013–14. Despite its charge to preserve habitats and
protect scenery, it has no line item in its budget for land acquisition and so
works in partnership with other divisions of DEC and private nonprofit
organizations. As is true of the Greenway, based on many discussions with
stakeholders the Estuary Program has set forth a vision for the future of
the river and works collaboratively with other conservation organizations
as well as counties, municipalities, businesses, industry, and private citizens throughout the watershed.[21]

Because it includes the Hudson's entire watershed, however, the Estuary Program embraces a vastly larger geographic area than do the three
principal conservation groups. It also can claim a greater commitment to
habitat protection and restoration. And the Estuary Program has taken
on climate change in a holistic way. *The State of the Hudson 2015* points

to significant increases in temperature in recent years, increased annual rainfall, and rising sea levels as the new reality that will shape the ecosystem as well as the lives of residents and animals in the next few decades. Flowering plants are blooming earlier in the spring than the historical norms, summer songbirds are also arriving earlier, and sea-level rises will surely have devastating consequences for the shallows and tidal marshes of the river. The huge storms of recent years—tropical storms Irene and Lee in 2011, Hurricane Sandy in late October 2012—have demonstrated the need for greater urgency in making the river and its environs more resilient and better prepared to address long-term climate change. Governor Andrew Cuomo has recognized this, and the Estuary Program is responding to the challenge. It has also benefited from the work of the Hudson River Foundation, which was established with $12 million from Consolidated Edison as part of the 1980 Hudson River peace treaty. The foundation produces scientific research on the river ecosystem that has proved invaluable to the Estuary Program as well as to other conservation groups and the Army Corps of Engineers.[22]

The success of these land trusts and other conservation organizations, along with what individuals and numerous other organizations have accomplished in preserving the landscape of the Hudson River Valley over the last half century, is truly remarkable. But as any developer will tell you, taking land off the market increases the price of the remaining acres. Scenic Hudson has identified the most important remaining land to be preserved, some sixty-five thousand acres, which will cost an estimated $500 million to secure through acquisition or easement. The state has identified areas of biological or scenic importance, in the Catskills, the Highlands, or the river's shallows, and has helped to preserve farmland throughout the valley, but much remains to be done to ensure that the Hudson continues to flow through mountains and farms and rolling countryside. Scenic Hudson's Draft Open Space Conservation Plan of 2014 has enumerated priority projects that will embrace 3.5 million acres. There simply isn't enough private-sector or public money available to complete the job.[23]

The great missing link to a vibrant, economically flourishing Hudson River Valley is its cities. To be sure, Scenic Hudson has been instrumental in the remarkable renaissance Beacon has experienced over the last decade, and the downtown of Hudson has art galleries and antiques shops

that attract people from metropolitan New York who have moved to summer or vacation houses in Columbia County. But poverty in Beacon and
Hudson, especially among racial minorities, remains entrenched.

Other, larger cities, especially Newburgh and Poughkeepsie, have
largely failed to reverse the decline that began in the 1950s, with the
influx of large numbers of African Americans from the South and with
disastrous urban renewal programs that destroyed thousands of historic
buildings and left large swaths of the riverfront a grassy, underused yet
potentially invaluable space for residential and commercial redevelopment. Newburgh's population in 2010 was 28,866, of whom 34.2 percent
lived below the poverty line. Dominant residential groups were Hispanic
or Latino (14,732) and African American (8,317). Poughkeepsie was
slightly larger, with 32,736 residents, of whom 24.1 were impoverished.
African American residents numbered 10,967, while 5,910 were Hispanic
or Latino.[24]

Reviving these cities and other riverfront communities is imperative.
With wide swaths of vacant riverfront property, if these cities became
more attractive as places to live and work, they could absorb much of
the population growth the valley will experience in coming years, thereby
reducing the pressures associated with suburban sprawl. To do so will
require significant investment, both from the state and the federal government, to upgrade infrastructure and address long-standing problems
caused by poverty and inequality. Poughkeepsie has been doing better
than Newburgh in securing funding from Albany. The New York State
Regional Economic Development Corporation recently announced the
award of $7 million to Poughkeepsie, which is a welcome step. Included is
financing to create the Kaal Rock Connector, a trail that will link the city's
northern and southern waterfront parks. Another grant awards $500,000
toward construction of the city's Southern Waterfront Promenade. Among
several smaller grants in 2015 and 2016, Newburgh received $100,000 to
locate the sources of its sanitary sewer overflows and identify solutions.
These state dollars, important as they are, do not address the causes of
poverty or the consequences of segregation for residents of the two cities.[25]

Enduring revitalization will require heroic efforts by elected officials to
equalize city and suburban taxes (because older cities have lost much if
not most of the industrial and commercial properties that once contributed to municipal finance, property taxes are much higher than in adjacent

suburbs), though this is unlikely. That the federal and state governments will substantially increase aid to cities is also unlikely. Essential, too, will be significant improvements in urban schools, because middle-class families with young children often make the quality of school districts a key consideration in where they choose to live. Again, the political will to invest heavily in urban school districts doesn't seem to exist.

Today Hudson River cities and suburbs are divided places, the cities largely inhabited by racial minorities, the suburbs overwhelmingly by more prosperous whites. Until these cities become magnets for redevelopment and attract the kinds of residents who throng new development along the banks of the Saw Mill River in Yonkers or the arts district in Beacon, the Hudson River Valley will never realize the sense of regional identity that proponents of the Greenway and the National Heritage Area hope to achieve.

Much good has occurred in the Hudson River Valley since Consolidated Edison announced its plan to construct a pumped-storage power plant at Storm King Mountain in 1962. Conservation and environmental groups have succeeded in defeating numerous proposals that would have diminished the scenic attributes of the Hudson and have preserved a significant amount of land through acquisition or easements. These are enormous gifts to future generations of residents. But we have become a suburban nation, as Columbia University historian Kenneth T. Jackson has so ably demonstrated, largely because of a cultural predisposition that celebrates the single-family home on its own plot of land and governmental policies that have effectively subsidized homeownership. The very policies that have made the suburban dream possible for millions of Americans in the years since World War II continue to threaten the quality of life in the Hudson River Valley and in other cherished places across the United States. In New York State the long-held and fiercely protected tradition of home rule has effectively prevented adoption of regional strategies to control development, though the efforts of the Greenway and the National Heritage Area have had some success in recent years in gaining inter-municipal cooperation in planning and zoning. But as the LG case demonstrates, some communities will decide to ignore their neighboring municipalities and approve plans that will ultimately damage the quality of life in their areas.[26]

We live in an era when taxes are moderate and antitax sentiment is high. Yet our needs—from investment in infrastructure to eliminate the combined sewage outflows that poison our river and lakes to adequate housing for our lower-income citizens to better schools for our children, and much-needed repairs to highways, bridges, and airports, for example—outpace our collective willingness to pay for them. Citizens in the Hudson River Valley, especially in the depressed river cities, are buffeted between trying to make ends meet and protecting the place where they live. A scenic vista, however beautiful, doesn't pay the rent or buy food.

There are several steps that can be taken immediately. One is for municipalities and counties along the river to strengthen zoning ordinances and appropriate the money to defend them in the courts. Another is significant investment, on the part of all levels of government, to upgrade the sewage treatment infrastructure of communities along the Hudson. The Environmental Protection Agency estimates that it will cost $36 billion nationwide over thirty years to upgrade wastewater treatment facilities, and while the price tag is high, this is an essential investment in our environment. The cost to New York State will be significant. Cities cannot afford these upgrades on their own, making it essential that the state and the federal government play a significant role. Still another step is to make public service a service to the public. Riverkeeper and other organizations have demonstrated, time and again, that some governmental officials, from the EPA and the state DEC to mayors, local councilmen and women, routinely protect polluters and subvert the public interest. Paul Gallay of Riverkeeper asserted in 2015 that New York had experienced a 64 percent decline in enforcement of the Clean Water Act over the previous five years. Our nation desperately needs, in New York and in other states, local officials and regulatory agencies to enforce the Clean Water Act and other environmental legislation from the 1970s.[27]

Residents of the Hudson River Valley and citizens across the nation require a stronger commitment from the government to protect the environment. The Department of Environmental Conservation's reluctance for too long to hold GE accountable for the PCBs it dumped in the river is only the most egregious example of the failure of regulatory agencies. Governmental agencies at all levels—local, state, and federal—need to join Scenic Hudson, Riverkeeper, and the Estuary Program, along with other environmental groups, and address the fundamental challenges a polluted river and a warmer earth and atmosphere present to our collective future. But as Pete Seeger said so often, and as experience has proven, we can't rely on bureaucrats and politicians to protect the Hudson River Valley. The Hudson is beloved by many residents and by the tourists who admire its scenery and visit its many historic and cultural sites. These residents need to take ownership of it and continue the fight to make it pristine once again. The same, of course, is true of the planet on which we live. René Dubos's famous mantra about acting locally still applies. The Hudson River is still worth fighting for, and yes, organizations and individuals matter.

NOTES

Introduction

1. I am following the two-river distinction used by the Hudson River Natural Resource Trustees in *PCB Contamination of the Hudson River Ecosystem: Compilation of Contamination Data through 2008* (January 2013).

2. See David Schuyler, *Sanctified Landscape: Writers, Artists, and the Hudson River Valley, 1820–1909* (Ithaca, N.Y., 2012).

3. Ibid.; John K. Howat, *The Hudson River and Its Painters* (New York, 1972).

4. Robert D. Lifset, "The Environmental Is Political: The Story of the Ill-Fated Hudson River Expressway, 1965–1970," *Hudson River Valley Review* 22 (Spring 2006): 28–53.

5. Albert K. Butzel, "Storm King Revisited: A View from the Mountaintop," *Pace Environmental Law Review* 31 (Winter 2014): 370–97; David Sive, "Environmental Standing," *Natural Resources & Environment* 10 (Fall 1995): 49–58.

6. Barnabas McHenry, letter to the author, Dec. 21, 2016.

7. Hudson River Estuary Program, *The State of the Hudson 2015* (n.p., 2015), 4; Riverkeeper, *How's the Water? 2015: Fecal Contamination in the Hudson River and Its Tributaries* (Ossining, N.Y., 2015).

8. Frances F. Dunwell, *The Hudson River Highlands* (New York, 1991), and *The Hudson: America's River* (New York, 2008).

9. J. Winthrop Aldrich, remarks in the panel discussion "Framing the Viewshed: The Bend in the River," Feb. 25, 2012, www.youtube.com/user/watch?v=8KQFKfFZqG8.

1. The Battle over Storm King

1. "Huge Power Plant Planned on Hudson," *New York Times* (hereafter cited as *NYT*), Sept. 27, 1962.

2. Robert Lifset made this connection in his excellent book, *Power on the Hudson: Storm King Mountain and the Emergence of Modern American Environmentalism* (Pittsburgh, 2014), 5–6. Other accounts of the Storm King case include Robert H. Boyle, *The Hudson River: A Natural and Unnatural History* (New York, 1969), 153–81; Allan R. Talbot, *Power along the Hudson: The Storm King Case and the Birth of Environmentalism* (New York, 1972); Frances F. Dunwell, *The Hudson River Highlands* (New York, 1991), 202–30; and John Cronin and Robert F. Kennedy Jr., *The Riverkeepers: Two Activists Fight to Reclaim Our Environment as a Basic Human Right* (New York, 1997), 22–49.

3. Washington Irving, *A History of New York, from the Beginning of the World to the End of the Dutch Dynasty . . . by Diedrich Knickerbocker* (1809; Philadelphia, 1871), 389–90. According to Benson J. Lossing, geologists believed that the Highlands were "a barrier to the passage of the waters [of the Hudson], and caused a vast lake which covered the present Valley of the Hudson" and which extended many miles to the north. Lossing, *The Hudson: From the Wilderness to the Sea* (1866; Hensonville, N.Y., 2000), 207–8.

4. Timothy Dwight, *Travels in New England and New York*, ed. Barbara Miller Solomon, 4 vols. (1822; Cambridge, Mass., 1969), 3:303–4, 313. For accounts of other travelers' reaction to the Hudson Highlands in the early nineteenth century see David Schuyler, *Sanctified Landscape: Writers, Artists, and the Hudson River Valley, 1820–1909* (Ithaca, N.Y., 2012), 8–27.

5. Thomas Cole, "Essay on American Scenery," *American Monthly Magazine*, n.s. 1 (Jan. 1836): 1–12; James Fenimore Cooper, *The Pioneers; or, Sources of the Susquehanna* (1823; New York, 1988), 292–94; Nathaniel Parker Willis, *American Scenery*, 2 vols. (London, 1840), passim; John K. Howat, *Frederic Church* (New Haven, Conn., 2005), 172–73. See also Schuyler, *Sanctified Landscape*, 8–68.

6. Vincent Scully, "Prepared Testimony of Vincent J. Scully, Jr.," typescript copy in Scenic Hudson Papers, Archives and Special Collections, James A. Cannavino Library, Marist College, Poughkeepsie, N.Y. (hereafter cited as Scenic Hudson Papers).

7. "Huge Power Plant Planned on Hudson."

8. "Con Ed Project on Hudson Gains," *NYT*, May 20, 1964; "Governor Backs Storm King Plant," *NYT*, Dec. 12, 1964. See also Lifset, *Power on the Hudson*, 37–49.

9. Albert K. Butzel, "Birth of the Environmental Movement in the Hudson River Valley," in *Environmental History of the Hudson River: Human Uses That Changed the Ecology, Ecology That Changed Human Uses*, ed. Robert E. Henshaw (Albany, N.Y., 2011), 279–90.

10. Doty is quoted in "U.S. Urged to Block Con Ed Power Plant," *NYT*, Oct. 9, 1964; Lifset, *Power on the Hudson*, 53–65; "Saving the Hudson Highlands," *NYT*, Nov. 17, 1964.

11. Lifset, *Power on the Hudson*, 50–65; "Preliminary Report of the Joint Legislative Committee on Natural Resources on the Hudson River Valley and the Consolidated Edison Company Storm King Mountain Project," Feb. 16, 1965, copy in the Hudson River Conservation Society Collection, box 2, Archives and Special Collections, James A. Cannavino Library, Marist College, Poughkeepsie, N.Y. For Boyle's significant role in the Storm King case and the organization of the Hudson River Fishermen's Association see Cronin and Kennedy, *Riverkeepers*, 22–49.

12. Lifset, *Power on the Hudson*, 50–65; "Preliminary Report of the Joint Legislative Committee on Natural Resources on the Hudson River Valley"; Robert Watson Pomeroy to Joseph C. Swidler, Feb. 16, 1965, Hudson River Conservation Society Collection, box 2. The joint committee report was also printed in *Hearings before the Subcommittee on National Parks and Recreation of the Committee on Interior and Insular Affairs*, House of

Representatives, 89th Congress, first session, July 24 and 25, 1965. Pomeroy's remarks are on pp. 200–203; the preliminary report of the Pomeroy joint committee was printed ibid., 203–11. See also "Con Ed River Plan Scored in Albany," *NYT*, Feb. 18, 1965.

13. Lifset, *Power on the Hudson*, 72–75; "Preliminary Report of the Joint Legislative Committee on Natural Resources on the Hudson River Valley"; "Legislator Asks President to Ban Storm King Plant," *NYT*, Mar. 3, 1965; John Sibley, "Waterborne Pickets Protest Hydroelectric Project That Might Mar the Beauty of the Hudson River Valley," *NYT*, Sept. 7, 1964.

14. Scenic Hudson Preservation Conference v. FPC, 354 F.2d 608, 1 ERC 1084 (2d Cir. 1965). See also Butzel, "Birth of the Environmental Movement," 283–84; "Storm King Plant Blocked by Court," *NYT*, Dec. 30, 1965, and Lifset, *Power on the Hudson*, 93–104.

15. Draft of Statement for Laurance S. Rockefeller, Chairman of the Hudson River Valley Commission, Jan. 1966, L. S. Rockefeller Papers, Rockefeller Archive Center, Tarrytown, N.Y.; Scenic Hudson Preservation Conference, board minutes, Feb. 20, 1968, Scenic Hudson Preservation Conference, Minutes and Ad Hoc Committee meeting minutes, 1967–1971, Scenic Hudson Collection: Records Relating to the Storm King Case, 1963–1981, Archives and Special Collections, James A. Cannavino Library, Marist College, Poughkeepsie, N.Y.; Alexander Saunders to Mr. and Mrs. Whitney North Seymour Jr., Dec. 26, 1969, Whitney North Seymour Papers, box 1, Archives and Special Collections, Cannavino Library.

16. Lifset, *Power on the Hudson*, 112–19, 151–54. The testimony of Eliot and Scully is in the Scenic Hudson Collection at Marist.

17. Lifset, *Power on the Hudson*, 115–19.

18. Ibid., 112–15.

19. These developments are summarized in Scenic Hudson Preservation Conference, et al. v. Federal Power Commission, et al., 453 F.2d 463 (2d Cir. 1971), and in Lifset, *Power on the Hudson*, 107–19.

20. Scenic Hudson Preservation Conference, et al. v. Federal Power Commission, et al., 453 F.2d 463 (2d Cir. 1971).

21. Ibid.

22. Ibid. For an excellent analysis of the Scenic Hudson decisions, and the ways the courts have backed away from the stringent standards established by Scenic Hudson I, see Albert K. Butzel, "Storm King Revisited: A View from the Mountaintop," *Pace Environmental Law Review* 31 (Winter 2014): 370–97.

23. Boyle, *Hudson River*, 153–81; Lifset, *Power on the Hudson*, 164–73; Butzel, "Birth of the Environmental Movement," 285–87; "Report Says Storm King Plant May Peril 75% of Bass in River," *NYT*, Dec. 16, 1973; "Con Edison: Endless Storm King Dispute Adds to Its Troubles," *Science*, n.s. 184 (June 28, 1974): 1353–58.

24. Robert H. Boyle, "A Stink of Dead Stripers," *Sports Illustrated*, April 26, 1965, 81–84; Boyle, *Hudson River*, 153–81; Lifset, *Power on the Hudson*, 174–85.

25. "A Peace Treaty for the Hudson," *NYT*, Dec. 20, 1980; Jill Smolowe, "Con Ed to Drop Storm King Plant as Part of Pact to Protect Hudson," *NYT*, Dec. 20, 1980; Statement by Russell E. Train on Hudson River Settlement, Scenic Hudson Collection, Marist; Allan R. Talbot, *Settling Things: Six Case Studies in Environmental Mediation* (Washington, D.C., 1983), 13–24; Lifset, *Power on the Hudson*, 174–85.

26. John K. Howat, *The Hudson River and Its Painters* (New York, 1972), 9, 51. See also David C. Huntington, *The Landscapes of Frederic Edwin Church: Vision of an American Eden* (New York, 1966). On the preservation of Olana see David Schuyler, "Saving Olana," *Hudson River Valley Review* 32 (Spring 2016): 2–26.

27. Boyle, *Hudson River*, 154; Lawrence Pringle, "Storm over Storm King," *Audubon* 70 (July–Aug. 1968): 60.

28. Lyndon B. Johnson, Annual Message to Congress on the State of the Union, Jan. 4, 1965; Johnson, Special Message to the Congress on Conservation and Restoration of Natural

Beauty, Feb. 8, 1965; William M. Blair, "President Asks Federal Power to End Pollution," *NYT*, Feb. 9, 1965.

29. John A. Andrew III, *Lyndon Johnson and the Great Society* (Chicago, 1998), 173–77 (quotation on 177); Martin V. Melosi, "Lyndon Johnson and Environmental Policy," in *The Johnson Years: Vietnam, the Environment, and Science*, ed. Robert A. Divine (Lawrence, Kans., 1987), 113–49.

30. Among the most important congressional documents are *A National Policy for the Environment*, a 1968 report of the Senate Committee on Interior and Insular Affairs, the *Congressional White Paper on a National Policy for the Environment*, also produced by the Senate Committee on Interior and Insular Affairs, and the *Joint House-Senate Colloquium to Discuss a National Policy for the Environment* (1968). Muskie's testimony and the text of the Environmental Quality Improvement Act of 1969 are in *Congressional Record—Senate*, June 12, 1969, 15544–53.

31. For the open space movement, Whyte, and Udall see Adam Rome, *The Bulldozer in the Countryside: Suburban Sprawl and the Rise of American Environmentalism* (Cambridge, UK, 2001), chap. 4.

32. See Adam Rome, *The Genius of Earth Day: How a 1970 Teach-In Unexpectedly Made the First Green Generation* (New York, 2013); Cronin and Kennedy, *Riverkeepers*, 45–46.

33. Lynton Keith Caldwell, *The National Environmental Policy Act: An Agenda for the Future* (Bloomington, Ind., 1998), 23–47; Daniel R. Mandelka, *NEPA Law and Litigation*, 2nd ed. (Saint Paul, Minn., 1996); and Matthew J. Lindstrom and Zachary A. Smith, *The National Environmental Policy Act: Judicial Misconstruction, Legislative Indifference, and Executive Neglect* (College Station, Tex., 2001). See also Lifset, *Power on the Hudson*, 239, n. 40.

34. Caldwell, *National Environmental Policy Act*, 20, 30; Leon Billings, e-mails to the author, July 1, 2015, July 24, 2015.

35. Butzel, "Birth of the Environmental Movement," 285; David Sive, "Environmental Standing," *Natural Resources & Environment* 10 (Fall 1995): 50; Scenic Hudson Preservation Conference et al. v. Federal Power Commission, 453 F.2d 463 (2d Cir., 1971).

36. Cronin and Kennedy, *Riverkeepers*, 37.

2. Politics and the River

1. Fred Smith, "The Future of the Hudson River Valley," undated speech, probably late Sept. or early Oct. 1965, copy in the Laurance S. Rockefeller Papers, box 138, Rockefeller Archive Center, Tarrytown, N.Y. (hereafter cited as L. S. Rockefeller Papers).

2. Udall is quoted in "Redevelopment of Hudson Urged," *NYT*, Oct. 25, 1964.

3. "New Congressman Joins Unit Fighting Storm King Project," *NYT*, Nov. 8, 1964; Hudson Highlands National Scenic Riverway Bill, H.R. 3012, in *Hearings before the Subcommittee on National Parks and Recreation of the Committee on Interior and Insular Affairs*, House of Representatives, 89th Congress, first session, July 24 and 25, 1965, 1–4 (there is a typescript copy of the bill in the Hudson River Valley Commission Files, box 2, New York State Archives, Albany); "Establishment of Hudson Highlands National Scenic Riverway, N.Y.," *Congressional Record—House*, Jan. 18, 1965, 812–14; "Congress Gets Bill to Bar 'Intrusions' along the Hudson," *NYT*, Jan. 19, 1965.

4. "New Congressman Joins Unit Fighting Storm King Project," *NYT*, Nov. 8, 1964; Hudson Highlands National Scenic Riverway Bill, in *Hearings*, 1–4.

5. Udall is quoted in McCandlish Phillips, "Nation and State Clash over River," *NYT*, July 26, 1965; "Historic Hudson National Scenic Riverway," *Congressional Record—House*, Feb. 11, 1965, p. 2560; "Plan for Hudson May Be Extended," *NYT*, Mar. 16, 1965.

6. Nelson A. Rockefeller, press release announcing appointment of Hudson River Valley Commission, Mar. 20, 1965, L.S. Rockefeller Papers, box 137; "Governor Offers Plan for Hudson," *NYT*, June 6, 1965; "The Role of the Federal Government in the Hudson River Project," unsigned and undated draft, probably late winter or early spring 1965, L.S. Rockefeller Papers, box 138; "An Organization to Do the Job," unsigned and undated draft, L. S. Rockefeller Papers, box 138; U.S. Department of the Interior, Bureau of Outdoor Recreation, *Focus on the Hudson: Evaluations of Proposals and Alternatives* (n.p., 1966), 15. Rockefeller's role in creating the Hudson River Valley Commission receives scant attention in Richard Norton Smith's *On His Own Terms: A Life of Nelson Rockefeller* (New York, 2014). My interpretation of the commission differs significantly from the one Sam Aldrich, the second executive director of the commission, presents in *Dancing with the Queen, Marching with King: The Memoirs of Alexander "Sam" Aldrich* (Albany, N.Y., 2011). On the attitude of Rockland and Orange County officials toward the commission see Henry L. Diamond to Richard Wiebe, Feb. 18, 1966, L. S. Rockefeller Papers, box 138.

7. Milbank Tweed Hadley & McCloy, Memorandum, the Hudson River Valley Commission, copy in the L. S. Rockefeller Papers, box 137. At my request, Richard T. Sharp, a partner at Milbank, has looked into the circumstances of this memorandum and believes, based on firm correspondence, that it was prepared at the behest of Laurance Rockefeller. Richard Sharp, e-mail to the author, Oct. 22, 2015.

8. "The Hudson River Fight Must Go On," statement by Leo G. Rothschild, Mar. 22, [1965], copy in L. S. Rockefeller Papers, box 138; "Governor Scored on Hudson Plans," *NYT*, Mar. 22, 1965; "State Spurs Plan to Guard Hudson," *NYT*, Apr. 25, 1965; Laurance Rockefeller is quoted in "Scenic Hudson Called a Job for State," *NYT*, Apr. 15, 1965.

9. *Fourteenth Annual Report of the Joint Legislative Committee on Natural Resources*, Legislative Document No. 26 (1965), copy in the L. S. Rockefeller Papers.

10. "Scenic Hudson Called a Job for State"; "Governor Offers Plan for Hudson"; for clear indications of Rockefeller insiders' perceptions of the politics involved in these various proposals for the Hudson Valley see Henry L. Diamond to L. S. Rockefeller, June 18, 1965, and Fred Smith to L. S. Rockefeller, Mar. 15, 1965, in L. S. Rockefeller Papers, box 137, and staff meeting minutes, Nov. 3, 1965, Record Group (RG) 15, Nelson A. Rockefeller Gubernatorial, Series 34, Diane Van Wie, Subject Files—Staff Meeting Material, 1965–1966, box 23, folder 555, Rockefeller Archive Center.

11. Statement by Governor Nelson A. Rockefeller Concerning a Proposed Hudson River Valley Scenic Corridor Linking the Hudson River to the Adirondack and Catskill Parks, June 5, 1965; "Hudson River Corridor Act of June 28, 1965," typescript copy in the Hudson River Valley Collection, folder B—Rosters, Rockefeller Archive Center.

12. Eleven Reasons Why the Hudson River Valley Needs a Permanent Commission, unsigned and undated memorandum; Fred Smith to L. S. Rockefeller, April 13, 1966, both in L. S. Rockefeller Papers, box 137. See also "The Hudson River Valley Commission: A Short History," typescript, Aug. 17, 1966, L. S. Rockefeller Papers, box 137; "State Spurs Plan to Guard Hudson," *NYT*, Apr. 25, 1965; "Governor Offers Plan for Hudson," *NYT*, June 6, 1965; "Governor Names 37 to Study River," *NYT*, June 12, 1965.

13. Wirth is quoted in Hudson River Valley Commission minutes, June 19, 1965, copy in L. S. Rockefeller Papers, box 137; Nelson A. Rockefeller to John Wilkie, Apr. 5, 1966, and Bruce Howlett to Ben H. Thompson, Nov. 23, 1965, both in L. S. Rockefeller Papers, box 137.

14. Hudson River Valley Commission, *Summary Report*, February 1, 1966 (n.p.), which is unpaginated.

15. Ibid.; Hudson River Valley Commission, "A Proposal for a Permanent Commission," typescript draft, Oct. 8, 1965; "Establishment of a Permanent Hudson River Valley Commission," typescript, Dec. 1, 1965.

16. Hudson River Valley Commission, *Summary Report*, February 1, 1966; Nelson A. Rockefeller, press release, Jan. 31, 1966, in L. S. Rockefeller Papers, box 137.

17. Ottinger to Nelson A. Rockefeller, Sept. 30, 1965, RG 15, Nelson A. Rockefeller Papers, Gubernatorial, Series 34; Ottinger to Conrad Wirth, Feb. 2, 1966, L. S. Rockefeller Papers, box 138; Gordon K. Cameron to Whitney North Seymour Jr., Mar. 14, 1966, Apr. 8, 1966, Whitney North Seymour Papers, box 1, Archives and Special Collections, James A. Cannavino Library, Marist College, Poughkeepsie, N.Y.

18. Bill Jacket, chapter 345, Laws of New York 1966, copy in the Hudson River Valley Commission Records, New York State Archives, Albany; Hudson River Valley Commission, minutes, Oct. 9, 1965, copy in the L. S. Rockefeller Papers, box 137; Hudson River Valley Commission, *Annual Report*, 1967 (n.p., 1967), 6; "Assembly Votes Hudson Program," *NYT*, May 5, 1966.

19. Ottinger to Nelson A. Rockefeller, Sept. 30, 1965, in RG 15, Nelson A. Rockefeller Gubernatorial, Series 34, Diane Van Wie, Subject Files—Staff Meeting Materials, 1965–1966, box 23, folder 555; Ottinger to Conrad L. Wirth, Feb. 2, 1966, and Ottinger to Stewart Udall, Feb. 2, 1966, in L. S. Rockefeller Papers, box 137; Ottinger, press release, Feb. 1, 1966, in L. S. Rockefeller Papers, box 138.

20. Bureau of Outdoor Recreation, *Focus on the Hudson*, passim; "Rockefeller Plan on Hudson Valley Scored by Udall," *NYT*, Oct. 9, 1966. On Rockefeller's proposed east bank expressway see Robert Lifset, "The Environmental Is Political: The Story of the Ill-Fated Hudson River Expressway, 1965–1970," *Hudson River Valley Review* 22 (Spring 2006): 28–53.

21. N. A. Rockefeller to John T. Connor, Sept. 9, 1965, and N. A. Rockefeller to Stewart Udall, Oct. 10, 1966, in Rockefeller Family Papers, box 137, L. S. Rockefeller Papers; "Rockefeller Plan on Hudson Valley Scored by Udall"; "Governor Scores Report by Udall," *NYT*, Oct. 10, 1966

22. An Act to Direct the Secretary of the Interior to Cooperate with the States of New York and New Jersey on a Program to Develop, Preserve, and Restore the Resources of the Hudson River and Its Shores . . . , Sept. 26, 1966; Nelson A. Rockefeller Papers, Gubernatorial Series 10.3, Counsel's Office, Robert R. Douglass, Authorities and Commissions, Hudson River Valley Commission, box 2, folder 26; Compact Creating the Hudson River Valley Commission, ibid.; Laurance S. Rockefeller to Nelson A. Rockefeller, Mar. 2, 1966, L. S. Rockefeller Papers, box 138; "Delay Proposed in Hudson Plans," *NYT*, Mar. 11, 1966; "New Phase Due in Hudson Valley," *NYT*, Sept. 16, 1966.

23. *Congressional Record—House*, Sept. 6, 1966, p. 21788; Stewart L. Udall to Wayne N. Aspinall, June 14, 1966, in Committee on Interior and Insular Affairs, Hudson River Basin Compact, Report No. 1917, p. 7; Maurice R. Dunie to Aspinall, July 27, 1966, ibid., 11–12; Lee C. White to Aspinall, June 27, 1966, ibid., 12–17.

24. *Congressional Record—House*, Sept. 6, 1966, pp. 21778, 21780; "Protecting the Hudson Valley," *NYT*, Aug. 2, 1966; "The Lagging Partner," *NYT*, Oct. 14, 1966; "3-Member Panel Urged for Hudson," *NYT*, Dec. 17, 1967. See also "Governor Scored on Scenic Hudson," *NYT*, July 30, 1965, and "Who Should Protect the Hudson Valley?," *NYT*, Aug. 2, 1965.

25. "Letter Imperils Truce of Hudson," *NYT*, Apr. 7, 1966.

26. Hudson River Valley Commission, minutes, Feb. 7, 1968, Mar. 6, 1968, Feb. 13, 1969, Dec. 10, 1970, Hudson River Valley Commission Records, box 2.

27. "Powerful Agency on Hudson Urged," *NYT*, June 12, 1966; "Governor Scores New Hudson Plan," *NYT*, June 15, 1966; "The Hudson Loses a Safeguard," *NYT*, Sept. 22, 1969; "Guarding the Hudson Valley," *NYT*, Nov. 22, 1969.

28. "U.S.-State Clash Looms on Hudson," *NYT*, June 18, 1967; "Aldrich Is Named to Hudson Panel," *NYT*, Dec. 12, 1966.

29. Alexander Aldrich to N. A. Rockefeller, July 13, 1966, Rockefeller, Personal Papers, Projects, Series L, box 5, folder 39, Rockefeller Archive Center; Hudson River Valley Commission, minutes, Oct. 4, 1967, Jan. 20, 1968, June 5, 1968, July 10, 1968; Aldrich, *Dancing with the Queen*, 148. For examples of Aldrich letters to Nelson Rockefeller about deliberations of the commission see those of Sept. 14 and Nov. 21, 1967. Aldrich's memoir, *Dancing with the Queen*, misrepresents his role in the Georgia-Pacific case. He asserts that he recognized that the proposed location was "in the most scenic heart of the Highlands" and urged his staff to find an alternative location, which turned out to be an industrial area in Haverstraw (148–49). See also "The Lagging Partner," *NYT*, Oct. 14, 1966, an editorial that conceded that political differences were at the base of the dispute between Udall and Rockefeller but concluded that "the Secretary has more right on his side of the argument than has Mr. Rockefeller."

30. Wade Greene, "What Happened to the Attempts to Clean Up the Majestic, the Polluted Hudson," *NYT*, May 3, 1970; David Bird, "Sewer Costs Imperiling State Pure Water Drive," *NYT*, Mar. 31, 1969.

31. The counsel, identified only by the surname Koenig, is quoted in Hudson River Valley Commission, minutes, Aug. 18, 1970. See also K. Harrington-Hughes, "Clearwater Sails for Cleaner Hudson," *Water Pollution Control Federation* 51 (Feb. 1979): 222.

32. Hearing Re Proposed Landfill Project of the Sagamore Pulp Corporation, South Glens Falls, Jan. 3, 1968; Hudson River Valley Commission, minutes, Jan. 8, 1968; Hudson River Valley Commission, *Newsletter* 5, no. 1 (Jan. 1971): 1, copy in the Hudson River Valley Commission Records.

33. Hudson River Valley Commission, minutes, July 5, 1968, Aug. 14, 1968.

34. Hudson River Valley Commission, minutes, Aug. 13, 1969; Aldrich, *Dancing with the Queen*, 149.

35. Hudson River Valley Commission, Review of Proposed Residential Subdivision by Ketchum Construction Corporation, minutes, May 11, 1970, Aug. 11, 1970, Aug. 18, 1970, Sept. 10, 1970.

36. Hudson River Valley Commission, minutes, Feb. 28, 1968.

37. Richard A. Persico and Ronald W. Pederson to Robert R. Douglass, Nov. 24, 1971, Rockefeller Papers, Gubernatorial Series 10.3, Counsel's Office, Robert R. Douglass, Authorities and Commissions, Hudson River Valley Commission, 1971–1972, box 2, folder 27.

38. Robert H. Boyle, *The Hudson: A Natural and Unnatural History* (1969; New York, 1979), 164. For Aldrich's role in the preservation of Olana see David Schuyler, "Saving Olana," *Hudson River Valley Review* 32 (Spring 2016): 1–26.

39. Fergus Reid III to Robert Douglass, Jan. 18, 1968; Robert Douglass to Fergus Reid III, Jan. 26, 1968, both in Nelson A. Rockefeller Papers, Gubernatorial Series, Counsel's Office, Series 10, box 533; the 1969 annual report of the commission is in the Rockefeller Papers, Gubernatorial, Press Office, Agency and Commission Reports, HRVC, Annual Report, July 9, 1970, RG 15, box 71, folder 1610.

40. Rockefeller, press release, July 8, 1970, Nelson A. Rockefeller Papers, Press Office, Agency and Commission Reports, Hudson River Valley Commission, Annual Report, July 8, 1970, RG 15, box 71, folder 1610; Fergus Reid II to N. A. Rockefeller, Mar. 26, 1971, in Rockefeller Papers, Gubernatorial Series, Counsel's Office, Robert R. Douglass, Authorities and Commissions, Hudson River Valley Commission, 1971–1972, box 2, folder 27.

41. Hudson River Valley Commission, minutes, April 8, 1971, May 13, 1971, Oct. 28, 1971, Nov. 18, 1971, Dec. 29, 1971; W. H. Whyte to L. S. Rockefeller, Mar. 29, 1971, L. S. Rockefeller Papers; Hudson River Sloop Restoration Inc., Board of Directors, minutes, Oct. 3, 1971, Fred Starner Collection, Archives and Special Collections, James A. Cannavino Library, Marist College, Poughkeepsie, N.Y. (hereafter cited as Starner Collection).

42. Bill Jacket, chapter 75, Laws of New York 1971, and Bill Jacket, chapter 45, Laws of New York 1980, both in Hudson River Valley Commission Records.

43. Boyle, *Hudson River*, 275, 282.

3. Pete Seeger and the *Clearwater*

1. "Clearwater Carrying Pollution Drive to Washington," *NYT*, Apr. 15, 1970; William C. Woods, "No Clear Water," *Washington Post*, Apr. 22, 1970; Woods, "Seeger's Song: Clear Water," *Washington Post*, Apr. 24, 1970.

2. Seeger is quoted in Woods, "No Clear Water."

3. Leslie Ware, "Pete Seeger: Keeping the Dream," *Sierra*, Mar./Apr. 1989, 82–83; David King Dunaway, *How Can I Keep from Singing? The Ballad of Pete Seeger* (New York, 1981), 133–35; and Allan M. Winkler, *"To Everything There Is a Season": Pete Seeger and the Power of Song* (New York, 2010).

4. Scenic Hudson, Administrative History, Minutes of Executive and Advisory Committee Meeting, May 10, 1966, Scenic Hudson Papers, Marist College. There is no follow-up to this committee discussion in surviving board minutes, and apparently no correspondence with Seeger. John Mylod, longtime executive director of Hudson River Sloop Clearwater Inc., also believes that Carmer was the person on Scenic Hudson's board who was adamantly opposed to any association with Seeger. Information provided by John Mylod, Oct. 30, 2015.

5. Proposal for the Construction, Use, and Maintenance of a Replica of a "Hudson River Sloop" (bears the pencil notation "Pete's Plan 1966"), Starner Collection, Marist College. See also Pete Seeger, "How the Clearwater Got Started," undated memoir in Scenic Hudson Administrative Files, Scenic Hudson Papers.

6. "Hudson Restoration Includes Boat," *NYT*, Sept. 30, 1966; "From the Field of Travel," *NYT*, Oct. 2, 1966; Hudson River Sloop Restoration, Board of Directors, minutes, Aug. 15, 1971; "Hudson River Sloop Restoration to Exhibit at N.Y. Boat Show" (press release, 1968); Notice of Special Meeting of the Members of the Hudson River Sloop Restoration Inc., c. Dec. 12, 1971; Starner, memorandum, Environmental Program of HRSR Inc., Feb. 14, 1971, all in Starner Collection, Marist College. Robert H. Boyle noted that the *Clearwater*, then under construction in Maine, was intended to be a "floating museum": Boyle, *The Hudson: A Natural and Unnatural History* (1968; New York, 1979), 50n.

7. Lisa Yane, "Take Me to the River," *New Age Journal*, July/Aug. 1990: 38–39, 93–96; the August 1970 interview is published in Libby Arnold, "Clearwater: A Living Reminder of the Days When the River Ran Clear," *Hudson Valley Profile* 1 (Aug. 1971): 39; Fred Starner, memorandum, Environmental Program of HRSR Inc., Feb. 14, 1971; Hal Cohen is quoted in Amy McDermott, "Seeger's Legacy Lives on Aboard Sloop Clearwater," State of the Planet, Earth Institute, Columbia University, http://blogs.ei.columbia.edu, May 13, 2014. Starner relates his conversation with Bob Boyle in a document titled "A Call for Action," 1971, Starner Collection.

8. Pete Seeger, *God Bless the Grass* (1964; Smithsonian Folkways Recordings, 2007).

9. Pete Seeger, "Reflections on a Boat Reviving the Hudson," *NYT*, Jun. 22, 1986; "Seeger and Others Sing to Help Hudson River Floating Museum," *NYT*, Oct. 3, 1966; John S. Wilson, "Pete Seeger Devotes Concert to the Hudson," *NYT*, Aug. 14, 1969; Parton Keese, "Sloop with a Mission to Sail the Hudson," *NYT*, Mar. 14, 1969; "Copy of Old Hudson Sloop Is Launched," *NYT*, May 19, 1969; Pete Seeger to Richard Wilkie, n.d. [early Oct. 1968], Starner Collection; "Copy of Old Hudson Sloop Is Launched," *NYT*, May 19, 1969; Arnold, "Clearwater," 37; "Hudson River Sloop Restoration to Exhibit at N.Y. Boat Show" (press release, 1968), Starner Collection; Alexander Saunders Jr., Pete Seeger, et al. to Dear Volunteer Crew, May 29, 1969, Starner Collection; Seeger, "How the Clearwater Got

Started." The lyrics of "Sailing down My Dirty Stream" are printed in Arnold, "Clearwater," 38, and in "Seeger and Others Sing to Help Hudson River Floating Museum," *NYT*, Oct. 3, 1966.

10. "Sloop Will Sail up the Hudson in Campaign for Clean Water," *NYT*, Aug. 2, 1969; "Sloop on Voyage to Purify Hudson Spreads Zeal and Song," *NYT*, Aug. 28, 1969.

11. "Hudson River Group Aide Quits in Protest on Seeger," *NYT*, Sept. 28, 1970; Donald R. Presutti to Board of Directors, Hudson River Sloop Restoration Inc., Sept. 23, 1970, Starner Collection.

12. "Clearwater Blocked at Cold Spring," *Beacon Evening News*, Apr. 13, 1978; Pete Seeger, "Song of the Clearwater," *Parade*, Nov. 26, 1978, 5; Hudson River Sloop Restoration, board of directors, minutes, Feb. 14, 1971, Starner Collection; Arnold, "Clearwater," 40.

13. Long Range Planning Committee, untitled memorandum on board decision-making structures, n.d. [1970–71], Starner Collection.

14. Dobson, President's Report, in Hudson River Sloop Restoration, Board of Directors, minutes, Aug. 15, 1971; Executive Committee, minutes, Apr. 25, 1975, both in Starner Collection.

15. Fred Starner to Dom Pirone, Sept. 13, 1971; Fred Starner to John Burns III, Nov. 23, [1971]; Reed Haslam to Board Members of Hudson River Sloop Restoration Inc., Sept. 19, 1972; David M. Seymour to Members of the Board of Directors, HRSR, Sept. 24, 1972; Executive Committee, minutes, May 30, 1975, May 24, 1979, all in Starner Collection.

16. "Notes: Six-Day Cruises on a Hudson River Sloop," *NYT*, Oct. 21, 1973; "Rot Threatening the Clearwater," *NYT*, Feb. 19, 1976; Progress Report on Repair of Clearwater for December, Jan. 3, 1976; "Hudson River Sloop Restoration," press release, Mar. 1, 1976, both in Starner Collection; information provided by John Mylod, Oct. 30, 2015.

17. Maynard Bray to Dear People, Apr. 19, 1976, Starner Collection; information provided by John Mylod, Oct. 30, 2015.

18. Arnold, "Clearwater," 39; "Wood, Field and Stream: Thousands Gathering at the River for Hudson Cleanup," *NYT*, Apr. 22, 1976; Leslie Ware, "Pete Seeger: Keeping the Dream," *Sierra*, March/April 1985, 39; Board of Directors, minutes, Aug. 15, 1971, Oct. 21, 1978; Walt Schwanne to Angela Magill, Dec. 11, 1976; Sloop Club Network to Clearwater's Board of Directors, Sept. 21, 1984; minutes, General Meeting, Sept. 27, 1984, all in Starner Collection; Mylod is quoted in Yane, "Take Me to the River," 96.

19. Board of Directors, minutes, Sept. 12, 1976, Starner Collection; information provided by John Mylod, Oct. 30, 2015; Seeger is quoted in Greg Aunapu, "The Clearwater at 21: Coming of Age," *UpRiver/DownRiver*, Mar.–Apr. 1991, 54.

20. Seeger is quoted in Arnold, "Clearwater," 42–43; Seeger reminisced about his youth and longtime association with the Hudson River in an audiotape produced as part of Thomas Whyatt and Robin MacFarlane's "The Troubled Hudson," a film and audiotape production by Educational Design, sponsored by the Hudson River Sloop Inc., 1976, copy in Clearwater Collection, Marist College.

21. Seeger expressed the importance of attachment to locality on numerous occasions. I am quoting from an interview with Howard Jay Rubin published in a North Carolina journal, the *Sun*, May 2014, 7, 9. See also Ware, "Seeger: Keeping the Dream," 88.

22. *Sun*, May 2014, 7, 9; Ware, "Seeger: Keeping the Dream," 88.

23. Seeger is quoted in "Clearwater Carrying Pollution Drive to Washington," *NYT*, Apr. 15, 1970. For the *Washington Post*'s coverage of events in the capital see "March on Interior to Highlight Earth Day Activities in D.C.," Apr. 22, 1970; "Demonstrations to Mark U.S. 'Earth Day' Today," ibid.; "Area Holds Cleanup with Rally," Apr. 23, 1970; Richard Harwood, "Earth Day Stirs Nation," Apr. 23, 1970. On Earth Day see Adam Rome's excellent

book, *The Genius of Earth Day: How a 1970 Teach-In Unexpectedly Made the First Green Generation* (New York, 2013).

24. Hudson River Sloop Clearwater, Board of Directors, minutes, Nov. 20, 1977, Dec. 4, 1977, Jan. 22, 1978, Jan. 29, 1978; Executive Committee, minutes, June 30, 1978; Board of Directors, minutes, May 5, 1979, all in Starner Collection. On the Shoreham voyage Seeger and Jackson Browne gave a concert in Boston that generated $10,000 for the *Clearwater*.

25. Aunapu, "Clearwater at 21," 52–53; Robert Hanley, "Story of Hudson Told to Students," *NYT*, May 21, 1972; "Wood, Field and Stream: Thousands Gathering at the River for Hudson Cleanup," *NYT*, Apr. 22, 1975; Pete Seeger describes the onboard educational program in "Reflections on a Boat Reviving the Hudson"; Hudson River Sloop Clearwater, Funding Proposal, June 1993, Clearwater Collection, Marist College.

26. Robert Sherman, "The Clearwater Is Bringing Song to the Shores," *NYT*, Oct. 25, 1981; Robert Sherman, "Mansion Melodies and Mini-Concerts," *NYT*, Oct. 22, 1989.

27. Eleanor Blau, "A Festival of Ethnicity and Ecology on the Hudson," *NYT*, June 22, 1979; Robert Sherman, "A Roaring Folk-Song Success," *NYT*, July 1, 1979; Andrew C. Revkin, "An Environmental Festival Returns to Its River," *NYT*, June 19, 1999; "Pollution Forces Relocation of Hudson River Festival," *Kingston Daily Freeman*, Mar. 2, 1988; Clearwater's Great Hudson River Revival, June 15 and 16, 1985, Starner Collection.

28. Board of Directors, minutes, Oct. 3, 1971; Burns is quoted in Hudson River Sloop Restoration, news release, Dec. 15, 1971; Revision of President's and New and Unscheduled Business Reports of Minutes of Annual Meeting, Hudson River Sloop Restoration (n.d., probably Sept. 1972); Board of Directors, minutes, Mar. 7, 1976, June 27, 1972, all in Starner Collection; "Clear Sailing," *NYT*, Dec. 19, 2004; information provided by John Cronin.

29. Hudson River Sloop Clearwater Inc., *2012 Annual Report*, 15; John Mylod and Sarah Johnston to the Clearwater Board of Directors, June 2, 1985, Hudson River Sloop Clearwater Collection, Marist College, Series 4—John Mylod's Projects and Interests; the various environmental efforts mentioned in this paragraph are described in various issues of *Clearwater Navigator*.

30. There is a large box of materials devoted to Springside in the Clearwater Collection at Marist College. Many documents in that box have informed my thinking about the *Clearwater*'s role in the preservation of Springside, but especially John Mylod's testimony, in behalf of Clearwater, in opposition to the change in zoning that the developer needed. I have also relied on information conveyed by Mylod in conversation and correspondence. See also Harvey Flad, "Matthew Vassar's Springside: '. . . the Hand of Art, When Guided by Taste,' " in *Prophet with Honor: The Career of Andrew Jackson Downing, 1815–1852*, ed. George B. Tatum and Elisabeth Blair MacDougall (Washington, D.C., 1989), 253–57, as well as Flad's "Springside: Preserving Downing's Last Landscape," which will be published in a forthcoming issue of the *Hudson River Valley Review*. On Downing's significance see David Schuyler, *Apostle of Taste: Andrew Jackson Downing, 1815–1852* (1996; Amherst, Mass., 2015).

31. Peter Applebome, "This Boat Is Your Boat, This Boat Is My Boat, and a River Beckons," *NYT*, Sept. 19, 2004.

32. "New Sloop for the River," *NYT*, Feb. 10, 1980; Josh P. Roberts, "A Floating Environmental School Gets Her Bottle of Champagne," *NYT*, Aug. 16, 1981; "A Sloop Bows In on the Hudson," *NYT*; "What Is Ferry Sloops," n.d., typescript copy in Clearwater Collection, Marist College, Series 4—John Mylod's Projects and Interests; "Ferry Sloops Setting Sail for Yonkers Waterfront," *NYT*, June 21, 1992; Lynne Ames, "Arson Suspected in Fire Aboard Sloop," *NYT*, July 23, 1995; Marek Fuchs, "Sloop That Sailed Hudson in Ruins," *NYT*, Sept. 22, 2002.

33. Board of Directors, minutes, Aug. 25, 1985; Seeger, "Reflections on a Boat Reviving the Hudson"; Hudson River Sloop Clearwater: Case for a New Sloop (c. 1987), copy in Starner Collection.

34. Hudson River Sloop Clearwater: Case for a New Sloop (c. 1987), Clearwater Collection, Marist College.

35. McLean, *Tapestry* (Mediarts, 1969); Seeger's foreword and McLean's poem ("for Pete") are printed in McLean, *Songs and Sketches of the First Clearwater Crew* (Croton-on-Hudson, N.Y., 1970), n.p.

36. *Clearwater Navigator*, Spring 2014; Hudson River Sloop Clearwater Inc., *Statements of Financial Position*, Nov. 30, 2014, and Nov. 30, 2013, 11, 15; Paul Post, "Restoring a Hudson Crusader, Plank by Plank," *NYT*, Dec. 14, 2015.

37. Hudson River Sloop Clearwater Inc., *Annual Reports*, 2012, 15, and 2011, 14.

38. I am grateful to David T. Conover, education director at Hudson River Sloop Clearwater Inc., for the estimates on the number of people who have sailed on the sloop or participated in its onshore educational programs since 1969. For Robert Kennedy Jr.'s statement about Seeger's significance see Michael Hall, "Legendary Hudson River Sloop Clearwater Undergoes Restoration," WNBC News (https://www.nbcnewyork.com/news/local/Clearwater-the-Hudson-River-Sloop-and-Environmental-Symbol-Undergoes-Restoration-Pete-Seeger-371158721.html); "Clearwater Revival: Overhauling Sloop a Symbol of Hudson's Revival," *Kingston Daily Freeman*, Mar. 3, 2016.

39. Jon Pareles, "Pete Seeger, Champion of Folk Music and Social Change, Dies at 94," *NYT*, Jan. 28, 2014; Joseph Berger, "For Seeger, Years of Singing and Sailing to Save His Hudson River," *NYT*, Jan. 28, 2014; Tom Staudter, "Pete Seeger: Folk Singer, Activist, American Treasure," *Hudson Valley Magazine*, April 2014.

40. "Clearwater Cancels 2016 Music Festival Founded by Pete Seeger," *Middletown Times Herald Record*, Jan. 21, 2016; Lynn Woods, "Clearwater Organization Looks to Right the Ship after Recent Turmoil," hv1, Feb. 4, 2016, http://hudsonvalleyone.com/2016/02/04/Clearwater-organization; Conover is quoted in Hall, "Legendary Hudson River Sloop Clearwater Undergoes Restoration"; Michael D'Onofrio, "Sloop Clearwater Back in Action," *Poughkeepsie Journal*, July 31, 2016.

41. Conover is quoted in Hall, "Legendary Hudson River Sloop Clearwater Undergoes Restoration."

4. The Fishermen and the Riverkeeper

1. Robert Juet's Journal, edited by Robert M. Lunny, in *Chronicles of the Hudson: Three Centuries of Travel and Adventure*, ed. Roland Van Zandt (1971; Hensonville, N.Y., 1992), 9–15; Robert H. Boyle, *The Hudson River: A Natural and Unnatural History* (1969; New York, 1979), 39.

2. Benson J. Lossing, *The Hudson: From the Wilderness to the Sea* (1866; Hensonville, N.Y., 2000), 144–46.

3. Edward K. Spann, *The New Metropolis: New York City, 1840–1857* (New York, 1981), 117–39; Lossing, *Hudson*, 414–64.

4. "Health, Department of," *Encyclopedia of New York State*, ed. Peter Eisenstadt et al. (Syracuse, N.Y., 2005), 702–3; "New-York's Water Supply: Report of the State Board of Health," *NYT*, Oct. 6, 1889; "Filth Found Everywhere: What a Tour of the Big Croton Watershed Revealed," *NYT*, Aug. 29, 1891.

5. The Survey Commission report is quoted in "Pollution of the Hudson River," State Department of Health typescript, Aug. 31, 1939, copy in the Hudson River Conservation Society Collection, box 2, Archives and Special Collections, James A. Cannavino Library, Marist College, Poughkeepsie, N.Y. The rest of this paragraph is also based on the Department of Health typescript.

6. Boyle, *Hudson River*, 98–99; John Cronin and Robert F. Kennedy Jr., *The Riverkeepers: Two Activists Fight to Reclaim Our Environment as a Basic Human Right* (New York, 1977), 18; Theodore Roosevelt, "Our Vanishing Wildlife," *Outlook*, Jan. 1913, 161–62.

7. Cronin and Kennedy, *Riverkeepers*, 43–44, passim; Boyle, *Hudson River*, 130–31.

8. Cronin and Kennedy, *Riverkeepers*, 22, 24–25.

9. Robert H. Boyle, "From a Mountaintop to 1,000 Fathoms Deep," *Sports Illustrated*, Aug. 17, 1964, www.si.com/vault/1964/08/17/608062/from-a-mountaintop-to-1000-fathoms-deep.

10. Robert H. Boyle, "America Down the Drain," and Stewart Udall, "'His Anger Is Fully Justified'—Udall," both in *Sports Illustrated*, Nov. 16, 1964, 80–90, and 84.

11. Robert H. Boyle, "A Stink of Dead Stripers," *Sports Illustrated*, Apr. 26, 1965, 81–84; Cronin and Kennedy, *Riverkeepers*, 32; Boyle, *Hudson River*, 159–65.

12. Boyle, "Stink of Dead Stripers."

13. Cronin and Kennedy, *Riverkeepers*, 40, 53. The importance of a local grounding for environmentalism goes back a century and a half, to Henry David Thoreau, to John Burroughs in the late nineteenth century, and many others in the years since. René Dubos's clarion call to think globally and act locally is the powerful modern statement of this belief. See my chapter on Burroughs in *Sanctified Landscape: Writers, Artists, and the Hudson River Valley* (Ithaca, N.Y., 2012), 133–50, and William Cronon's "The Trouble with Wilderness: Or Getting Back to the Wrong Nature," in *Out of the Woods: Essays in Environmental History*, ed. Char Miller and Hal Rothman (Pittsburgh, 1997), 28–50.

14. Boyle, "My Struggle to Help the President," *Sports Illustrated*, Feb. 16, 1970, 32ff; Boyle, *Hudson River*, 102–3; the Fishermen's Association statement of purpose is quoted in Boyle, *Hudson River*, 278; Cronin and Kennedy, *Riverkeepers*, 43–44.

15. Boyle, "My Struggle to Help the President"; Boyle, *Hudson River*, 97–102; Cronin and Kennedy, *Riverkeepers*, 42–44.

16. Boyle, "My Struggle to Help the President"; Boyle, *Hudson River*, 102.

17. Cronin and Kennedy, *Riverkeepers*, 159–62; information provided by Albert K. Butzel and John Cronin; "Riverkeeper: An Incomplete History," Riverkeeper, *Annual Journal 2016*, 9. See also William W. Buzbee, *Fighting Westway: Environmental Law, Citizen Activism, and the Regulatory War That Transformed New York City* (Ithaca, N.Y., 2014), 67–69 and passim.

18. Scenic Hudson et al. v. Callaway, 370 F 2d (S.D. N.Y. 1973); River Defense Committee et al. v. Thierman, 380 F. Supp. 91 (S.D. N.Y, 1974); Thomas Whyatt to Hon. Michael DiBert, Aug. 5, 1974, copy in the Hudson River Conservation Society Collection, box 2.

19. Boyle, *Hudson River*, 276–77.

20. Michael Roddy, "The Hudson River Is His Beat: Conservationists Name Whyatt," *Tarrytown Daily News*, June 21, 1973, copy in the Hudson River Conservation Society Collection, box 2; Boyle, *Hudson River*, 289.

21. Cronin and Kennedy, *Riverkeepers*, 56; information provided by Thomas Whyatt; Suzanne DeChillo, "A Watchdog on the Hudson," *NYT*, Sept. 9, 1984.

22. Nelson Bryant, "New Riverkeeper to Patrol Hudson," *NYT*, Feb. 27, 1983; "Safeguarding the Hudson," *NYT*, May 15, 1983; Cronin and Kennedy, *Riverkeepers*, 51, 71–76; "It All Began with Fishermen," Riverkeeper, *Annual Journal 2016*.

23. Cronin and Kennedy, *Riverkeepers*, 94–110.

24. Ibid., 187–88; information provided by John Cronin.

25. For Gallay's remarks see *Riverkeeper Journal 2015*, 1.

26. Riverkeeper, *Fractured Communities: Case Studies of the Environmental Impacts of Industrial Gas Drilling* (Ossining, N.Y., 2010), 3, passim.

27. Cronin and Kennedy, *Riverkeepers*, 195–98; "Riverkeeper's 11 Biggest Wins in 2011," https://www.riverkeeper.org/news-events/news/riverkeeper/riverkeepers-11-biggest-wins-in-2011-2/; information provided by John Cronin; Robert F. Kennedy Jr., *DEP's Watershed Police: Cops in Cuffs* (Ossining, N.Y., Feb. 1999), 1–3, 7, 28, passim; John Parker, "Protecting Our Precious Drinking Water," Riverkeeper, *Annual Journal 2016*, 14.

28. John Verleun, "Riverkeeper Enforcement Update," *2011 Annual Journal*, 23–24.

29. "Gowanus Canal," www.nyc.gov/html/harborwater/gowanus_canal_superfund.shtml; "Riverkeeper, 2010 Achievements," https://www.riverkeeper.org/news-events/news/riverke eper/2010-achievements/; "Riverkeeper's 11 Biggest Wins in 2011"; Josh Verleun, "River-keeper Enforcement Update," *2011 Annual Journal*; "Boat Patrol Targets Pollution," *2015 Journal*; "Riverkeeper's Biggest Victories of 2013," https://www.riverkeeper.org/blogs/docket/riverkeepers-biggest-victories-of-2013/.

30. Riverkeeper, *Annual Journal 2014*; Dan Shapley, "How's the Water Where You Live," Riverkeeper, *Annual Journal 2014*, 5; Paul Gallay, "Going Big, for Clean Water and Safe En-ergy," Riverkeeper, *2013 Annual Journal*, 5, and "Change Makers and Game Changers," Riverkeeper, *2013 Annual Journal*, 16–17; Pisces Conservation Ltd., *The Status of Fish Pop-ulations and the Ecology of the Hudson*, April 2008, unpaginated; Josh Verleun, "Work-ing to Protect the Hudson River's Dwindling Fish Population," Riverkeeper, *2010 Annual Journal*, 7.

31. Shapley, "How's the Water?," 5; Gallay, "Going Big" and "Change Makers."

32. Riverkeeper, *How's the Water? 2015* (Ossining, N.Y., 2015), 6, 8, 9, 30–34, passim.

33. Hudson River Estuary Program, *The State of the Hudson 2015* (Albany, N.Y., 2015), 4; Riverkeeper, *Sustainable Raindrops* (Ossining, N.Y., 2008); Basil Seggos, "A Greener New York Makes for a Cleaner Harbor," Riverkeeper, *Annual Journal 2008*, 6.

34. "Riverkeeper's Biggest Victories of 2013"; "Riverkeeper's Biggest Victories of 2014," https://www.riverkeeper.org/blogs/the-watchdog/riverkeepers-biggest-victories-of-2014/; infor-mation provided by Lea Rae and Paul Gallay.

35. Victor Tafur, "Special Report: Hudson River Fish in Peril," Riverkeeper, *2008 Annual Report*, 11–12; Daniel Wolff, "The State of the River, 1609–2019," Riverkeeper, *2009 An-nual Journal*, 19; information provided by Paul Gallay.

36. Riverkeeper statement on EPA/NY agreement regarding Tappan Zee and Clean Water funds, undated press release.

37. Information on these volunteer efforts is derived from Riverkeeper's website, www.riverkeeper.org.

38. Robert Worth, "Eight at Riverkeeper Resign over Kennedy's Hiring of a Rare-Egg Smuggler," *NYT*, June 22, 2000; Boyle is quoted in Worth, "A Kennedy and His Mentor Part Ways over River Group," *NYT*, Nov. 5, 2000.

39. Cronin and Kennedy, *Riverkeepers*, 117–36; www.waterkeeper.org.

40. *NYT*, Jan. 7, 2017; Paul Gallay, "Riverkeeper, New York State, and Entergy Sign a Landmark Agreement to Close Indian Point by 2021," news release, Jan. 9, 2017; Scenic Hudson, "Entergy to Close Indian Point Nuclear Plant in Landmark Agreement," press re-lease, Jan. 9, 2017.

41. Information in the paragraph is drawn from www.riverkeeper.org and from informa-tion provided by Paul Gallay.

5. The Continuing Battle against Power Plants

1. Rod Vandivert, "Utilities and the Hudson River," special report presented to the New York State Conservation Council annual meeting, Sept. 27, 1969, typescript copy in the Sce-nic Hudson Administrative Collection, box 61, Scenic Hudson Papers, Marist College.

2. Alfonso A. Narvaez, "State Is Planning to Construct Nuclear Plant on Hudson by '82," *NYT*, Mar. 1, 1974; "Upstate Area Divided by Atomic Project," *NYT*, Apr. 14, 1974; Stone and Webster Engineering Corp., "Metropolitan Transportation Authority Plant Site Study," progress report, which is summarized in "Final Environmental Statement by the U.S. Nuclear Regulatory Commission for Greene County Nuclear Power Plant Proposed by Power

240   *Notes to Pages 105–111*

Authority of the State of New York" (hereafter "Final Environmental Statement"), January 1979, p. 3–1, table 9–14, p. 9–54.

3. Harold Faber, "A Nuclear Plant for Subways Due," *NYT*, May 22, 1975; "Contract Awards," *NYT*, June 14, 1974; "Final Environmental Statement," p. 3–1, table 9–14, p. 9–54; information provided by Loretta Simon. On the preservation of Olana see David Schuyler, "Saving Olana," *Hudson River Valley Review* 32 (Spring 2016): 1–26.

4. My thinking about public authorities has been influenced by Robert A. Caro, *The Power Broker: Robert Moses and the Fall of New York* (New York, 1974). On the FitzPatrick nuclear plant see "State Power Authority's First Nuclear Plant Starts Operating," *NYT*, Aug. 19, 1975.

5. Hauspurg is quoted in Harold Faber, "Con Ed Picks 2 Mid-Hudson Areas as Possible Sites for a Power Plant," *NYT*, Nov. 18, 1976; Carl H. Petrich, "EIA Scoping for Aesthetics: Hindsight from the Greene County Nuclear Power Plant EIS," in *Improving Impact Assessment: Increasing the Relevance and Utilization of Scientific and Technical Information*, ed. Stuart L. Hart et al. (Boulder, Colo., 1984), 58.

6. Alan Gussow, "Prepared Testimony on Aesthetic Impact of Green County Nuclear Power Plant," Mar. 2, 1979, copy in possession of Harvey K. Flad. See also Gussow, "Beauty in the Landscape: An Ecological Viewpoint," in *Landscape in America*, ed. George F. Thompson (Austin, TX, 1995, 223–40.

7. Gussow, "Prepared Testimony." See also testimony by Harvey K. Flad and David C. Huntington on the aesthetic impact of the proposed nuclear plants, copies in possession of Harvey K. Flad.

8. "Nuclear Power Plant to Be Built," [Olana] *Crayon* 4 (Mar. 1974): 1; "Upstate Area Divided by Atomic Project."

9. Scott and Bruner are quoted in "Upstate Area Divided by Atomic Project"; "Final Environmental Statement," p. 2–8; Faber, "Nuclear Plant for Subways Due." For a complete listing of local government acts in opposition to the Cementon plant see "Final Environmental Statement," appendix J. Harvey Flad places the Cementon battle in a broad context in "The Influence of the Hudson River School of Art in the Preservation of the River, Its Natural and Cultural Landscape, and the Evolution of Environmental Law," in *Environmental History of the Hudson River: Human Uses That Changed the Ecology, Ecology That Changed Human Uses*, ed. Robert E. Henshaw (Albany, N.Y., 2011), 291–311.

10. "Final Environmental Statement," pp. 2–9, 4–16 to 4–20, 4–42, 4–46, 4–54, 5–54. See also Elizabeth Peelle, "Socioeconomic Impact Assessment and Nuclear Power Plant Licensing," in *Improving Impact Assessment*, 93–117; "Brief selected chronology" of the Greene County nuclear power plant licensing action is in Peelle, "Socioeconomic Impact Assessment," 100–101; information provided by Loretta Simon.

11. "Final Environmental Statement," passim; "Brief selected chronology" of the Greene County nuclear power plant licensing action, 100–101.

12. Testimony of Donald N. Stone, Robert W. Graves, and Bruce E. Podwal on Land Use and Aesthetics Contentions, June 27, 1977, in Joint Proceedings in United States of America Nuclear Regulatory Commission before the Atomic Safety and Licensing Board and the State of New York Department of Public Services Board on Electric Generation Siting and the Environment; Power Authority of the State of New York, Greene County Nuclear Power Plant, Environmental Report (1975), chapter 11, copy in the possession of Harvey K. Flad.

13. Testimony of Stone, Graves, and Pownal; PASNY, Green County Nuclear Power Plant, Environmental Report, chapter 11.

14. Information provided by J. Winthrop Aldrich and Loretta Simon; "Final Environmental Statement," p. 1–1; Petrich, "EIA Scoping for Aesthetics," 59–61. Loretta Simon

describes her involvement in opposition to the Cementon plant in "The Fight to Save Olana and Its Environs," in a pamphlet published by the Olana Partnership, *Framing the Viewshed: A Bend in the River* (Greenport, N.Y., 2012).

15. National Environmental Policy Act of 1969 (Jan. 1, 1970), Public Law 91–190, sect. 101, 83 Stat. (Washington, D.C., 1970), 852.

16. Petrich, "EIA Scoping for Aesthetics"; Petrich, "Assessing Aesthetic Impacts in Siting a Nuclear Power Plant: The Case of Greene County, New York," *EIA Review* 3, no. 4 (1982): 311–32; Petrich, "Aesthetic Impact of a Proposed Power Plant on an Historic Wilderness Landscape," paper presented at the National Conference on Applied Techniques for Analysis and Management of the Visual Resource, Incline Village, Nev., Apr. 23–25, 1979, http://www.fs.fed.us/psw/publications/documents/psw_gtr035/psw_gtr035_11_petrich.pdf.

17. Petrich, "EIA Scoping for Aesthetics"; Petrich, "Assessing Aesthetic Impacts"; Petrich, "Aesthetic Impact of a Proposed Power Plant"; the photographs and the visual preference survey are reproduced in "Final Environmental Statement," appendix N.

18. Petrich, "The Historical and Cultural Context of the Proposed Greene County Nuclear Power Plant," 37, draft copy, Olana Archive, Olana State Historic Site, Greenport, N.Y.; John K. Howat, *The Hudson River and Its Painters* (New York, 1972), 174 (this is quoted in "Final Environmental Statement," p. 5–62); J. Winthrop Aldrich, statement in *Framing the Viewshed*, Feb. 25, 2012 (the panel discussion, by Aldrich, Carl Petrich, and Rick Benas and moderated by Dorothy Heyl, has not been transcribed but was videotaped and is available at www.youtube.com/user/watch?V=8KQFKfZqG8); Jervis McEntee diary, July 22, 1872, Jervis McEntee Papers, Archives of American Art, Smithsonian Institution, Washington, D.C.; Vincent Scully, "Palace of the Past," *Progressive Architecture*, May 1965, 184–89.

19. The letters that Petrich solicited from Novak and Wilmerding are quoted in "Final Environmental Statement," pp. 5–70 and 5–71. For Petrich's statement about Huntington's influence on his understanding of the significance of Olana and its viewshed see *Framing the Viewshed*. Petrich gave Church's painting the title *Winter Scene, Olana* in the "Final Environmental Statement."

20. Testimony of Dr. Stephen S. Bernow before the Joint Hearings of the Nuclear Regulatory Commission and the New York State Board on Electric Generation Siting and the Environment, Mar. 2, 1979, copy in Scenic Hudson Preservation Conference Administrative Files, box 53, Scenic Hudson Papers; J. P. Rod and M. L. Lamping, Action Plan—Power Authority of the State of New York (PASNY) Proposed Nuclear Plant in Cementon, Greene Co., N.Y., July 10, 1979, copy in Scenic Hudson Administrative Files, Scenic Hudson Papers.

21. Copies of the testimony by Gussow, Huntington, and Flad, courtesy of Harvey K. Flad.

22. Testimony of Harvey K. Flad, courtesy of Harvey Flad; Harvey Flad, e-mail to the author, May 3, 2017; Flad explained the methodology used in preparing the photo-simulations in appendix A of his testimony. The Public Service Commission staff member's estimation of Flad's testimony is quoted in J. Winthrop Aldrich to the Members of the Hudson River Conservation Society, Apr. 1979, copy in the Olana Partnership files, Greenport, N.Y. See also Flad, "Analysis of Aesthetic Impacts of a 1200 MW Greene County Nuclear Power Plant Proposed by the Power Authority of the State of New York," Feb. 26, 1979, which he submitted along with his prepared testimony on Mar. 2, 1979, courtesy of Harvey K. Flad, and Katherine Ghilain, "Improving Community Character Analysis in the SEQRA Environmental Impact Review Process," *NYU Environmental Law Journal* 17 (2009). Flad gratefully acknowledged the significant help he received from Ruth Piwonka of the Columbia County Historical Society in identifying significant historic sites and scenic views he presented in his testimony.

23. Petrich made this statement about NRC's reluctance to publish the "Final Environmental Statement" in *Framing the Viewshed.*

24. Testimony of Donald N. Stone, Robert W. Graves, and Bruce E. Podwal, Joint Proceedings before the Atomic Safety and Licensing Board and the Board on Electric Generation Siting and the Environment, June 27, 1977, copy in the possession of Harvey K. Flad; "Final Environmental Statement," pp. 5–62 to 5–68, iv.

25. Petrich, "EIA Scoping for Aesthetics," 58; Petrich, "Assessing Aesthetic Impacts," 312; "Final Environmental Statement," table 9–14, p. 9–54; for Rick Benas's assessment of the importance of the "Final Environmental Statement" see *Framing the Viewshed.*

26. For Aldrich's statement of how leaders at Clearwater urged the Hudson River Conservation Society to abandon aesthetics as an issue see *Framing the Viewshed*; "Brief selected chronology" of the Greene County nuclear power plant licensing action, 100–101; Peter Kihss, "New York Power Agency Drops Nuclear-Energy Project Upstate," *NYT*, Apr. 6, 1979; Anthony J. Parisi, "Nuclear Reactors under Close Study," *NYT*, Apr. 3, 1979; R. Drummond Ayres Jr., "Three Mile Island: Notes from a Nightmare," *NYT*, Apr. 16, 1979.

27. Robert H. Boyle, *The Hudson River: A Natural and Unnatural History* (1969; expanded ed., New York, 1979), 294; Robert C. Stover to Harvey Flad, Feb. 4, 1980, enclosing copy of the Order Enclosing Proceeding, copy in the possession of Harvey K. Flad; John Winthrop Aldrich to Dear Friend, June 1979, Hudson River Conservation Society Collection, Archives and Special Collections, James A. Cannavino Library, Marist College, Poughkeepsie, N.Y.

28. "Coal Terminal to Locate along River," *Scenic Hudson News*, Fall 1985, 6–7; Scenic Hudson, *Annual Report 1990* (Poughkeepsie, N.Y., 1991), 6; Scenic Hudson, *Annual Report 1991* (Poughkeepsie, N.Y., 1992).

29. Robert D. Lifset, *Power on the Hudson: Storm King Mountain and the Emergence of Modern American Environmentalism* (Pittsburgh, 2014), 11, 178–79; Faber, "Con Ed Picks 2"; "Drive Opens against Con Ed Atomic Plants," *NYT*, Mar. 6, 1977; Boyle, *Hudson River*, 177.

30. Energy Research and Development Authority, Lloyd Site Master Development Plan: Concept Phase Report, Nov. 1975, 7; Brown is quoted in Faber, "Con Ed Picks 2"; Boyle, *Hudson River*, 177.

31. Energy Research and Development Authority, Lloyd Site Master Development Plan: Concept Phase Report, Nov. 1975, 2–4, 7, 9.

32. Ibid., 2, 7, 9, 13–14, 22, 44.

33. Ibid.

34. "Town Votes to Oppose Nuclear Plant," *NYT*, June 3, 1974; information provided by Peter D. G. Brown; Peter D. G. Brown and Stephen J. Egemeier, eds., *Nuclear Power in the Hudson Valley: Its Impact on You* (Highland, N.Y., 1976), i, passim; "Drive Opens against Con Ed Atomic Plants," *NYT*, Mar. 6, 1977.

35. Faber, "Con Ed Picks 2."

36. Flad, "Visual Pollution of the Proposed Nuclear Reactor Site in the Town of Lloyd, Ulster County, New York," in *Guidebook to Field Excursions*, ed. John H. Johnsen, 48th Annual Meeting of the New York State Geological Association, Oct. 15–17, 1976, B9—12, B9—18–22.

37. Information provided by Peter D. G. Brown.

38. Center for Governmental Research Inc., "Athens Generating Project: An Assessment of the Project's Value to the Community and the Owner," June 1978, 1, 3, 4.

39. Ibid., 3, 7–8.

40. Richard Pérez-Peña, "Big Power Plant on the Hudson Wins Approval," *NYT*, Jun. 3, 2000; Harvey K. Flad, Prepared Testimony on Aesthetic Impact of Greene County Nuclear Plant, March 2, 1979.

41. New York State Department of State, *Scenic Areas of Statewide Significance* (Albany, 1993), 88, 102; Scenic Hudson Preservation Conference, "Scenic Hudson Settles Athens Generating Lawsuit," press release, Jan. 3, 2001, courtesy of Scenic Hudson; Tom Anderson, "Power Play on the Hudson," *Journal News* (White Plains, N.Y.), July 2, 2000.

42. "Cleaner Power in New York," *NYT*, June 7, 2000; "Right Decision on Power Plant," *Poughkeepsie Journal*, June 10, 2000; information provided by Ned Sullivan and J. Winthrop Aldrich. The case was Scenic Hudson Inc. and the Scenic Hudson Land Trust Inc. v. Alexander F. Treadwell as Secretary of State, the New York Department of State, and Athens Generating Company, L.P., which had been filed in federal court in the Northern District of New York.

43. This chronology is based on the New York Department of Public Service website: www3. dps.ny.gov/W/PSCWeb.nsf/ArticleByTitle/F58F9043CFC25FAC8525257687006F3916?.

44. Scenic Hudson, unpublished statement about the withdrawal of its federal lawsuit against the New York Department of State, Dec. 22, 2000; "Scenic Hudson Settles Athens Generating Lawsuit," press release, Jan. 3, 2001; "State, Athens Generating Announce $1 Million in Grants for Historic Preservation Projects in Greene, Columbia," *Kingston Daily Freeman*, Feb. 12, 2003; "Catskill-Olana Grants Awarded by Foundation," *Hudson Register Star*, June 28, 2007.

45. David W. Kaiser, federal consistency coordinator, NOAA, letter to James P. King, general counsel, New York Department of State, [Dec. 8, 2000,] courtesy of Scenic Hudson; information provided by Ned Sullivan, J. Winthrop Aldrich, and Sara Griffen, former president of the Olana Partnership.

46. Boyle, *Hudson River*, 272.

6. Scenic Hudson's Expanding Mission

1. I have relied on information provided by David Redden and Albert K. Butzel in my description of Scenic Hudson in the 1970s. On the increasing importance of ecology in environmental law in the 1970s see Robert D. Lifset, *Power on the Hudson: Storm King Mountain and the Emergence of Modern American Environmentalism* (Pittsburgh, 2014) and Albert K. Butzel, "Birth of the Environmental Movement in the Hudson River Valley," in *Environmental History of the Hudson River: Human Uses That Changed the Ecology, Ecology That Changed Human Uses*, ed. Robert E. Henshaw (Albany, N.Y., 2011), 279–90.

2. Scenic Hudson Preservation Conference, Board of Directors, minutes, Dec. 18, 1975, Sept. 16, 1976, Jan. 20, 1977, Mar. 13, 1977, Apr. 21, 1977, Aug. 18, 1977, Aug. 17, 1978, Scenic Hudson Papers, Marist College; Scenic Hudson, *Annual Report*, 1999 (Poughkeepsie, N.Y., 2000), lists the organization's achievements between 1973 and 1983 (p. 3).

3. Scenic Hudson, *Annual Report*, 1999, 3–4 (note that most of the annual reports are unpaginated).

4. The figure on the economic value of the tourism industry is from Scenic Hudson, *Important Victories and a Call to Action, 2015 Annual Report*. It is based on data from federal agencies (Labor and Commerce) and covers the river counties north of New York City.

5. Pataki is quoted in Tracie Rozhon, "Plans for Industrial Revival Divide Hudson River Towns," *NYT*, Mar. 13, 2000; Scenic Hudson, *Annual Report*, 2000; Moe is quoted in Winnie Hu, "Industrial Growth Threatens Scenic Hudson River Valley, Group Warns," *NYT*, June 27, 2000.

6. Erin M. Crotty, Commissioner, Department of Environmental Conservation, St. Lawrence Cement Company, LLC—Determination, September 8, 2004 (hereafter Crotty—Determination, September 8, 2004); Rozhon, "Plans for Industrial Revival"; Miriam D. Silverman, *Stopping the Plant: The St. Lawrence Cement Controversy and the Battle for Quality of Life in the Hudson Valley* (Albany, N.Y., 2006), 6–7; Marc S. Gerstman, In the Matter of the Application of St. Lawrence Cement Company, Reply to Appeal from Issues Rulings,

courtesy of Scenic Hudson. Sam Pratt explains why he believes Scenic Hudson was reluctant to join the opposition to St. Lawrence Cement, and what he considers its effort to claim credit for the victory, in "Metroland: Where Credit Is Due," *Metroland* (Summer 2005), http://hudson.typepad.com/stp/files/scenichudson.html.

7. Information provided by Ned Sullivan, Sam Pratt, and J. Winthrop Aldrich; for opposition to the plant in New England see, for example, "Ill Wind from New York," *Boston Sunday Globe*, Nov. 16, 2003, and "Stop Cement Plant on Hudson," *New Haven Register*, Nov. 28, 2003; Silverman, *Stopping the Plant*, 6–9.

8. Information provided by Sara Griffen and J. Winthrop Aldrich; Silverman, *Stopping the Plant*, 6–9.

9. Monkash and Posner are quoted in New York State Department of Environmental Conservation, In the Matter of the Application of St. Lawrence Cement Co., LLC, hearing before ALJ Helene Goldberger, Columbia-Greene Community College, June 21, 2001 (http://hudson.typepad.com/stp/files/hearing2001raw.html); information provided by Sam Pratt.

10. Crotty—Determination, September 8, 2004; New York State Department of Environmental Conservation, St. Lawrence Cement Company, LLC—Initial Ruling, December 7, 2001 (hereafter DEC—Initial Ruling, December 7, 2001); Silverman, *Stopping the Plant*, 9–16.

11. DEC—Initial Ruling, December 7, 2001; DEC, In the Matter of the Application of St. Lawrence Cement Co., LLC, June 21, 2001; Silverman, *Stopping the Plant*, 10–13.

12. DEC—Initial Ruling, December 7, 2001; information provided by Sam Pratt and Ned Sullivan.

13. DEC—Initial Ruling, December 7, 2001; DEC, Notice of Determination to Review Prevention of Significant Deterioration, 2001; DEC, Announcement of Public Comment Period and Combined Notice of Complete Application. Notice of Completion of Draft Environmental Impact Statement (DEIS), May 2, 2001. Benas is quoted in Caffry, In the Matter of the Application of St. Lawrence Cement Company, Reply of the Olana Partnership to the Applicant's and DEC Staff's Appeals from the ALJs Rulings on Party Status and Issues, Mar. 15, 2002, courtesy of Scenic Hudson; information provided by Harvey Flad; "SLC Industrial Nightmare Defeated; New Economic Vision Advances," Scenic Hudson, *Annual Report*, 2005 (Poughkeepsie, N.Y., 2006), 7.

14. Crotty—Determination, September 8, 2004; "Cement Plant Shutout Continues, Key Turning Point Ahead," Scenic Hudson, *Annual Report*, 2004 (Poughkeepsie, N.Y., 2005), 4; Silverman, *Stopping the Plant*, 14–16.

15. Caffry, In the Matter of the Application; Gerstman, In the Matter of the Application; New York State Department of State, *Scenic Areas of Statewide Significance* (Albany, July 1993), 11–106.

16. Silverman, *Stopping the Plant*, 9–16. Daniels's ruling is reprinted ibid., 119–55 (quotations on 124, 126, 128, 132).

17. Daniels, in Silverman, *Stopping the Plant*, 147–54 (quotations on 149, 150, 152).

18. Silverman, *Stopping the Plant*, 105, 109.

19. *Scenic Hudson News*, Spring 1980, 1; information provided by Ned Sullivan.

20. Klara B. Sauer, "Scenic Hudson: 25 Years and Still Going Strong," *Scenic Hudson News*, Spring 1988, 4; Scenic Hudson, *Annual Report 1984*; *Annual Report*, 1987–88; *Annual Report*, 1990, 3–4; *Annual Report*, 1990–91; information provided by Steve Rosenberg, executive director, Scenic Hudson Land Trust Inc., and Albert K. Butzel; Harold Faber, "Group Buys Private Land in Putnam County for a Public Park," *NYT*, Sept. 22, 1991.

21. Scenic Hudson, *Annual Report*, 1984, 1987–88, and 1990–91; Harold Faber, "New York Is to Buy Acreage on Hudson for Recreational Use," *NYT*, Jan. 10, 1988; information on Sloop Hill provided by John Doyle, who was executive director of the Heritage Task Force.

22. Scenic Hudson, *Annual Report*, 1991–92, 4; *Annual Report*, 1992–93, 5–6; *Annual Report*, 1993–94, 5; *Annual Report*, 1994–95; *Annual Report*, 1995–96; *Annual Report*, 1996–97; *Annual Report*, 1997–98; *Annual Report*, 2000; *Annual Report*, 2001; *Annual Report*, 2004, 10; information provided by Ned Sullivan.

23. Scenic Hudson, *Annual Report*, 1992–93, 5–6; *Annual Report*, 2000; *Annual Report*, 1997–98; "In Accepting Val-Kill Medal, Scenic Hudson Announces Bold Land-Saving Campaign," press release, Oct. 14, 2007, courtesy of Scenic Hudson.

24. Faber, "Group Buys Private Land in Putnam County"; Ralph Blumenthal, "13 Institutions Obtain Control of Vast Bequest," *NYT*, May 4, 2001. I am grateful to Ned Sullivan, Frederic C. Rich, and Barnabas McHenry for helping me understand the complexities of the Wallace Fund and the 2001 resolution.

25. Scenic Hudson, *Saving the Land That Matters Most: Protecting the Hudson Valley's National Treasures* (Poughkeepsie, N.Y., 2007).

26. Scenic Hudson, *Annual Report*, various years, 2002–2015.

27. Carol Sondheimer and Glenn Hoagland, "A Need to Preserve the Olana Landscape," *Scenic Hudson News*, Fall 1986, 5; Scenic Hudson, *Annual Report*, 1991–92, 4; *Annual Report*, 2011; *Annual Report*, 2012; information provided by Ned Sullivan.

28. Data from the American Farmland Trust is presented in Scenic Hudson, *Securing Fresh, Local Food for New York City and the Hudson Valley* (2013), 3; Scenic Hudson, *Saving the Land That Matters Most*; Scenic Hudson, *Farmland Conservation: Supporting Family Farms and Rural Economies Providing Fresh, Local Food* (c. 2000); Scenic Hudson, *Annual Report*, 2015. See also Tom Daniels and Deborah Bowers, *Holding Our Ground: Protecting America's Farms and Farmlands* (Washington, D.C., 1997).

29. Scenic Hudson, *Securing Fresh, Local Food*, 3; Scenic Hudson, *Saving the Land That Matters Most*; Scenic Hudson, *Farmland Conservation*; information provided by Steve Rosenberg and Ned Sullivan.

30. Scenic Hudson, *Securing Fresh, Local Food*, 4, 3; "Connecting the Dots: Ramping up Farmland Protection," Scenic Hudson, *Annual Report*, 2013.

31. Scenic Hudson, *Securing Fresh, Local Food*, 10–13.

32. "Land Rush Threatens Access to the Public's Waterfront," Scenic Hudson, *Annual Report*, 2004, 8; "Connecting People to Their River," *Annual Report*, 2007; "We're Working to Guarantee a Healthy, Economically Vibrant Hudson Valley," *Annual Report*, 2008; "Connecting People to the River," *Annual Report*, 2010.

33. "Teetering on the Edge," *Annual Report*, 2006; "Land Rush Threatens Access to Public's Waterfront"; "Connecting People to Their River."

34. Scenic Hudson, *Revitalizing Hudson Riverfronts: Illustrated Conservation and Development Strategies for Creating Healthy, Prosperous Communities* (Poughkeepsie, N.Y., 2010), 7, 21–41.

35. "Pushing the Envelop to Revive Beacon's Natural Assets" and "Saving Land, Creating Parks That Preserve Our Valley," Scenic Hudson, *Annual Report*, 1994; "Beacon: Emerging Model of Riverfront Renaissance," *Annual Report*, 2005, 4.

36. "Daring to Imagine a Yonkers River Uncovered, a Downtown Reborn," Scenic Hudson, *Annual Report*, 2005, 9; "Yonkers: Strong Advocacy, New Funding Bring Back the Saw Mill River," *Annual Report*, 2006, 5; "Revitalizing Waterfronts and Downtowns," *Annual Report*, 2013; information provided by Reed Sparling.

37. "Tarrytown: A Riverfront Eyesore Transformed into a New Park," Scenic Hudson, *Annual Report*, 2005, 5; "Building Parks That Connect People to the River," *Annual Report*, 2009; "We're Working to Guarantee a Healthy, Economically Vibrant Hudson Valley," *Annual Report*, 2008; "Connecting People to the River," *Annual Report*, 2011; "Connecting People to Nature," *Annual Report*, 2012.

38. "Fueling the Green Economy with New Parks and Protected Lands," Scenic Hudson, *Annual Report*, 2009; "Ensuring the Valley's Economic Future," *Annual Report*, 2010; "Connecting the Dots: Spreading Walkway's Success," *Annual Report*, 2012; Harold Faber, "Worthless Bridge; Priceless View," *NYT*, July 26, 1993; Michael Malone, "Rusty Bridge, Great Views and Soon, a Walkway?," *NYT*, Jan. 1, 2007; information provided by Harvey Flad.

39. "PCB Cleanup: Even Now, Not a Done Deal," Scenic Hudson, *Annual Report*, 2004, 10; "Break Comes in PCB Stalemate; Further Vigilance Needed," *Annual Report*, 2005, 6; "PCBs—GE, Stop the Stall," *Annual Report*, 2006, 10; "PCBs: A Major Step Forward," *Annual Report*, 2007; Robert H. Boyle, "Poison Roams Our Inland Seas," *Sports Illustrated*, Oct. 26, 1970, 71–84; Environmental Defense Fund and the New York Public Interest Research Group Inc., *Troubled Waters: Toxic Chemicals in the Hudson River* (New York, 1977).

40. "Building an Environmental Army," Scenic Hudson, *Annual Report*, 2006, 9–10.

41. Ibid.

42. "Blocking Needless and Costly Transmission Lines," Scenic Hudson, *Annual Report*, 2015.

43. Amanda J. Purcell, "Scenic Hudson Receives Grant to Purchase Land for Preservation," *Poughkeepsie Journal*, July 31, 2016; "Creating a Climate-Resilient Valley," Scenic Hudson, *Annual Report*, 2016.

44. Information provided by Ned Sullivan.

7. Linking Landscapes and Promoting History

1. Charles E. Little, *Greenways for America* (Baltimore, 1990), 26; Tessa Melvin, "State Adopts Greenway Concept for Hudson Valley," *NYT*, July 21, 1991; the congressional act creating the Hudson River Valley National Heritage Area (Public Law 104–333) is printed as an appendix to *Hudson River Valley National Heritage Area Management Plan* (Albany, N.Y., 2002); information provided by Mark Castiglione.

2. Frederick Law Olmsted, "Report upon a Projected Improvement of the Estate of the College of California, at Berkeley, Near Oakland," June 29, 1866, in Victoria Post Ranney et al., eds., *The Papers of Frederick Law Olmsted*, vol. 5, *The California Frontier, 1863–1865* (Baltimore, 1990), 546–73; Olmsted, Vaux & Company, "Report of the Landscape Architects," Jan. 24, 1966, in *Papers of Frederick Law Olmsted, Supplementary Series I*, ed. Charles E. Beveridge and Carolyn F. Hoffman (Baltimore, 1997), 105–6; Olmsted, Vaux & Company, "Report of the Landscape Architects and Superintendents," Jan. 1, 1868, ibid., 134–41 (quotation on 138).

3. Little, *Greenways for America*, 15–25. For my thoughts on Howard and the influence of his writing see Kermit C. Parsons and David Schuyler, eds., *From Garden City to Green City: The Legacy of Ebenezer Howard* (Baltimore, 2002), 1–8. MacKaye proposed the Appalachian Trail in an article, "An Appalachian Trail: A Project in Regional Planning," *Journal of the American Institute of Architects* 9 (October 1921): 325–30.

4. Little, *Greenways for America*, 99–104.

5. Information on Franny Reese's importance to the evolution of the Greenway was provided by John Cronin; Klara Sauer, Summary of Greenway Creation as I Remember, undated typescript, courtesy of Mark Castiglione.

6. Sauer, Summary of Greenway Creation; Scenic Hudson Inc. and the National Park Service, *Building Greenways in the Hudson River Valley: A Guide for Action* (1989); information provided by Karl Beard.

7. Cuomo is quoted in Little, *Greenways for America*, 67.

8. Henry L. Diamond, "For a Hudson Greenway," *NYT*, Jan. 2, 1988. The report of the President's Commission on Americans Outdoors is quoted in Henry L. Diamond and Douglass Lea, *Greenways in the Hudson River Valley: A New Strategy for Preserving an American Treasure* (Tarrytown, N.Y., 1988), 9; the recommendations of the Regional Plan Association are described on 10, 21–22.

9. Diamond and Lea, *Greenways in the Hudson River Valley*, 10–12.

10. Ibid., 13, 15.

11. Ibid., 16.

12. Ibid., 13–15.

13. Ibid., 27–34.

14. Ibid., 41; New York State Department of Environmental Conservation, *The Hudson River Valley: A Heritage for All Time* (Albany, 1979), n.p.; Heritage Task Force for the Hudson River Valley, *1989 Annual Report* (New Paltz, N.Y., 1989), 1–8; John Doyle, Testimony before the Assembly Standing Committee on Environmental Conservation Regarding the Protection of the Hudson River Valley, n.d., courtesy of John Doyle; Westat (for the National Park Service), *Hudson River Valley National Heritage Area Evaluation Findings* (Rockville, Md., 2012), 2–26.

15. Diamond and Lea, *Greenways in the Hudson River Valley*, 45–46.

16. Robin W. Winks, *Laurance S. Rockefeller: Catalyst for Conservation* (Washington, D.C., 1997), 177–80; "Cuomo Signs a Bill Creating Parks Panel," *NYT*, Aug. 19, 1988; information provided by Barnabas McHenry.

17. New York (State), Legislature, Hudson River Valley Greenway Act of 1991 (www.esf.edu/efb/limburg/Hudson/HR_Greenway_ Legislation.pdf); Hudson River Greenway Council, *A Hudson River Valley Greenway* (Albany, N.Y., 1991), 12–13.

18. Hudson River Valley Greenway Act of 1991; Tessa Melvin, "River Pact Urged for 154-Mile Greenway," *NYT*, May 13, 1990; Harold Faber, "A Protected 'Greenway' Proposed along the Hudson," *NYT*, Oct. 1, 1990; Tessa Melvin, "State Adopts Greenway Concept for Hudson Valley," *NYT*, July 21, 1991; Winks, *Laurance S. Rockefeller*, 180; John Ferro, "How a New Year's Eve Call to Mario Cuomo Saved Greenway," *Poughkeepsie Journal*, July 3, 2015. A number of developers and builders who expressed opposition to the Greenway Act are quoted in Melvin, "State Adopts Greenway Concept for Hudson Valley."

19. Hudson River Valley Greenway Act of 1991. The U.S. Department of the Interior had recommended that a regional agency have the power to overturn local planning or zoning ordinances that it considered inadequate, in *Focus on the Hudson: Evaluating Proposals and Alternatives* (Bureau of Outdoor Recreation, U.S. Department of the Interior, 1966).

20. Hudson River Valley Greenway Act of 1991.

21. Information on Dutchess County's initiatives provided by Mark Castiglione; Orange County Greenway Compact, approved by the Greenway Communities Council June 12, 2013, 5, 7. Links to this, Dutchess County's, and the other completed plans are available at hudsongreenway.ny.gov/Planning/Greenway_Compact.aspx.

22. Information provided by Mark Castiglione.

23. Hudson River Valley Greenway Act of 1991; information provided by Mark Castiglione; Hudson River Access Forum, *Between the Railroad and the River: Public Access Issues and Opportunities along the Tidal Hudson* (n.p., 1989).

24. Westchester County Department of Planning, https://planning.westchestergov.com/westchester-riverwalk; information provided by Mark Castiglione.

25. Hudson Highlands Fjord Trail Draft Master Plan, April 29, 2015, www.hudson fjordtrail.org/master-plan.

26. Scenic Hudson, "Hyde Park Trail River Overlook," www.scenichudson.org/parks/hydeparktrail; information provided by Mark Castiglione; Hudson River Greenway Water Trail, hudsonrivergreenwaywatertrail.org.

27. "Governor Cuomo Announces Next Step in Plan to Build Hudson River SkyWalk," press release, May 31, 2016.

28. Information provided by Mark Castiglione.

29. Information provided by Mark Castiglione; hudsonrivervalleyramble.com.

30. *Hudson River Valley National Heritage Area Management Plan*, 3, passim; information provided by Mark Castiglione; *Biographical Directory of the United States Congress, 1774–Present*, bioguide.congress.gov/scripts/biodisplay.pl?index=H000627. A copy of the relevant section of the Omnibus Parks and Public Lands Management Act of 1966 is included in an unpaginated appendix to National Park Service, *Hudson River Valley Special Resource Study Report* (Boston, 1996).

31. National Park Service, *Hudson River Valley Special Resource Study Report*, 8–9.

32. Ibid., 32–33. See also David Schuyler, *Sanctified Landscape: Writers, Artists, and the Hudson River Valley, 1820–1909* (Ithaca, N.Y., 2012).

33. National Park Service, *Hudson River Valley Special Resource Study Report*, 38–42.

34. *Hudson River Valley National Heritage Area Management Plan*, 3, 16, 28–33; David Schuyler, "Pencil and Pen in Defense of Nature: Thomas Cole and the American Landscape," *Hudson River Valley Review* 31 (Autumn 2014): 16-37.

35. *Hudson River Valley National Heritage Area Management Plan*, 41–44, passim; QL Consulting Inc. and the Office of Thomas J. Martin, *Regional Tourism Strategy Final Report*, vol. 1, *Findings and Recommendations* (1995), 7.

36. QL Consulting Inc. and the Office of Thomas J. Martin, *Regional Tourism Strategy Final Report*, vol. 1, *Findings and Recommendations*, 9–15.

37. Ibid.

38. *Hudson River Valley National Heritage Area Management Plan*, 32; information provided by Jim Johnson.

39. Thomas Cole National Historic Site, *The Hudson River School Art Trail Guide*, 2nd ed. (Catskill, N.Y., 2013).

40. Ann Davis, *Report of Interviews at Heritage Sites in the Hudson River Valley National Heritage Area, Summer and Fall 2002* (Poughkeepsie, N.Y., 2004), 5; J. Winthrop Aldrich, *Heritage Sites 2004: A Report to the Management Committee of the Hudson River Valley National Heritage Area* (Albany, N.Y., 2004), 1–5.

41. *Tourism Economics: The Economic Impact of Tourism in New York; 2014 Calendar Year, Hudson Valley Focus* (n.p., n.d.), 3, 4, 9, 30, 31, 35, 40, passim; information provided by Mark Castiglione.

42. Information provided by Mark Castiglione; Westat (for the National Park Service), *Hudson River Valley National Heritage Area Evaluation Findings* (Sept. 2012), 4–64 to 4–65.

43. Westat, *Hudson River Valley National Heritage Area Evaluation Findings*, 3–61, 3–48.

8. A Poisoned River

1. Hudson River Valley Commission, Minutes, Dec. 29, 1971, Hudson River Valley Commission Records, New York State Archives, Albany; Dr. K. R. Murphy to Pyranol Task Force, June 5, 1970, http://www.timesunion.com.default.article/Dredging-up-the-truth-5294643.php.

2. Thomas Cairns and Emil G. Siegmund, "PCBs: Regulatory History and Analytical Problems," *Analytical Chemistry* 53 (Sept. 1981): 1183–92; Thomas R. Head III, "PCBs—the

Rise and Fall of an Industrial Miracle," *Natural Resources & Environment* (Spring 2005): 15–19; Brendan J. Lyons, "Dredging Up the Truth: Records Show GE Was Warned about Health Threats of PCBs Decades before the Anti-Dredging Campaign," *Albany Times Union,* Mar. 8, 2014. For the effects of PCBs on human health see David O. Carpenter, "Polychlorinated Biphenyls (PCBs): Routes of Exposure and Effects on Human Health," *Reviews on Environmental Health* 21 (Feb. 2006): 1–23; David O. Carpenter, "Exposure to and Health Effects of Volatile PCBs," *Reviews on Environmental Health* 30 (Feb. 2015): 1–12; and National Research Council, *A Risk-Management Strategy for PCB-Contaminated Sediment* (Washington, D.C., 2001), 5, 32–33.

　　3. Lyons, "Dredging Up the Truth"; J. F. Nelson to J. F. McAllister, Oct. 30, 1969; and Nelson, "PCB: An Industry Problem?," Oct. 30, 1969, all accessible at http://www.timesunion.com/default/article/Dredging-up-the-truth-5294643.php.

　　4. Robert H. Boyle, "Poison Roams Our Coastal Seas," *Sports Illustrated,* Oct. 26, 1970, 70–84; Boyle, *The Hudson River: A Natural and Unnatural History* (1969; expanded ed., New York, 1979), 295–300.

　　5. Cairns and Siegmund, "PCBs: Regulatory History," 1183; Head, "PCBs—the Rise and Fall," 15–19; "Hudson River PCBs," http://www.riverkeeper.org/campaigns/stop-polluters/pcbs/; David Stout, "G.E. Agrees to Clean Part of Tainted River in Massachusetts," *NYT,* Sept. 25, 1998. Nelson, "PCB: An Industry Problem?," and K. R. Murphy to Pyranol Task Force, June 5, 1980 (the accompanying documents from GE were available at http://www.timesunion.com/default/article/Dredging-up-the-truth-5294643.php but have since been removed. Copies are available in the author's files or through the *Albany Times Union.*

　　6. Rinker Buck, "As G.E. Goes, So Goes Economy of 2 Counties," *NYT,* Feb. 15, 1976; Brian Nearing, "GE Workers Facing Fort Edward Job Loss Push PCB Health Studies," *Albany Times Union,* Jan. 22, 2016; Nearing, "When General Electric Leaves Fort Edward, Pollution Remains," *Albany Times Union,* Mar. 6, 2014.

　　7. "A Failure Here," *NYT,* Sept. 10, 1975; Lyons, "Dredging Up the Truth"; Boyle, *Hudson River,* 299.

　　8. Richard Severo, "State Says Some Striped Bass and Salmon Pose a Toxic Peril," *NYT,* Aug. 8, 1975; "U.S. Scores Pollution of Hudson with PCB," *NYT,* Nov. 25, 1975; Severo, "G.E. Testifies on PCB-Discharge Cuts," *NYT,* Dec. 9, 1975; Boyle, *Hudson River,* 299.

　　9. Information provided by John Cronin; Walter Schwanne to Russell Train, Aug. 11, 1975; Seeger is quoted in executive committee minutes, Sept. 11, 1975; minutes, Annual Sloop Restoration Meeting, 1976, both in Starner Collection, Marist College.

　　10. Lyons, "Dredging Up the Truth"; K. H. Harvey to Ind. & Power Capacitor Department, Sept. 23, 1968, http://www.timesunion.com/default/article/Dredging-up-the-truth-5294643.php. Monsanto claims to have been unaware of the toxicity of PCBs before 1968.

　　11. Ibid.

　　12. K. H. Harvey to Ind. & Power Capacitor Department, Sept. 23, 1968; Richard Severo, "Interior Aide Urges Curbs in Use of PCB Chemical," *NYT,* Nov. 22, 1975; Severo, "E.P.A. Chief Plans to Curb PCB Pollution," *NYT,* Dec. 23, 1975.

　　13. Severo, "Interior Aide Urges Curbs"; Richard Severo, "Reid Visits Fishermen on the Hudson and Warns Them of PCB Pollution," *NYT,* Oct. 18, 1975.

　　14. "U.S. Scores Pollution of Hudson with PCB," *NYT,* Nov. 25, 1975; Severo, "Reid Visits Fishermen"; Carl Carmer, *The Hudson* (New York, 1939), 402–6.

　　15. Kevin Sack, "G.E. to Stop Flow of PCBs into the Hudson River," *NYT,* July 18, 1993.

　　16. National Research Council, Committee on the Assessment of Polychlorinated Biphenyls in the Environment, *Polychlorinated Biphenyls: A Report* (Washington, D.C., 1979), xiii, 1, 3, 39, 101, passim; U.S. Environmental Protection Agency, Hudson River PCBs Site

New York, Record of Decision (2002), i; Hudson River Natural Resource Trustees, *PCB Contamination of the Hudson River Ecosystem, Compilation of Contamination Data through 2008* (Silver Spring, Md., Jan. 2013), 1, 3, 18–19; "U.S. Scores Pollution of Hudson with PCB"; Severo, "Reid Visits Fishermen"; Raymond Hernandez, "Pataki Administration Calls for Dredging of the Hudson River to Clean Up PCB's," *NYT*, Nov. 17, 2000.

17. U.S. Environmental Protection Agency, Hudson River PCBs Superfund Site, "Hudson River Cleanup," https://www3.epa.gov/hudson/cleanup.html; Angela Magill to Russell Train, Sept. 10, 1976, Starner Collection; Hudson River Natural Resource Trustees, *PCB Contamination of the Hudson River Ecosystem*, 9–19.

18. [GE], "Status Report and 1991 Strategy," Jan. 17, 1991, http://www.timesunion.com. default.article/Dredging-up-the-truth-5294643.php; Joshua Cleland, *Advances in Dredging Contaminated Sediment: New Technologies and Experience Relevant to the Hudson River PCBs Site* (Poughkeepsie, N.Y., 1997), 1, 5; U.S. Environmental Protection Agency, Hudson River PCBs Site New York, Record of Decision (2002), 1–8. For a cogent rebuttal of GE's claims, especially its overoptimistic estimate of sediment recovery rates and the length of time it would take for Hudson River fish to recover from exposure to PCBs see L. Jay Field, J. W. Kern, and L. B. Rosman, "Re-visiting Projections of PCBs in Lower Hudson River Fish Using Model Emulation," *Science of the Total Environment*, July 2016: 489–501; information provided by Ned Sullivan. See also EPA administrator Carol M. Browner's repudiation of GE's public relations campaign, as reported in Andrew C. Revkin, "U.S. Environmental Chief Attacks G.E. Pollution Ads," *NYT*, July 10, 1998.

19. U.S. Environmental Protection Agency, Hudson River PCBs Site New York, Record of Decision (2002), 54–62, 94–98.

20. Jay Field, John Kern, and Lisa Rosman, *Re-Visiting Model Projections of Lower Hudson River Fish PCBs Using Model Emulation and Recent Data* (New York, May 19, 2015); Enck is quoted in David Sirota, "Federal Agencies Demand General Electric Continue Cleaning Up Its Hudson River Pollution," *International Business Times*, Sept. 29, 2015.

21. Peter Lehner, letter to the editor, *Schenectady Sunday Gazette*, Jan. 21, 2001; Rich Schiafo, *Citizens' Guide to Hudson River Natural Resource Damage Assessment and Restoration* (Poughkeepsie, N.Y., 2004), 5; information provided by John Mylod.

22. Boyle, *Hudson River*, 296.

23. U.S. Environmental Protection Agency, Hudson River PCBs Superfund Site, Phase 1 Dredging Factsheet, November 2009; EPA, Phase 2 Overview Factsheet, 2015.

24. Todd Bridges et al., *Hudson River Phase 1 Dredging Peer Review Report* (Washington, D.C., 2010), iii–viii, 1–2, 6, 13, 29, 31, 38, 48, 84–86.

25. Andrew C. Revkin, "Dredging of Pollutants Begins in Hudson," *NYT*, May 16, 2009; Immelt is quoted in "GE Completes Hudson River Dredging," GE press release, Oct. 5, 2015; Statement from EPA on Hudson River Cleanup, Oct. 1, 2015; Judith A. Enck, "EPA Removal of PCBs from Hudson Worked," *Albany Times Union*, Jan. 30, 2016, and the response by Ned Sullivan and Aaron Mair, "Hudson Cleanup Far from Complete," *Albany Times Union*, Feb. 8, 2016.

26. Hudson River Natural Resource Trustees, *PCB Contamination of the Hudson River Ecosystem*, passim; Environmental Protection Agency "Responses to NOAA Manuscript Entitled: 'Re-Visiting Projections of PCBs in Lower Hudson River Fish Using Model Emulation' (Field, Kern, Rosman, 2015)," white paper, Mar. 2016; Hudson River Natural Resource Trustees, "Federal Trustees Correct General Electric's Misinformation in Latest Hudson River PCB Report," press release, Feb. 3, 2014.

27. Hudson River Natural Resource Trustees, "Federal Trustees Correct General Electric's Misinformation in Latest Hudson River PCB Report"; Brian Nearing, "Coalition Asks GE Mandate to Dredge PCBs from Tainted Champlain Canal on Hudson River," *Albany Times Union*, Apr. 14, 2015.

28. "Decision Time on the Hudson," editorial, *NYT*, May 25, 2015; "G.E., Finish the Job on the Hudson," editorial, *NYT*, Sept. 4, 2015.

29. "GE Completes Hudson River Dredging," press release, Oct. 5, 2015; Scenic Hudson, NRDC, Riverkeeper, and Hudson River Sloop Clearwater, petition to the United States Environmental Protection Agency for Evaluation and Expansion of Remedial Action Selected in the 2002 Record of Decision for the Hudson River PCBs Site, Dec. 17, 2015, courtesy of Scenic Hudson; Enck, "EPA Removal of PCBs from Hudson Worked."

30. Scenic Hudson, NRDC, Riverkeeper, and Hudson River Sloop Clearwater, petition to the United States Environmental Protection Agency for Evaluation and Expansion of Remedial Action; Enck, "EPA Removal of PCBs from Hudson Worked."

31. Enck, "EPA Removal of PCBs from Hudson Worked"; Sullivan and Mair, "Hudson Cleanup Far from Complete."

32. Cuomo is quoted in Sirota, "Should General Electric Clean Up Its Pollution in New York? Gov. Andrew Cuomo Isn't Sure," *In These Times* (www.inthesetimes.com), Sept. 18, 2015; Sirota, "Federal Agencies Demand General Electric Continue Cleaning Up Its Hudson River Pollution."

33. EPA, Hudson River PCBs Superfund Site, Hudson River Cleanup, https://www3.epa.gov/hudson/cleanup.html; Carmer, *Hudson*, 402–6.

34. Seggos's letter to Judith Enck and his interview with the *New York Times*, along with the statement of EPA spokeswoman Deirdre Latour, are quoted in Jesse McKinley, "G.E. Spent Years Cleaning Up Its Mess in the Hudson; Was It Enough?," *NYT*, Sept. 9, 2016.

35. Information provided by Ned Sullivan.

36. Boyle, *Hudson River*, 289.

37. EPA, Proposed Second Five-Year Review Report for Hudson River PCBs Superfund Site, May 31, 2017; Scenic Hudson and Riverkeeper, "Flawed Data & Analysis Fatally Undermine EPA's Finding That Hudson PCB Cleanup Will Protect Environment & Public Health," press release, Sept. 5, 2015; Kevin J. Farley et al., *An Independent Evaluation of the PCB Dredging Program on the Upper Hudson and Lower Hudson River*, June 2017, http://www.hudsonriver.org/download/2017-06-01Report-HRFDredgingProgramEvaluationFinal.pdf.

38. Boyle, *Hudson River*, 289.

39. Ibid., 296–300; Boyle, "Poison Roams Our Coastal Seas": Environmental Defense Fund and the New York Public Interest Research Group Inc., *Troubled Waters: Toxic Chemicals in the Hudson River* (New York, 1977), xiv–xvi, III-2, passim; Bill Wegner, "Drugs in Our Drinking Water: The Problem of Pharmaceutical Pollution," Riverkeeper, *2010 Annual Journal*, 14–15; information provided by Paul Gallay; Amy Pochodylo and Damian E. Helbling, "Target Screening for Micropollutants in the Hudson River Estuary during the 2015 Recreational Season," New York State Water Resources Institute, Cornell University.

40. New York State Department of Environmental Conservation, *The State of the Hudson, 2015* (Albany, 2015), 4; Pisces Conservation, *The State of Fish Populations and the Ecology of the Hudson*, Apr. 2008, unpaginated.

41. See "Clean Water Jobs Coalition Urges Lawmakers to Renew Clean/Waste Water Funding Legislation as Clean Water Infrastructure Needs Escalate in Lower Hudson Valley," Oct. 19, 2016, which quotes Sullivan and Gallay, www.prweb.com/releases/2016/10/prweb13774665.htm.

42. Environmental Protection Agency, "Contaminants of Emerging Concern Including Pharmaceuticals and Personal Care Products," https://www.epa.gov/wqc/contaminants-emerging-concern-including-pharmaceuticals-and-personal-care-products; Environmental Protection Agency, "Aquatic Life Criteria for Contaminants of Emerging Concern: Part I, General Challenges and Recommendations," draft, June 3, 2008, 1–3.

9. A River Still Worth Fighting For

1. Robert Boyle, *The Hudson River: A Natural and Unnatural History*, expanded ed. (1969; New York, 1979), 22, 296, passim; Hudson River Estuary Program, *State of the Hudson 2015* (Albany, N.Y., 2015), 4.

2. "Halting the Threat from Crude Oil Shipments," Scenic Hudson, *Annual Report*, 2015; "Albany's Perilous Oil Boom," editorial, *NYT*, Apr. 2, 2014; Jad Mouawad, "New Oil Train Rules Are Hit from All Sides," *NYT*, May 2, 2015; Eleanor Randolph, "A Railway Catastrophe in the Making," *NYT*, Mar. 12, 2015; Marcus Stern, "How to Prevent an Oil Train Disaster," *NYT*, May 19, 2015; "How Reckless Energy Transport Costs the Hudson—and How We Fight Back," Riverkeeper, *Annual Journal 2016*, 22; "Oil and Water Shouldn't Mix," *Riverkeeper Journal 2015*, 12.

3. "Halting the Threat from Crude Oil Shipments," Scenic Hudson, *Annual Report*, 2015; Gallay is quoted in Dan Shapley, "Facing the Real Risks from New York's Crude Oil 'Virtual Pipeline,'" Riverkeeper, *Annual Journal 2014*, 12.

4. Shapley, "Facing the Real Risks," 12; National Academies of Sciences, Engineering, Medicine, *Spills of Diluted Bitumen from Pipelines: A Comparative Study of Environmental Fate, Effects, and Response* (Washington, D.C., 2016).

5. Information provided by John Cronin; Scenic Hudson, "Take Action: We Can't Let the Hudson Become a Waterborne Crude Oil Facility," press release, Aug. 8, 2016; Lisa W. Foderaro, "Plan to Let Barges Park on the Hudson Draws Ire from 'River Towns,'" *NYT*, Aug. 16, 2016.

6. Allison Dunne, "Elected Officials Criticize USCG Proposal on Anchorage Sites in the Hudson," WAMC Northeast Public Radio, Aug. 2, 2016; Lipscomb is quoted in Foderaro, "Plan to Let Barges Park on the Hudson Draws Ire"; "No Parking on the Hudson," editorial, *NYT*, Sept. 19, 2016.

7. Andrew Tangel, "LG Buys Huge Office Building in Englewood Cliffs," *Bergen Record*, Dec. 10, 2010.

8. For my analysis of the first battle for the Palisades see *Sanctified Landscape: Writers, Artists, and the Hudson River Valley, 1820–1909* (Ithaca, N.Y., 2012), 156–62; Diedrich Knickerbocker [Washington Irving], *A History of New York, from the Beginning of the World to the End of the Dutch Dynasty. . . .* (1809; New York, 1871), 386; William Cullen Bryant and James Silk Buckingham are quoted in John K. Howat, *The Hudson River and Its Painters* (New York, 1972), 135, 136; John Burroughs, "Primal Energies," in *Time and Change: The Writings of John Burroughs*, Riverby edition (Boston, 1904–1922), 7:173; "Save the Palisades from Ruin," *NYT*, Sept. 29, 1895.

9. Schuyler, *Sanctified Landscape*, 156–62; "Who Cares for the Palisades?," *NYT*, Mar. 20, 1897; "The Palisades of the Hudson," *NYT*, July 29, 1895; "To Save the Palisades," *NYT*, Aug. 27, 1895; "Preserve the Palisades," *NYT*, Oct. 8, 1895; "New Plan for Palisades," *NYT*, Oct. 9, 1895; "Preserve the Palisades," *NYT*, Oct. 10, 1895; "The Palisades," *NYT*, Nov. 27, 1897.

10. Tangel, "LG Buys Huge Office Building"; Michael Kimmelman, "More Opposition to Palisades Building," *NYT*, May 13, 2014; for comments of residents who feared that the LG project would change the character of their community see Minutes, Special Public Meeting of the Englewood Cliffs Planning Board, Apr. 30, 2014.

11. Much of this information is presented in Phillips Preiss Grygiel, LLC, Amendment to the Land Use Element of the Borough of Englewood Cliffs Master Plan Creating a New B-5 Corporate Zone Classification for Block 207, Lot 6 (Feb. 2016) and in Carol Jacoby, Plaintiff-Respondent, v. Zoning Board of Adjustment of the Borough of Englewood Cliffs and LG Electronics USA, Inc., Defendants-Respondents, and the New Jersey Federation of

Women's Clubs, Scenic Hudson, Inc., et al., Plaintiffs-Appellants, v. Board of Adjustment of the Borough of Englewood Cliffs and LG Electronics USA, Inc. Defendants-Respondents (Oct. 21, 2015), both courtesy of Scenic Hudson.

12. Carol Jacoby, Plaintiff-Respondent, v. Zoning Board of Adjustment of the Borough of Englewood Cliffs and LG Electronics USA, Inc. (Oct. 21, 2015), courtesy of Scenic Hudson. Judge Fasciale's opinion was included in Carol Jacoby v. Zoning Board of Adjustment of the Borough of Englewood Cliffs, Oct. 21, 2015.

13. Fasciale, in Carol Jacoby v. Zoning Board of Adjustment of the Borough of Englewood Cliffs, Oct. 21, 2005; information provided by Albert K. Butzel.

14. Englewood Cliffs Planning Board, Special Meeting, Feb. 24, 2016; information provided by Ned Sullivan.

15. Englewood Cliffs Planning Board, Special Meeting, Apr. 25, 2016; Case Settlement Agreement, June 17, 2015, courtesy of Scenic Hudson.

16. See, for example, Scenic Hudson, "Historic Victory atop the Palisades," press release, June 23, 2015; Jennifer Smith, "LG Lowers Height of Palisades Complex," *Wall Street Journal*, June 23, 2015; Ned Sullivan, "A Win for All atop the Palisades," *Huffpost Green*, June 29, 2015; "Saving the Palisades," editorial, *NYT*, July 3, 2015.

17. Hudson Valley Green, the hudsonvalleygreen.com; Hudson River Environmental Society, www.hres.org/joomla.

18. Much of this paragraph is based on presentations by Steve Rosenberg of Scenic Hudson, Joseph Martens of the Open Space Institute, Glenn Hoagland of the Mohonk Preserve, and Cara Lee of the Nature Conservancy at the symposium "Landscape Conservation in the Hudson River Valley: Past, Present, Future," organized by Mark Castiglione of the Hudson River Valley Greenway, held at the Henry A. Wallace Center, Franklin Delano Roosevelt Home and Library, Hyde Park, N.Y., Nov. 7, 2016; Frances F. Dunwell, *The Hudson: America's River* (New York, 2008), 296.

19. Information on the various land trusts has been drawn from their web pages as well as conversations with Harvey Flad of the Mohonk Preserve board and Ellen Henneberry of the Winnakee Land Trust.

20. On Minnewaska State Park Preserve see www://parks.ny.gov/parks/127/details.aspx/; Hudson River Estuary Management Act (Environmental Conservation Law 11-0306), www.dec.ny.gov/lands/43251.html; *State of the Hudson 2015*, passim; information provided by Harvey Flad, Frances Dunwell, and John Cronin.

21. *State of the Hudson 2015*, 12–13; information provided by Frances Dunwell.

22. *State of the Hudson 2015*, 12–13; information provided by Frances Dunwell.

23. Information presented by Steve Rosenberg at the symposium "Landscape Conservation in the Hudson River Valley."

24. Population statistics are from www.factfinder.census.gov.

25. "Mid-Hudson Awarded $83.3 M, Dutchess Projects Planned," *Poughkeepsie Journal*, Dec. 8, 2016; New York State, Regional Economic Development Councils, Awards 2015, Awards 2016 (Albany, 2015, 2016); Harvey Flad and Clyde Griffen, *Main Street to Mainframes: Landscape and Social Change in Poughkeepsie* (Albany, N.Y., 2009), 353–79.

26. Kenneth T. Jackson, *Crabgrass Frontier: The Suburbanization of the United States* (New York, 1985).

27. Paul Gallay, president's letter, in *Riverkeeper Journal* 2015, 1.

INDEX